WALTER LANGLEY RI

1852 - 1922

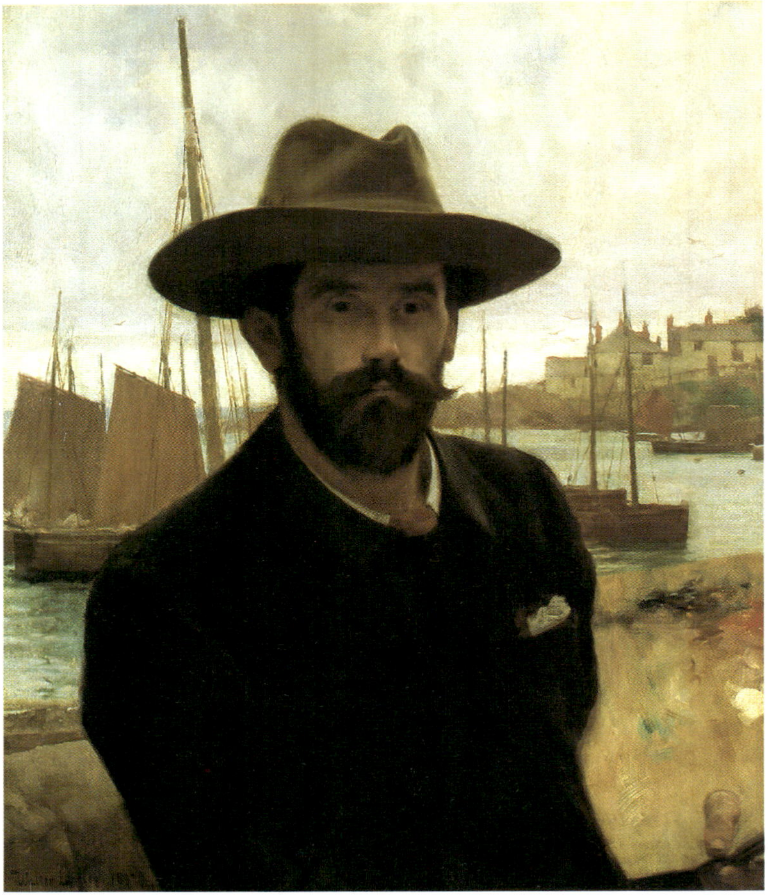

Walter Langley
Pioneer of the Newlyn Art Colony

ROGER LANGLEY *edited by Elizabeth Knowles*

Sansom & Company

in association with

Penlee House
Gallery & Museum

Front cover
The Greeting 1904
oil, 107 x 152cm

Frontispiece
Self Portrait 1897
oil, 77 x 64cm
(Uffizi Gallery, Florence)

First published in 1997 by Sansom and Company, Clifton, Bristol in association with Penlee House Gallery and Museum, Penzance.

ISBN 1 900178 45 1 (softbound) and ISBN 1 900178 31 1 (case-bound).
British Library cataloguing in Publication Data. A catalogue record for this book is available from the British Library.

Designed and typeset by Tessa and Phil Gendall and printed by Bath Press Colourbooks.
Text set in Monotype Sabon 10/16pt.

Contents

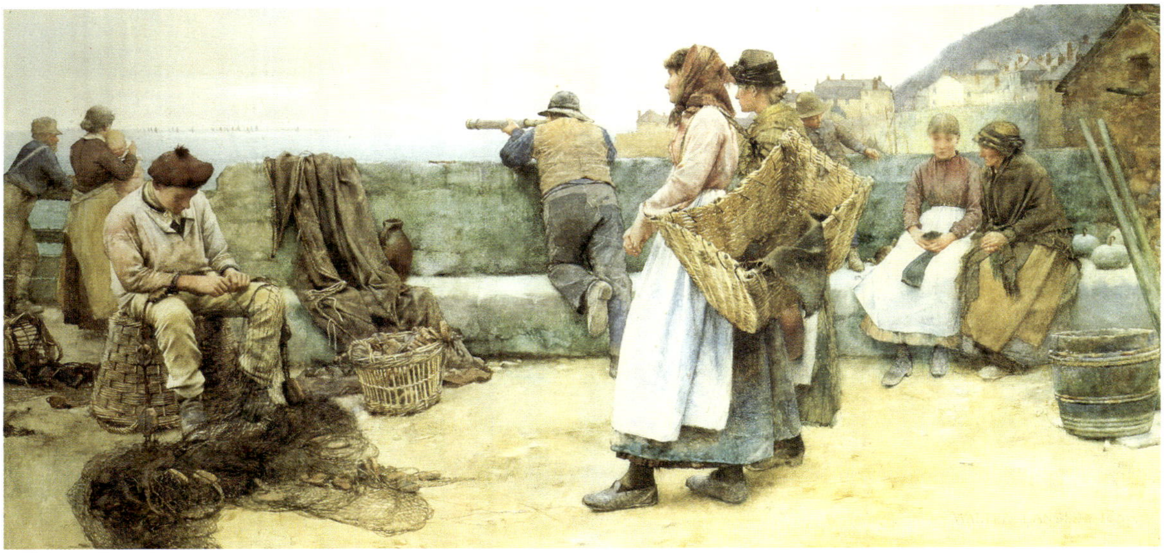

Foreword

My first meaningful encounter with the work of Walter Langley was provided by a touring exhibition, 'Newlyn School in Camera', organised by Jonathan Holmes in 1990-91 and shown at The Royal Cornwall Museum in Truro, where I then worked. The exhibition was full of interest but it was to the Langleys that I was drawn time after time, fascinated and moved by their combination of technical mastery and controlled emotional content. The accompanying photographs of the artist, seated in his studio, showed him as an attractive, modest figure who seemed to radiate a quiet authority - someone I felt I would have enjoyed meeting. His Midlands origins and socialist sympathies also interested me. Altogether, he seemed apart from the rest of the Newlyn School and yet his work in many ways represented the most essential and enduring appeal of Newlyn painting. His was an individual voice and a very particular talent, about which I longed to know more.

I was therefore delighted to learn, when I was appointed as Director in Penzance, that this book and the exhibition it accompanies were in preparation for Penlee House following the major redevelopment of 1996-97, and that I would be able to play a part in bringing it to fruition. I can think of no more appropriate project with which to establish the Gallery as a major centre for the study of art in West Cornwall, and of the remarkable work of the Newlyn School in particular.

The exhibition has been arranged by Jonathan Holmes of this museum. It will be shown at Birmingham Museum and Art Gallery, and at Warrington Art Gallery as well as here in Penzance. This book

PAGE 6
In a Cornish Fishing Village — Departure of the Fleet for the North
1886
watercolour, 61 x 122cm
(Penlee House Gallery and Museum, Penzance)

The scale and serenity of this painting mark it out as the most perfectly resolved of Langley's major exhibition pieces. His cool and controlled palette expresses the figures against the straight wall, the open sea and the clutter of baskets and nets with clarity and precision. It was shown at the RI in 1886 and an anecdotal account of its content appeared in a *Birmingham Post* article in which Langley's success was marked with local pride.

has been edited by Elizabeth Knowles. She, and indeed all of us, have had the benefit of earlier work on the Newlyn School, the first of it for John Halkes' Newlyn exhibitions in 1979 and 1985 by Caroline Fox and Francis Greenacre. There is also the work undertaken by Tessa Sidey for Birmingham and by Laura Wortley for David Messum.

We are grateful for help from Meg Duff and the Tate Gallery Library, Sue Lambert of the Victoria and Albert Museum, Susan Kent of Sotheby's and Sotheby's in Sussex, Graham Southern and his staff at Christie's, and Melissa Hardie of the West Cornwall Art Archive. David and Millie Messum, Richard Hagen of Broadway and Annamaria Petrioli Tofani of the Uffizi in Florence have been especially generous with their help.

Much of the photography for the book was by Colin Mills. We are indebted to the owners of the paintings for their permission to illustrate the works. Museums and galleries up and down the country have kindly provided photographs of the works in their own collections and we are most grateful for their co-operation.

Grateful thanks are also due to the private sponsors and to the Friends of Penlee House who have made generous contributions towards the cost of this publication.

This book and the exhibition it accompanies would not have been possible but for Walter Langley's grandson Roger, who has written the story of Langley's life and produced a meticulously researched catalogue raisonné of his work. We are deeply indebted to him for giving us the opportunity to present here, at last, a comprehensive review of Walter Langley's achievements.

Hazel Burston
Director
Penlee House Gallery
and Museum, Penzance

Author's Acknowledgements

I am much indebted to Jonathan Holmes of the Penlee House Gallery and Museum, whose interest and enthusiasm helped bring this book to fruition, and to countless people from within and outside the art world who made the research for it a real pleasure. They include the staff of many art galleries, auction houses and dealers, and of the Public Record Office at Kew, the British Library at Colindale, the Guildhall Library, London, the Local Studies Section of Birmingham Reference Library and the Institute of Contemporary British History. Too numerous to name individually, I hope they will accept instead my general, but no less warmly felt gratitude.

Maureen McCusker's researches in Birmingham gave me valuable insights into Langley's background, which was also illuminated by contributions from my late mother Dorothy Langley, Mrs Jo Senior, Denis and Walter Langley, and Herbert Whitburn.

To none of the foregoing should any errors or omissions in the text be attributable.

A heartfelt 'thank you' is due to my wife, Elizabeth, for her patience and support over the many years it took to draw together the threads of Langley's life and work.

This book has its genesis in the collation of Walter Langley's records by my father, John Langley. He was a staunch advocate of his father's work and it is a matter of great regret to me that he did not live to see even the beginning of the revival of popular appreciation of Newlyn art. I hope my work would have met with his approval.

Roger Langley

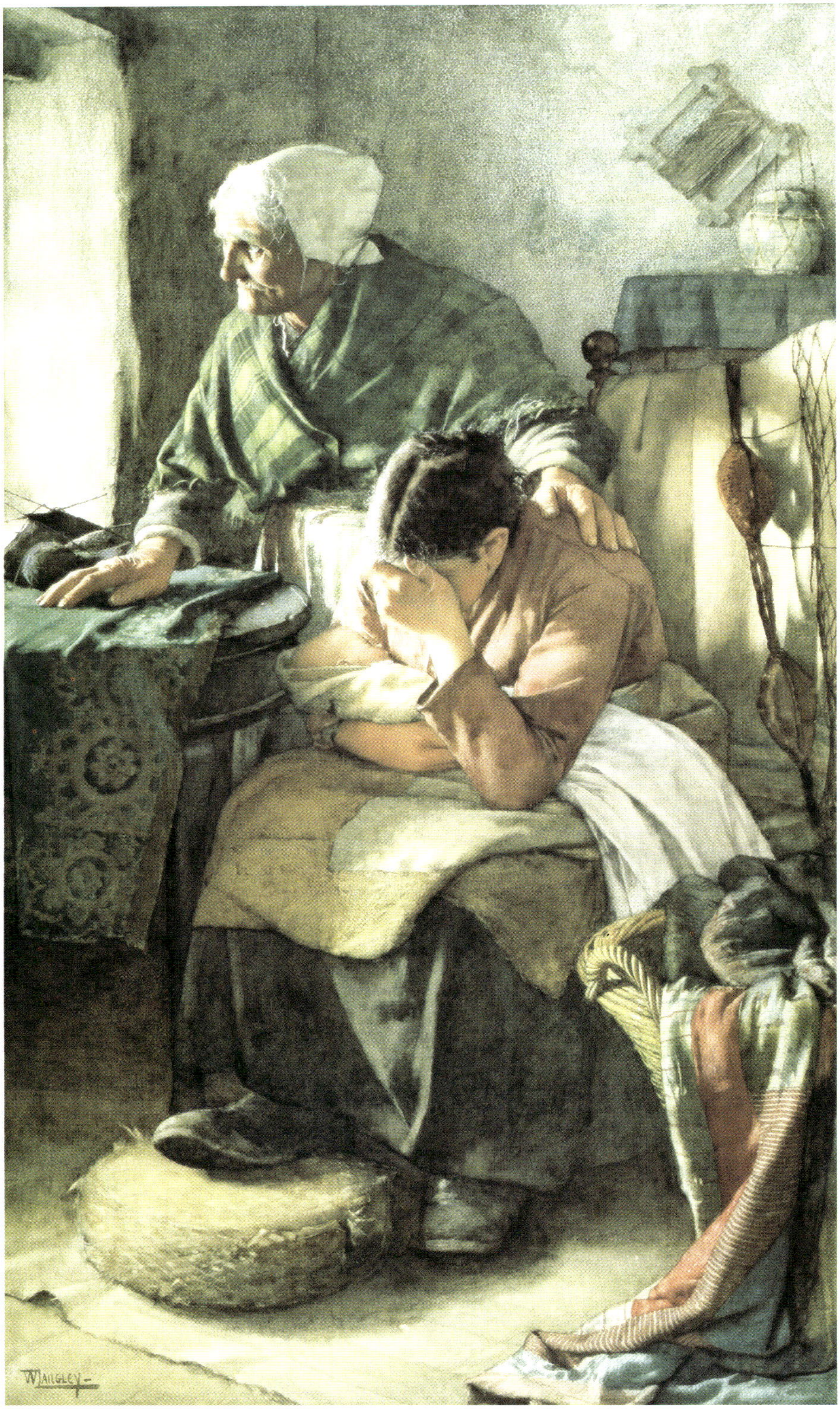
WLANGLEY

Introduction

When his large watercolour *Time moveth not, our being 'tis that moves* was shown at the Dudley Gallery in London in January 1883 it staked an impressive claim for Walter Langley among the painters of his day. Later that year, *But men must work and women must weep* at the Royal Institute of Painters in Watercolours secured his position. These successes had followed ten years of hard work to develop a watercolour painting technique powerful enough in painterly terms to convey Langley's expressive intentions and to be taken seriously as a primary medium.

For many decades the Royal Academy had dominated the London exhibition season with its huge, institutionalised showings. It was the leading gallery, not only for those who were knowledgeable about art but also for a large public, upwards of two or three hundred thousand of whom paid a shilling a time for a visit. Paintings had to survive hanging frame to frame, and careers were graded up and down as artists' works were hung 'on the line' or not. Watercolours, when they were shown, were invariably treated as drawings and hung in a separate room. Among the paintings, monumental canvasses sent by the leading artists of the day were the centrepieces of each year's show.

Langley, having found in watercolour the medium best suited to his own expression and which best suited the market he was beginning to find for his work, chose the less oppressive and only slightly less prestigious arena of the watercolour painters' Royal Institute. There, in successive years from 1883 to 1891, he showed nine major watercolours, each in its turn the pinnacle of his annual

PAGE 10
But men must work and women must weep, Though storms be sudden and waters deep, And the harbour bar be moaning 1882
watercolour, 90.5 x 53cm
(Birmingham Museums and Art Gallery)

The first major painting Langley showed at the RI in its prestigious gallery in Piccadilly in 1883. Besides a smaller watercolour from Leicester there are two drawings, one black and white and one sepia (also in Birmingham). The lines are from 'The Three Fishers' by Charles Kingsley, where they run as a refrain through three verses. The same lines were used by more than one other artist of the 1880s — the poem was a favourite at the time.

This is the first of Langley's works in which a tragedy at sea is presented indirectly, in its impact on the family at home. It became a theme to which he returned for some of his most ambitious works.

output, before he first showed an oil painting at the Academy in 1892. He had, in fact, during his first ten years of exhibiting in London, produced a few oils and shown them at the Oil Painters' Institute (in 1883, 1885 and 1886) but it was as a watercolour painter that his reputation was made.

The climate in art in the late 1870s and very early 1880s was broadly divided into what was considered high art, mostly costume pieces of high moral tone, and the new and more approachable genre painting. This last was epitomised by Dutch painting of the time, generally known as the Hague School.[1] Lying behind this

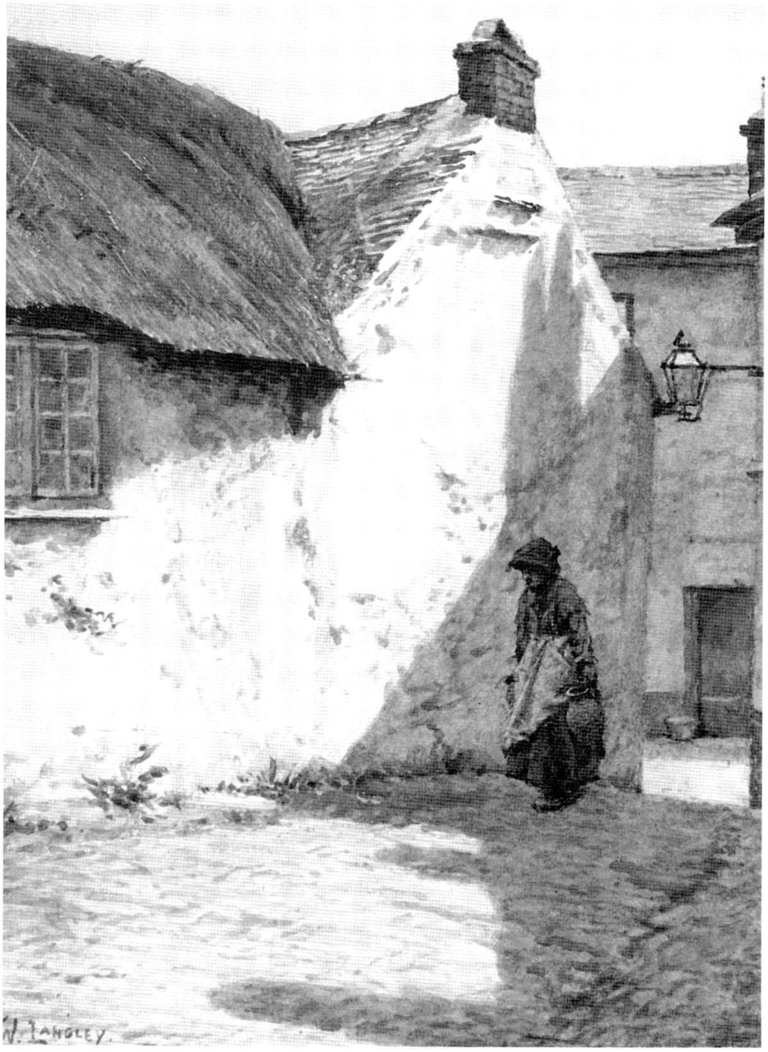

broad division was the far more fundamental difference between the approaches to painting represented by Whistler on the one hand and Ruskin (and by extension, the Pre-Raphaelites) on the other. While Whistler stood for romantic and purely aesthetic concerns in painting, Ruskin proposed an aesthetic governed by ideas and a quasi-scientific exactitude. Their confrontation in the notorious court case was in 1878.[2] At the time, however, though both were influential figures, their differences were a much less obvious strand in the pattern of contemporary art than that represented by the paintings of the Hague School. The Dutch artists opened a wide range of possibilities for an art in which the lives of hard-working people were taken to carry certain ideas about art and authenticity. A leading figure among them was Jozef Israels, who in 1855 began to take subjects from the fishing community at Zandvoort. His *Ida, the Fisherman's Daughter* enjoyed great success and was widely known through its reproduction in an engraving in 1860, while his *Cottage Madonna* of 1867 is typical of the religious tone he often applied. The three Maris brothers were important for the Hague School, not least because of their links with Paris and French plein air painting. The School emerged in Holland, in Paris and in London in the 1870s, establishing the idea that contemporary art should concern itself with the sea, with landscape and with working people.

The tradition of landscape painting in Britain had been refreshed in the 1850s, notably by David Cox, who attracted painters to follow him to Bettws-y-Coed, and by Millais and Ruskin at Brig o' Turk in the Trossachs. Ruskin's influential *Modern Painters* was published between 1843 and 1860; Dickens' *Bleak House* and *Hard Times*, the most pointed of his social commentaries, appeared between 1852 and 1854; these could be taken as points of reference in the development of new meanings for landscape and for genre art. William Powell Frith, himself a famous figure at the time, reported to a Parliamentary Committee in 1866 that landscape and genre art were the only kind that existed in England.[3] This somewhat over-simplified view was presumably based on Frith's own vision but it points up the importance of subject as a statement of intent at that time. The

PAGE 12
Sunshine and Shadow c1890
watercolour, 36 x 25cm

Jozef Israels
The Cottage Madonna c1867
(Detroit Institute of Arts, bequest of Nell Ford Torrey)

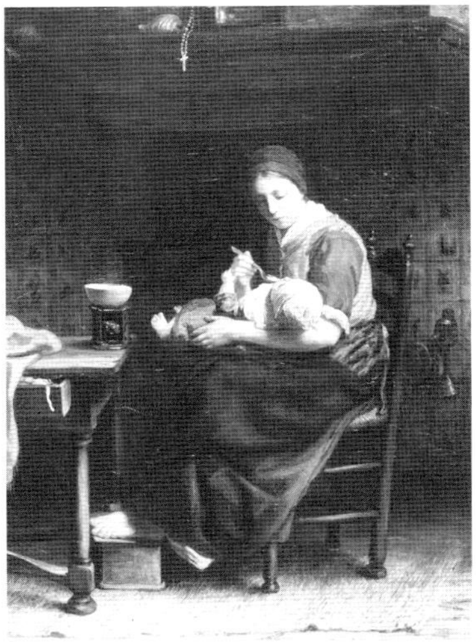

PAGE 15
Time moveth not, our being 'tis that moves 1882
watercolour, 19.7 x 11.5cm

One of at least two preliminary studies for the major watercolour. See page 60.

idea of a worthy subject for art was changed, in that worth itself, rather than being inherent in the subject alone — as in, say, a moment from the Bible — was seen as being conferred by the art upon its subject, and thus also by the fulfilment of a moral duty to portray poor people's plight.

The influence of French painting, and that of Jules Bastien-Lepage in particular, was important not only for a direct influence on style and subject but also for the painters who, after Lepage's inspiration, brought his message through into English painting in a number of different ways. Besides Stanhope Forbes, whose *Street in Brittany* was a success at the Academy in 1882, there were Clausen, Guthrie, La Thangue, Lavery and a number of future Newlyn School artists.[4] Following his first success at the Academy in 1878 Lepage's reiteration of a classic genre ideal was in the ascendant and the argument became polarised into history painting versus genre, much as the argument between abstraction and figuration stagnated into rhetoric in mid-twentieth century art criticism. The message carried by French painting's style and subject matter was spread out and down through many levels by reputation as well as by showings in London, as an increasing number of mostly gentlemanly painters came back from their studies in mostly conservative Parisian ateliers and comfortable Brittany hotels.

In the circles in which he found himself in Birmingham and London at the beginning of the 1880s, Langley was surrounded by a great variety of contemporary work. He was well aware of the importance of seeing the work of other artists. For him, as for many, one important opportunity had been through the spread of illustrated magazines, notably the *Graphic*, founded in 1869. From its pages the work of Herkomer, Fildes and Holl reached a wide audience. It could perhaps be argued that work seen in the form of engravings and to the scale of a page gave added weight to the importance of subject as. It must also have distorted a painter's style, especially the light painterly touch of a plein air painter, and probably his intention also. The magazine's illustrations promulgated a whole world of images: 'It is not too much to say that there was a visible change in the selection of subjects by

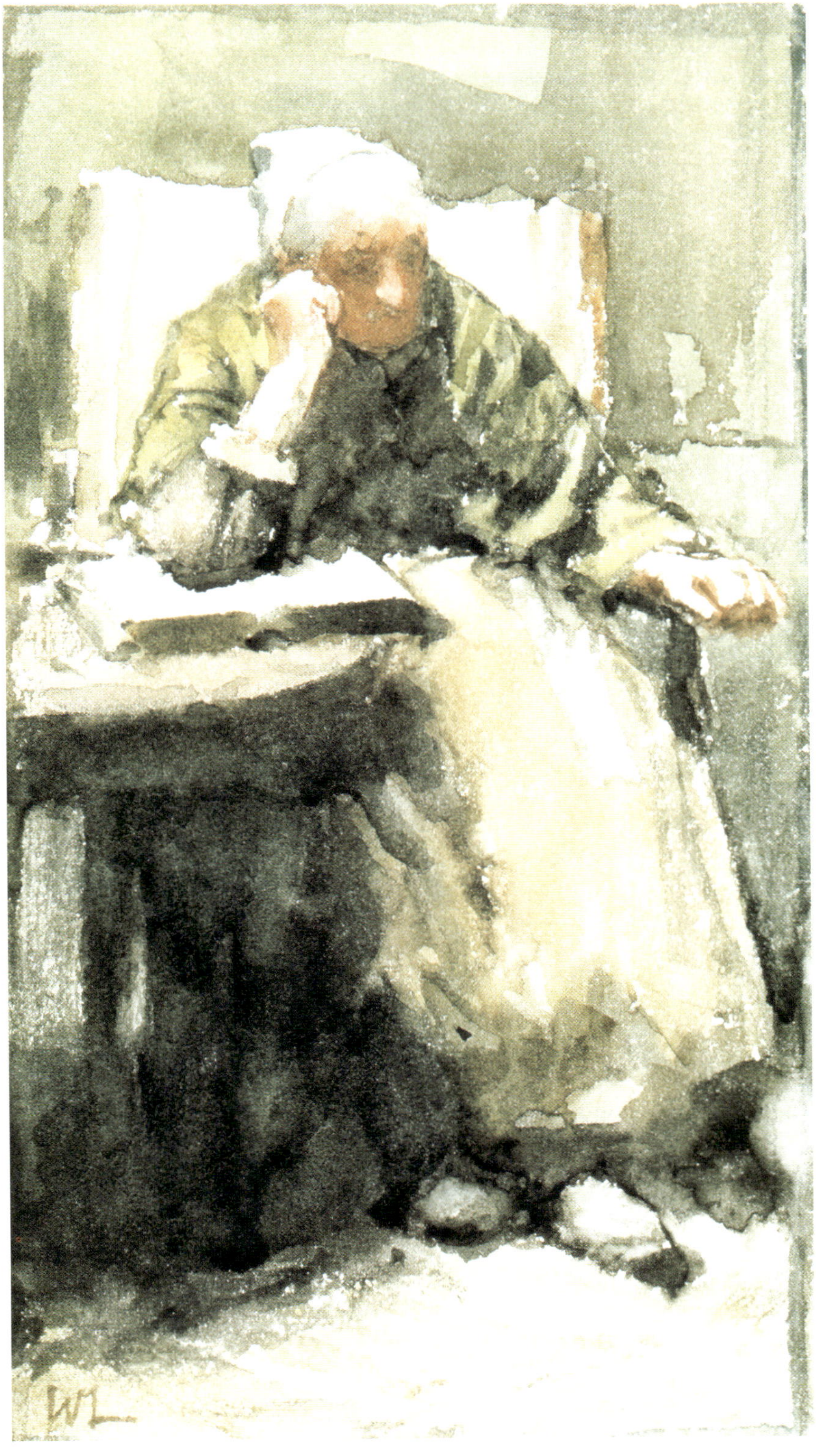

Among the Missing — Scene in a Cornish Fishing Village 1884
watercolour (reproduced from a contemporary print)

In Newlyn, a notice of boats and men lost in the far-off North Sea herring fishery would be put up outside the telegraph station at the old Post Office. This watercolour was shown at the RI in the spring of 1884, where it was proclaimed 'a hit'.

It was reproduced in the *Illustrated London News* and the *Graphic*, and hinted of as a Chantrey Bequest purchase, though this did not happen.

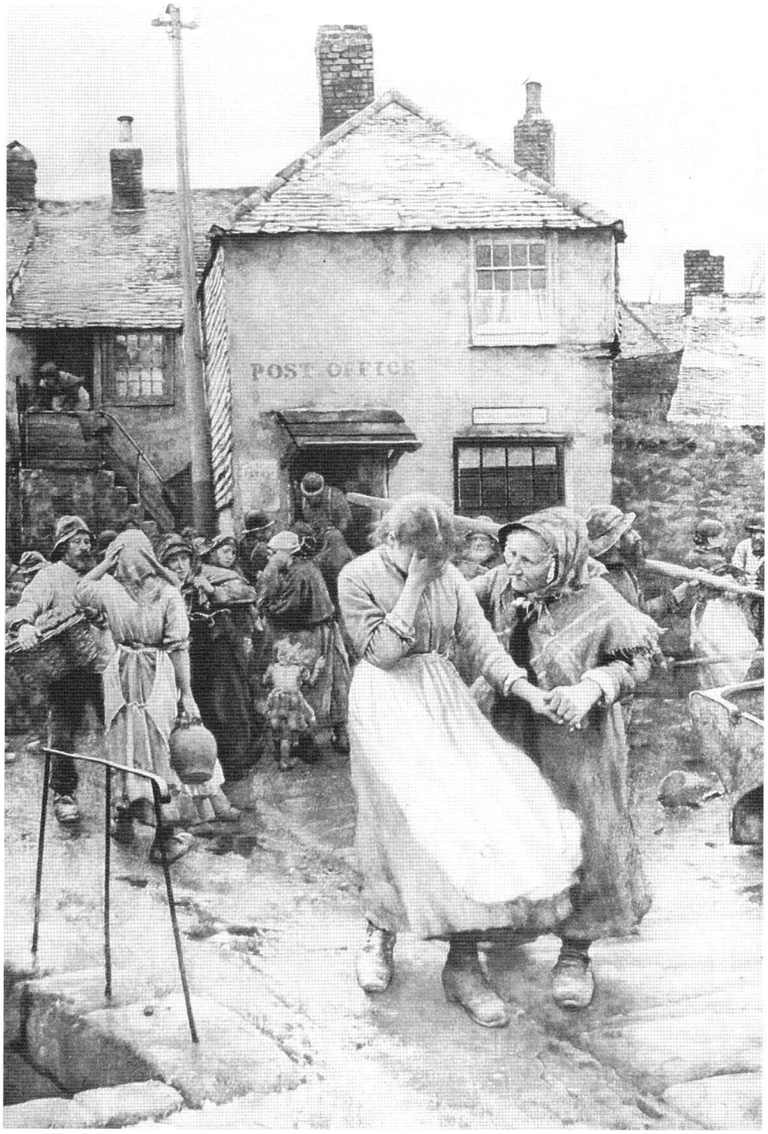

painters in England after the advent of the *Graphic* ... it was a lesson in life and a lesson in art.'[5]

The expansive climate of the mid-nineteenth century had provided civic leaders with both the good intentions and the means to initiate museums and art galleries for the benefit of their citizens, and all over the country new institutions were established in which fine and applied art was displayed with pride. Art societies formed in the early years of the century played a part and it was often an individual benefactor who brought the gallery into being. In Birmingham, the Royal Birmingham Society of Artists, the Midland Institute and the city's municipal art gallery all provided galleries where young artists could see paintings and where they could aspire to show their own work.

From the middle of the nineteenth century the art trade grew in importance and expanded to provide a layer of trade expertise and salesmanship between artists and clients. A dealer became an important partner for an artist, often publicising his work by arranging for reproductions (generally engravings before the rapid expansion of other technical means got under way) to be made and distributed. He was able to underwrite an artist's time, as J W Thrupp did for Langley, by commissioning work as well as making sales to private buyers that had previously been conducted only from the walls of the Academy and other grand venues, or by discreet private contacts between buyer and artist. In London, the Grosvenor Gallery opened in 1877 and became the famous and fashionable showplace of the Aesthetic Movement through the 1880s. It showed a great range of work in far better conditions than hitherto and must have begun to break down the hegemony of the Academy and Institute shows. In 1880-81, it mounted an exhibition of watercolours by contemporary artists which improved the reception of, and opportunities for, watercolour painters. The Dudley, where Langley had his first success in London, had opened in 1865 in the Egyptian Hall in Piccadilly and showed work by new artists before they became absorbed into a society or institute. Such galleries and other dealers were often the means by which paintings from other countries could be seen. Their interests led to French painting, as well as Hague School works, being shown in London in the 1870s.

Dealers, working in the prosperous industrial cities as well as in London, brought about a new era of collecting by people never previously seen to involve themselves with such things as art. These new clients' tastes inevitably pushed the balance towards affordable, approachable and generally conservative works, though the hot competition of the most avid of them often raised sale prices at the very top of the market. One titled lady reportedly

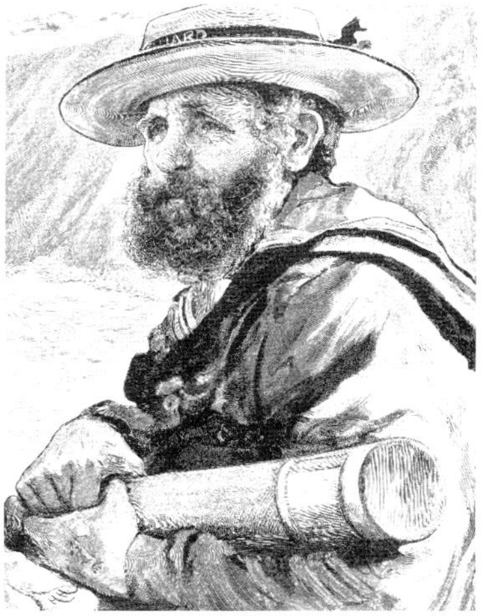

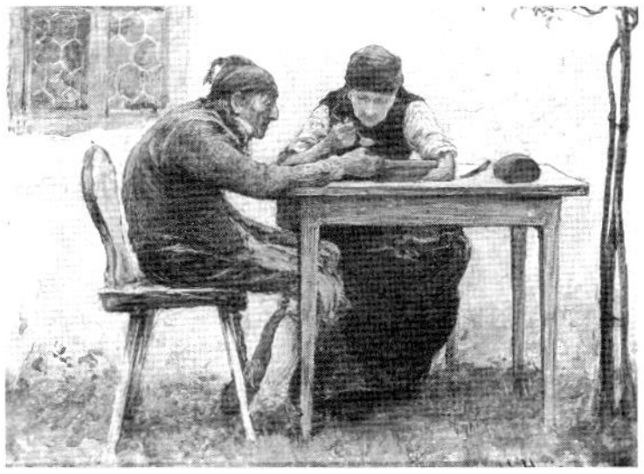

Hubert von Herkomer
Abendbrot 1872
(Watford Museum)

TOP
Hubert von Herkomer
The Coastguard
as engraved for the *Graphic* September 1879 (National Art Library, Victoria and Albert Museum)

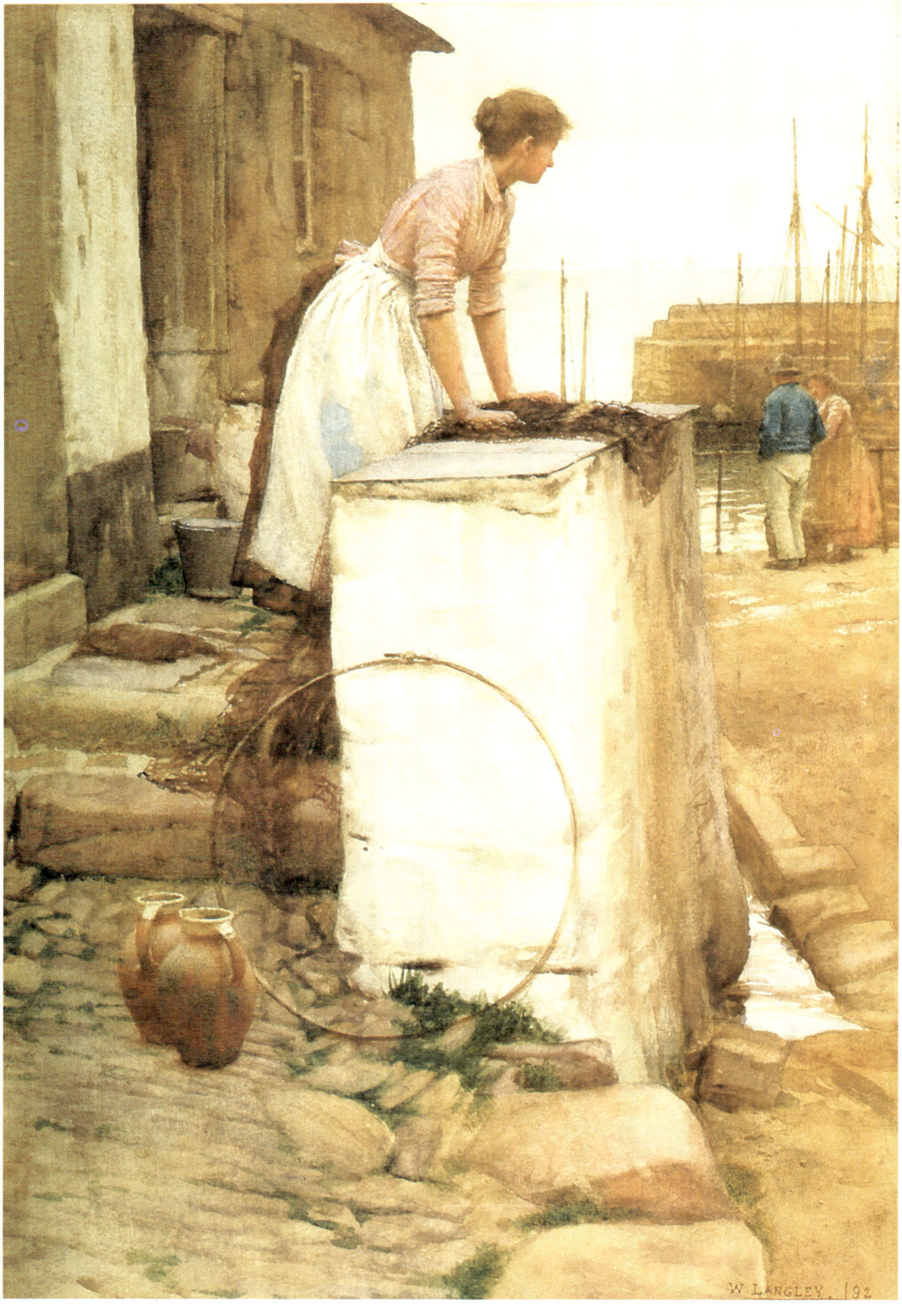
W. LANGLEY. '92

commented on the higher prices and the lowlier names in recorded sales lists.[6] It was also the era of artists who could live respectably by their art and whose social position was newly acceptable in consequence. Artists moved into large houses and their studios became comfortable bourgeois settings in which subjects could pose among upholstered sofas, soft drapery and carpets. Langley himself may be an extreme case — possibly the most extreme — of an artist who created his own social position by sheer hard work, but many others were carried, by affluence, a few rungs up the class-structured social ladder of the time.

When he began to exhibit in London Walter Langley was already involved in Birmingham's art world, showing at the Society of Artists and founding, with a group of young contemporaries, the Birmingham Art Circle. A Birmingham 'School' was described as such from about the middle of the century and by 1866 the Society found itself showing an increasing number of locally based artists alongside the work brought in from London and elsewhere. At that time there was a separate spring exhibition of watercolours, mostly in the tradition of English landscape painting like that of Cox and De Wint. The Pre-Raphaelites were seen there especially because Burne-Jones was a Birmingham man. A well known Birmingham watercolour of 1867, William Jabez Muckley's *The Song of the Shirt*, is interesting for its prevision of the idea of art taking up the cause, with modest but telling means, of a working woman. The Society also found buyers for the new home-grown artists like Langley. He had emerged from the back-to-backs in a city where liberal, reformist, public-spirited principles were gaining upon the old order, under such men as George Dawson and Joseph Chamberlain. Nonconformist principles were brought to practical effect in schools and the creation of opportunities for young people. Langley's family were Unitarians, a nonconformist sect who, together with the Quakers, had an influence on the city's affairs far out of proportion to their actual numbers. Birmingham was a fast-expanding city, a seed-bed of independent thought, where many small businesses, like Biermann's lithography workshop which employed Langley, formed a working community

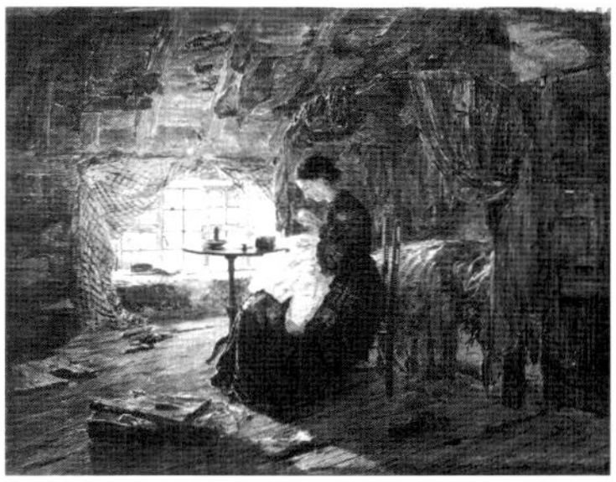

William Jabez Muckley
The Song of the Shirt 1867
(Birmingham Museums and Art Gallery)

PAGE 18
Woman looking down to a harbour 1892
watercolour, 45.7 x 30.5cm

This may be a Mousehole scene, though it has been known as 'Newlyn Harbour'.

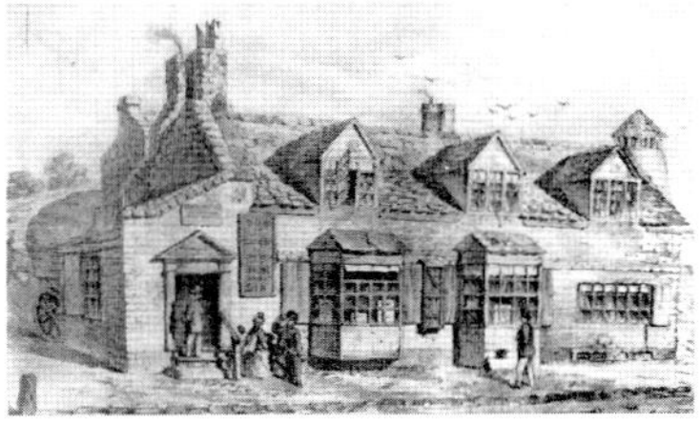

The Dog and Duck Inn, Birmingham 1871
medium and size not known, reproduced from a newspaper photograph

quite different to that of other industrial centres where only a few big employers held sway. Moreover, there were enough manufactories of goods that had to be well designed and stylish for the look of things to be important to trade as well as the sheer quantities produced. Against this background, Langley's training was a model of the ideals spearheaded by Prince Albert and his Great Exhibition, which sought to create a climate of opportunity and promote the highest standards of excellence in applied art (which today, of course, would be called design). When Langley went to the National Art Training School in South Kensington in 1872 it was founded upon the principle of drawing as 'a language of accurate description'[7] and the provision of the best possible examples of decorative arts for the students to study.

While he was still in effect a student of art in the service of industry, however, Langley was pursuing his own work as a painter. He travelled out from the teeming streets of the city into the countryside to paint and draw. He was responding not only to his own obvious inclination and to a desire to set himself aside from the commercial art absolutely necessary to his financial survival in those days, but at the same time to an idea about what constituted serious art. By finding country subjects he was aligning himself within the tradition of English landscape painting, and as he began to succeed with watercolours he established for his work a principle in which subject and aesthetic dovetail in a very straightforward way. Later, in remaining determined to make watercolour his primary medium, Langley was building upon an early aptitude for drawing and years of patient development of his technique. The ability he showed when he began to mature as an artist had been brought out by classes in applied as well as in fine art, and years of hard work in Biermann's lithography workshop.

Between his early etching *The Dog and Duck Inn* and Langley's designs for silverware the attainment of skill is considerable, as can also be seen in the gulf between *The Picture Book* and *A Fisher Girl*. But between these early works and Langley's first Newlyn watercolours there is a more serious difference. When he first went to Newlyn in 1880 and 1881, he was no doubt thinking along conventional lines about views and portraits (that is, not formal portraits but studies of people) and in his sketchbooks and watercolours done on the spot, Langley proceeded as any artist would, exploring the picturesque in the streets and the harbour as well as in the figures round about. In his studio watercolours he worked from models with props to produce an equivalent for what he had seen of the life of the place. He was already a professional artist and his arrival in Newlyn in fact coincided with his maturity as a painter; he was able to bring to bear on the subjects that most attracted him there a painterly vision of great expressive power.

Two words often applied to Langley's Newlyn watercolours require some qualification from today's perspective. They are 'reality' and 'freshness'. Both were liberally used in contemporary reviews by writers who did not hesitate to cite standards of reality when they were dealing with matters of style. The idea of fidelity to nature was confused between realistic presentation (that is, correctly represented light, shade, colour and tone), and realism in the sense of a warts-and-all depiction of a mundane subject. While the Pre-Raphaelites' close-focus realism was hailed as scientific perception, they 'mingled their intensely observed particular with portentous moments from history and religion',[8] and it gave way before Lepage's unvarnished truth, so called because of its subject as much, if not more, than for his treatment of it. 'Fresh' as a term was also applied indiscriminately to paint and subject. This was a particularly well worn term for Newlyn painters, with such a concentration of artists looking at the same beguiling set of subjects. In Langley's case his choices, and the material and structure of the major watercolours, underline the essentially graphic nature of his painterly approach. It was his nature to paint clearly. The subtlety in his work is not obtained by blurring edges nor by the use of fashionable painterly conventions such as were spawned by the Brittany square-brush technique. Interest in the picturesque (another word frequently brought into play) had graduated down, broadly speaking, from the grand Romantic scale to the incidental. The range of subjects that could be considered picturesque was extended, to the bleakest landscape

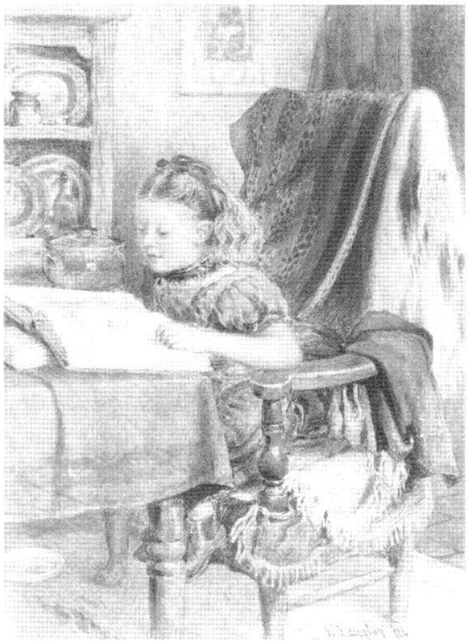

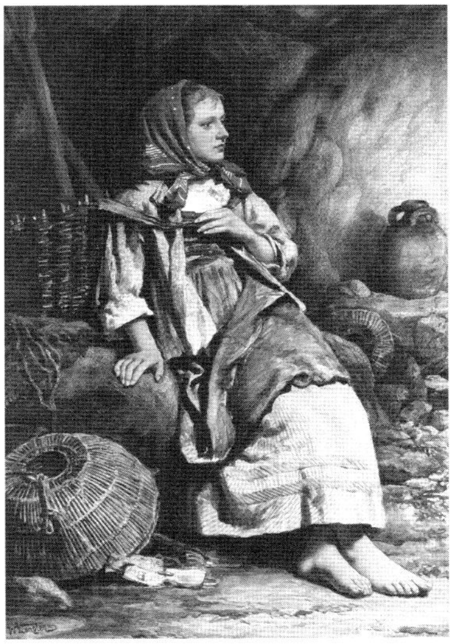

A fisher-girl c1877
watercolour, 64.1 x 44.2cm

Evidently a costumed model posed with props, probably intended as an Italian fisher-girl, Mediterranean and exotic subjects being much in vogue at the time.

TOP
The Picture Book 1876
watercolour, 31.8 x 22.2cm

on the one hand and to small domestic details on the other, though all were taken to express ideas about the human condition.

Langley, then, was working at a time when Realism, meaning the presentation of working people and working countryside, was at the heart of an avant garde that had begun in Holland and France. In England the argument for this kind of realism was based upon its use as a symbol of a new truth set in opposition to earlier academic precepts about what was or was not Art. Its most obvious protagonists were perhaps Leighton and Alma-Tadema, both hugely successful since the 1870s. They and other well known and well publicised history painters brought forward a new kind of Symbolism to add moral clothing to their essentially fleshy paintings. Although far removed from Symbolism of their kind, Langley's work does seem to carry a charge of symbolic meaning, albeit couched in relatively modest narrative terms, that adds a certain gravity to his major paintings. The overt narrative content of some, such as *In a Cornish Fishing Village — Departure of the Fleet for the North*, indeed seems to anticipate the cinema; the wide horizontal format he occasionally employed makes one think of the wide screen and the heroism of the figures in his major works also sometimes calls to mind the language spoken by film.

Brittany probably gave Langley a taste of the camaraderie to be found in a colony of artists away from their homes, and from his Birmingham days he knew how enlivening life in a group of like-minded painters could be. When he went to west Cornwall with Edwin Harris, however, he can hardly have known they would be the precursors of the pack of artists that descended on the place in their wake. Harris and Langley found in Newlyn what they hoped would be their Zandvoort, their Pont Aven, and Stanhope Forbes wrote of it later as 'a sort of English Concarneau'.[9] Above all, Langley wanted an extension of the landscape he had gone out from Birmingham to find, where he could fulfill the idea he had for painting figures and their setting, for an authentic mis-en-scene. He and Harris immediately embraced the working possibilities so plentifully provided by the place and their choice marked it out for others at a propitious moment.

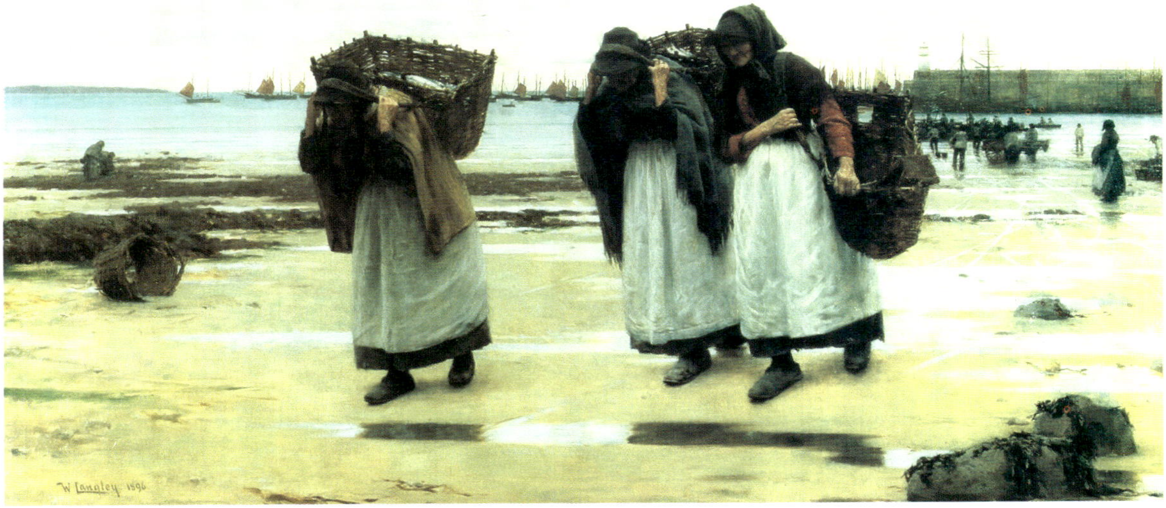

Breadwinners 1896
oil, 117 x 216cm

There are a number of studies for the women carrying fish creels on their backs and a watercolour version of this picture is in the Penlee House Gallery and Museum collection (see page 103).

Breadwinners is set on the beach at Newlyn with the end of the South Pier beyond. It is debatable whether the North Pier (opened in 1894) should be visible and therefore whether Langley has quite radically altered the scene for the purposes of this painting. It remains among the simplest and most monumental of his major compositions, reminiscent more of much earlier French plein-air painting of peasant subjects than of Newlyn subjects in general. There is a later and less telling work on this subject, *The Woman's Part* 1905.

The sequence of arrivals through the 1880s has been well documented here in Roger Langley's biography and elsewhere,[10] and the arrivals in St Ives likewise.[11] From the outset the two fishing communities, one each side of the narrow Penwith peninsula, were set apart in terms of art as well as by six miles of narrow road. In St Ives the emphasis was more towards marine painting and coastal landscape; in Newlyn figure painting was the main concern, even if the harbour and the boats still played an important part. As the decade went on, people came and went in a free flowing development of personalities and painting activity that cannot have failed to provide Langley with a nourishing background for his own work. He seems to have taken part with reasonable enthusiasm, or perhaps one should say as much enthusiasm as the tensions and stresses of a working artist would allow, in the round of suppers, picnics, theatricals and cricket. His mind was on his work and on the problems of exhibiting and selling, and he may have taken the social side for what it was worth in terms of keeping up with the game, as it were, as well as for relaxation.

In January 1884, Stanhope Forbes arrived, and immediately

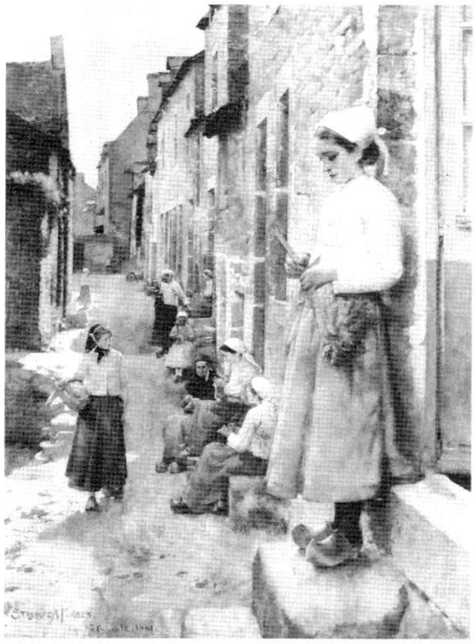

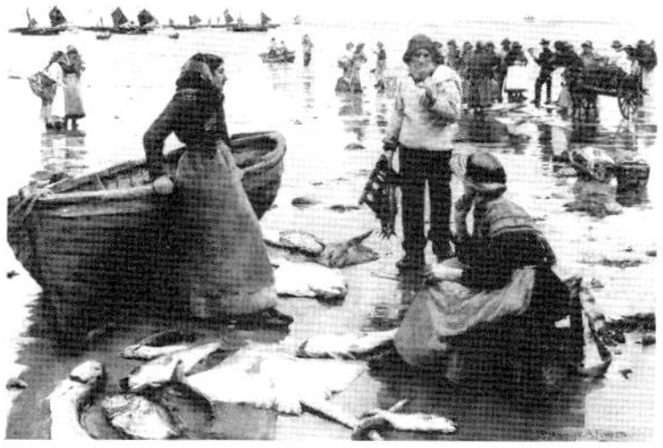

Stanhope Forbes
A Fish Sale on a Cornish Beach
1885
(Plymouth City Museum and
Art Gallery)

TOP
Stanhope Forbes
A Street in Brittany 1881
(National Museums and Galleries on
Merseyside, Walker Art Gallery)

took a leading role in the Newlyn artists' colony. He was well educated, from a cultured family, had travelled and worked in Brittany. The success of his *Street in Brittany* at the Academy in 1882, the charm of which was seen to overcome its technical flaws,[12] brought him to decide on plein-air painting and to seek out a Cornish context for his work. The success of firstly his *Fish Sale on a Cornish Beach* in 1885 and then *The Health of the Bride* in 1889 placed him at the head of the Newlyn brigade in the eyes of commentators and of the public. His central role in Newlyn affairs can, in retrospect, be seen to have been partly due to his natural assumption of that position and partly the fact that the emphasis of so much Newlyn history hitherto has been based upon his writings — including the daily chronicle provided by his letters to his mother — and those of his great friend Norman Garstin, among others. The opening of his School of Painting and, it might be argued, his marriage to Elizabeth Armstrong, consolidated his position.

There can be no harm in looking at the shape of things in Newlyn from the point of view that Stanhope Forbes provides, but it would be as well to remain conscious of this particular perspective. His relationship with Langley was not apparently a real friendship, though they rubbed along together well enough. Langley's position as a watercolour artist made a clear distinction between himself and those, like Forbes, for whom the Academy was the context. The difference in medium points up differences in style and also in intention. This is not to say that other artists' work is unimportant in relation to Langley's but simply that a comparison with Stanhope Forbes, as representing the main stream of Newlyn painting, may offer some insights. For the most part Langley's figures are closer to themselves in life and are set in cooler, more straightforward compositions. In works like *Disaster! Scene in a Cornish Fishing Village* of 1889 with its elaborate tumble of rain-soaked material and the central woman with her indoor apron thrown up over her hair, Langley comes closest to the figures set to play comparable roles in the work of Bramley, Forbes and others, whose intention was more to paint a scene and place their figures in it with elaborate care. Their work seldom holds the drama of *Disaster!*, while Langley achieves the monumental balances and breadth of Forbes' *Fish Sale* or Garstin's *The Rain it Raineth*, for instance, in such works as *Village Idyll* and *Breadwinners*. Frank Bramley's *A Hopeless Dawn* of 1888, generally regarded as the outstanding painting of his career and certainly his most successful at the time, deals with a woman's grief but its more obvious gesture of despair sets it apart from Langley's treatments both in terms of style and composition. A later painting of Langley's, *Between the Tides* of 1901, could be compared with Stanhope Forbes' *The Old Pier Steps*, 1911; Langley's crisper, fresher style provides a more sharply focused composition than do the rather heavy-handed painterly conventions of Forbes' later work, as can be seen in the light on the water and the directional brushstrokes modelling the clothes.

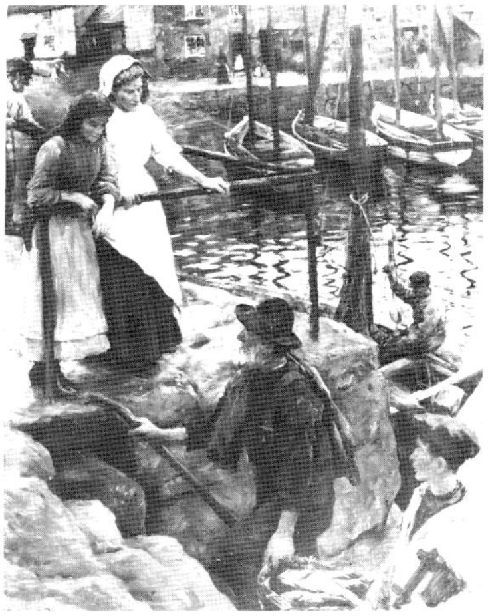

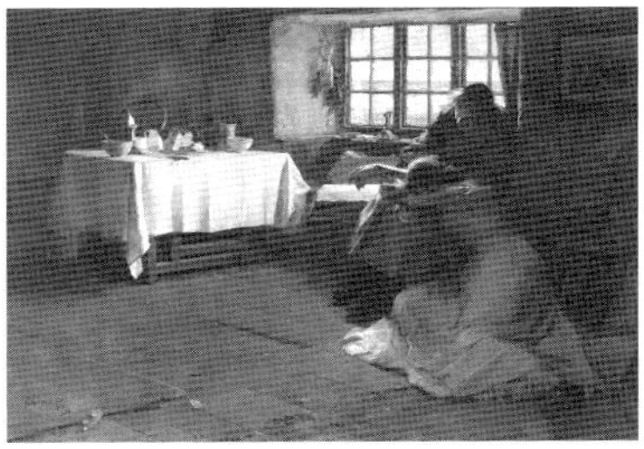

Frank Bramley
A Hopeless Dawn 1888
(Tate Gallery)

TOP
Stanhope Forbes
The Old Pier Steps 1911
(Bradford Art Galleries and Museums)

Through the 1880s and 1890s in Newlyn it was Langley's practice, conventionally enough, to make small sketches and working drawings, often with notes, on the spot in pocketable sketch books. Besides lively observations of things around him these include little studies for compositions where the idea for a major painting is set out. From these might emerge more substantial drawings and studies, sometimes on the spot and sometimes in the studio, as he developed an idea. These reveal how he orchestrated a figure, a setting, the light and shadow to bring about the expression of the painting he had in mind. Most significant are the monumental paintings with which he sought to make his most important statements, but the most diverse and the work by which he is best appreciated are the painting she made from life. They formed the bulk of his exhibited work each year. Some have the character of studies and indeed were made as preliminaries to more formal compositions. They often were heads or single figures set in a believable natural setting, in an interior or in the open air, and with the big exhibition pieces that were his most impressive successes at the time they undoubtedly represent the best of his work to us now, a century later. In the painterly language in which these more modest paintings were put

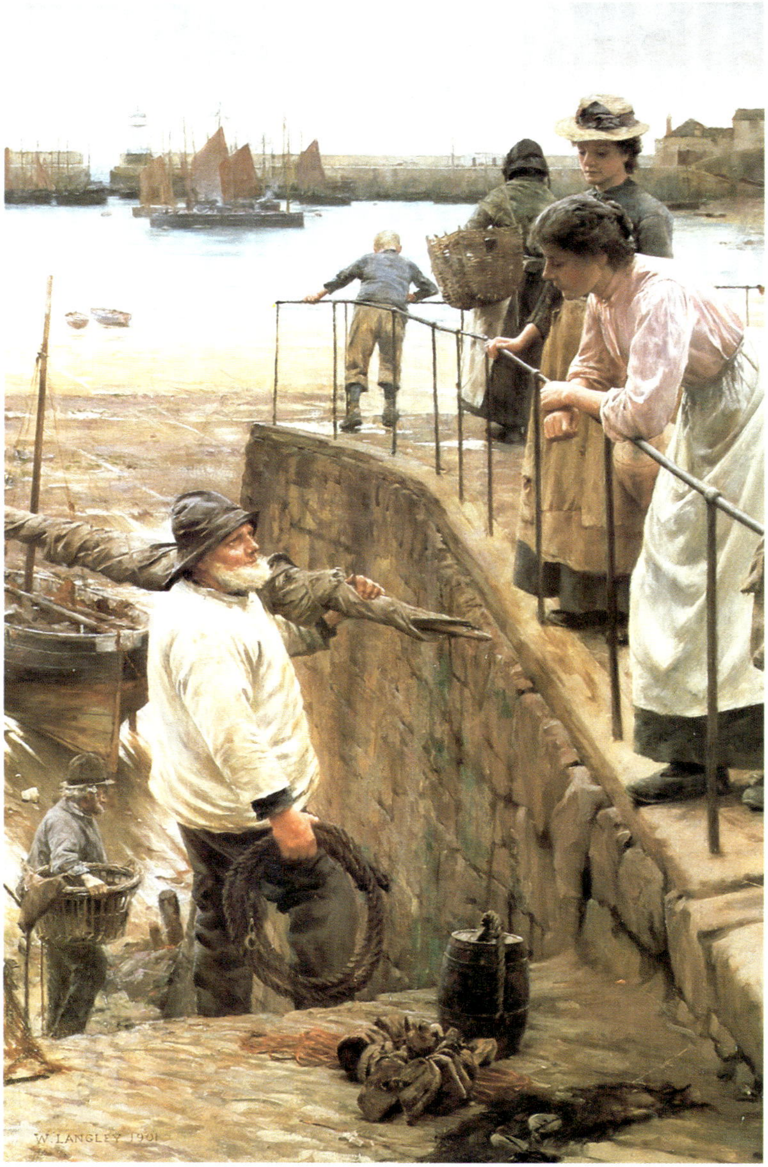

Between the Tides 1901
oil, 152.4 x 101.6cm
(Warrington Museum and
Art Gallery)

With the turn of the century and his new marriage to Ethel Pengelly, Langley turned to calmer and sunnier subjects. Paintings such as this and *A Cornish Idyll* 1902 (see page 114) are in contrast to harbour scenes like *Disaster* (see page 74) and *Never Morning wore to evening* (see page 110).

down on paper, lies the most profound expression, the essential character of Langley's painting.

When he was painting directly from a model, outside or in the studio, Langley's control of a loaded brush, of fluid watercolour paint, allowed extraordinary accuracy in expressing the look and feeling of the figure. The clarity of his vision could be laid down immediately. Though drawing lies behind this directness it does not mitigate the painting. Langley's aim seems to be to lay the paint down without contrivance, though the contrivance of the whole work is part of its rationale. The thought and preparation with which he set out for himself the pre-conditions for such work included the idea, the composition, the figure, the setting, the props and the light. All these were taken as he needed them, mostly from things seen (and usually sketched). He used a wooden palette painted white and watercolour with body colour, sometimes scratching through the paint surface to the paper tone. The chairs and tables of his interiors were softened as the composition demanded, with drapery, often an old quilt, and the white-washed cottage walls had pictures cut from magazines pinned up, or drying herbs or some utensil. Flowers, geraniums in pots or a jar of nasturtiums, or odd pieces of china would provide telling references to diurnal life and growth as well as points of colour. His feeling for the people he took as models seems unvaryingly warm and his response to them was clearly an important factor in the ultimate realisation of his work. Although the results are not portraits, Langley's models are not figures either. Their forms and faces are not elements in compositions but the central subject of the work. In the major watercolours such as *Village Idyll* these individuals are brought together into the broader and more ambitious compositions in which Langley sought to extend his visual language. His major watercolours must have represented for langley an expression of his allegiance to the world of watercolours and drawing rather than opposition to the medium that Langley himself began to use more as his career progressed. That they might remind someone today of film has already been touched on and may be merely superficial, but their relationship to photography is undoubtedly important in the pursuit of an understanding of how imagery works. For Langley himself, however, the visual language he developed was one in which telling (narrative) and presenting (formalism) were tied absolutely to the act of painting.

When Walter Langley died in 1922 his widow Ethel remained in their house in Penzance. She emptied the studio, leaving its contents packed away and turning piles of frames to the wall in her sitting room. At her death during the Second World War, the family found themselves in possession of an archive that recorded Langley's long working life but it was not until the mid-1980s that the attention of a new public for the Newlyn School caused his work to receive serious consideration again. With another decade since then and a calmer and more discerning market prevailing, Langley's paintings are getting the breathing space they need to stake again the claim that *Time moveth not* made for him in 1882. His position among his contemporaries has been endorsed by the enduring qualities of his paintings. His major exhibition paintings remain admirable in the context of late-nineteenth century art but now, perhaps, we can best witness his achievements and his steadfast integrity, in the watercolours Langley painted of the Newlyn people, straight from life.

Elizabeth Knowles

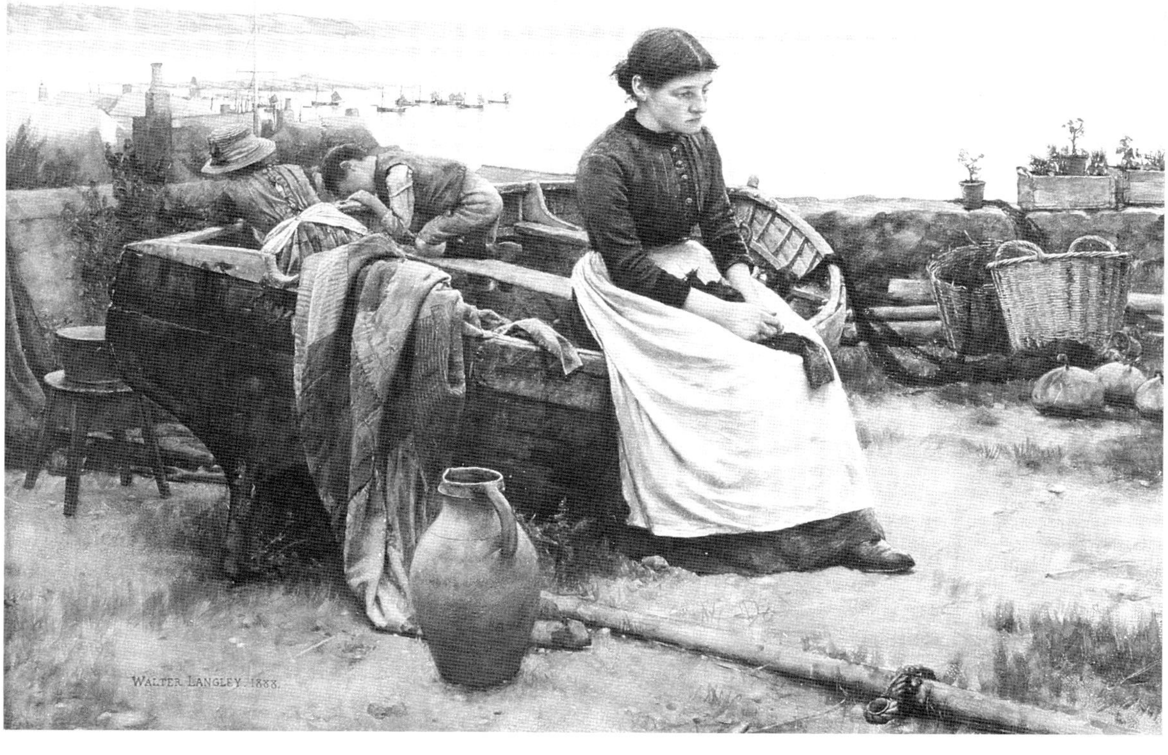

Notes

1 See the catalogue *The Hague School: Dutch Masters of the 19th Century* Grand Palais, Paris, the Royal Academy and the Gemeentemuseum, The Hague 1983.

2 A Whistler 'Nocturne' exhibited at the Grosvenor Gallery in 1877 had provoked Ruskin's response that he was '...flinging a pot of paint in the public's face' and Whistler sued for libel. The arguments were rehearsed in court and widely reported.

3 See the Report of the Select Committee on Art Union Laws 1866 no332, quoted in Paula Gillett *The Victorian Painter's World,* 1990 p4 and note 12 on p243.

4 See Caroline Fox and Francis Greenacre *Painting in Newlyn 1880-1930,* Barbican Art Gallery 1985 pp13-16 and Caroline Fox *Stanhope Forbes and the Newlyn School,* 1995 pp8-9.

5 Herkomer, in the obituary of the magazine's founder William Luzon Thomas, quoted in Paula Gillett, op.cit. p104. The *Graphic* was a fortnightly illustrated news magazine of enormous scope, bringing images of world events, inaccessible places, celebrities and home news items as well as reproductions of paintings and thus presenting art in the milieu of reportage.

6 Lady Eastlake, quoted in Paula Gillett, op.cit. p4.

7 Richard Redgrave, who had set up a system of numbered stages through which students were required to work and which allowed specialisations to be followed, quoted in Christopher Frayling *The Royal College of Art: One Hundred and Fifty Years of Art and Design,* pp41-42. Prince Albert's initiative for a museum and an art school was carried through by Henry Cole though not without opposition at the time, notably from Ruskin.

8 Ian Jeffrey, essay in *Landscape in Britain* catalogue, Arts Council, Hayward Gallery 1983 and tour, p26.

9 Stanhope Forbes, letter, early 1884, in the Tate Gallery Archive, quoted in Caroline Fox, op.cit. and elsewhere.

10 See Caroline Fox and Francis Greenacre, op.cit and the unsigned letter published in the *Magazine of Art* 1898 referred to on p8.

11 See *St Ives 1939-64* catalogue, Tate Gallery 1985 and the chronology revised by David Brown for the subsequent Japanese version of the exhibition.

12 These being the poor reconciliation of the foreground figure with those behind it in terms of the perspective of the houses and the street.

PAGE 28

O! For the touch of a vanish'd hand And the sound of a voice that is still 1888
watercolour, 67.3 x 95.5cm
(Birmingham Museums and Art Gallery)

Among the most widely shown of Langley's watercolours, it was illustrated in the *Magazine of Art* (April 1889) and published as a print by the *Penny Magazine* (date unknown). The title is from Tennyson's 'Break, Break, Break'. The view is from Newlyn with the far side of Mount's Bay and the Lizard on the horizon. This was one of three major watercolours painted during 1888, one being *Disaster*, see page 74, and the other a large horizontal painting set on the same stone-walled vantage point with rooftops below at the left and Mount's Bay beyond, entitled *Village Idyll — After the buoyant happy days of youth comes the calm eventide of age.*

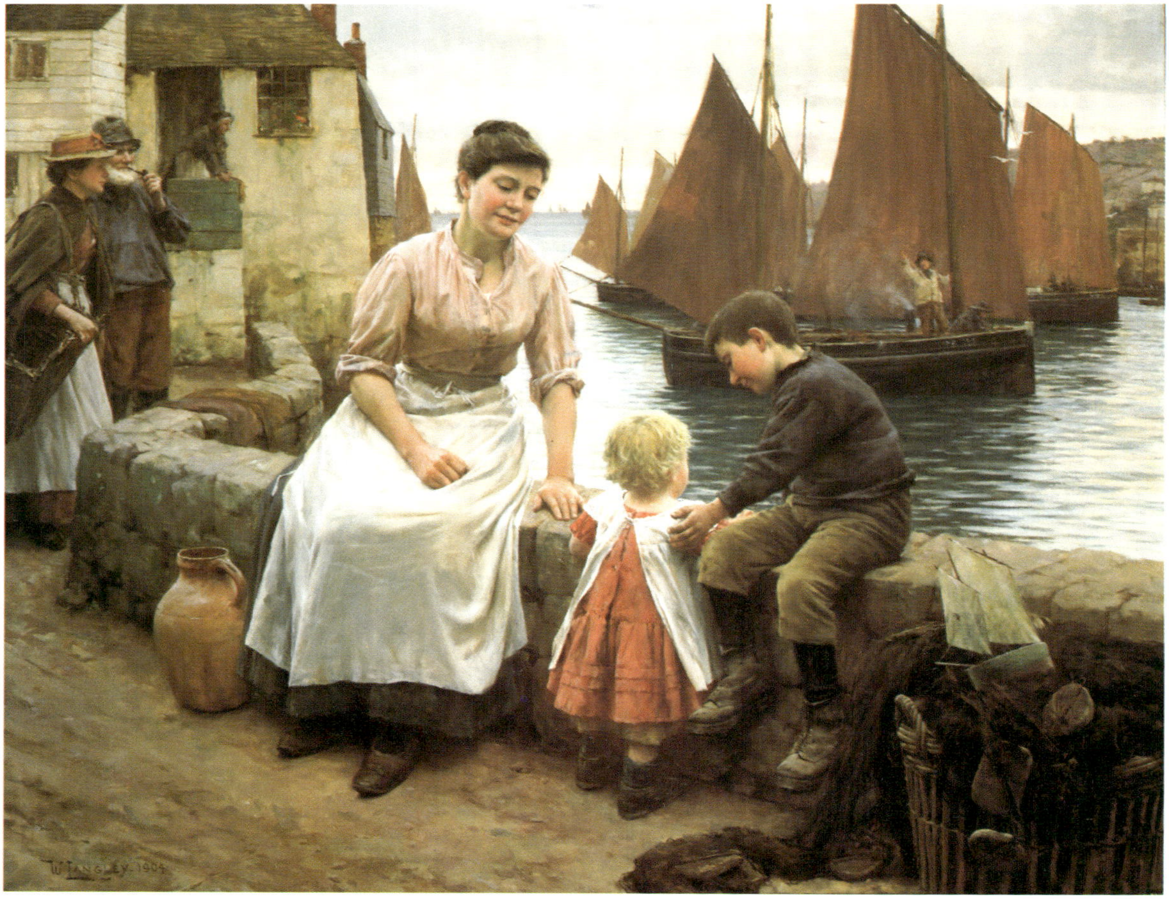

1852-1878 Early Days & Lithography

CHAPTER ONE

To most art collectors, the name Walter Langley doubtless conjures up a picture of Cornwall and its fisherfolk, yet his first thirty years were spent in Birmingham and it was there, and in the nearby hamlets of Nether and Over Whitacre, that his forbears had made their homes for some hundreds of years.[1] Walter's father, William Langley, grew up in Nether Whitacre, in a toll-house manned by his parents and uncle, but was sent at the age of fourteen to live with his grand-parents in Birmingham. There he was apprenticed to John Robinson, a tailor.

William seems to have learned his job well but he had little time in which to prepare himself for his future responsibilities. At the age of eighteen, and while still an apprentice, he married John's sixteen year-old grand-daughter, Mary Ann Robinson, who was then expecting their first child, Ellen. The young couple's early taste of hardship set the pattern for their future as Ellen was swiftly followed by twins Ann and Lucy, then Charlotte, Alfred, Mary, Alice, Walter, who was born on June 8, 1852, Minnie, Amy and Harriet. It is likely, too, that the eleven survivors tell only part of the story — Birmingham's infant mortality rate was higher than the national average and there are significant gaps between the recorded births.

The burgeoning family eked out a precarious existence in a succession of rented back-to-back courtyard houses in Irving Street, in the parish of St Thomas. Irving Street was part of a planned buffer-zone between the spacious estates of Edgbaston to the south and the slums of central Birmingham. The Langleys' near neighbours included a malthouse, a brass foundry and workshops

PAGE 30
The Greeting 1904
oil, 107 x 152cm

When shown at Newlyn Art Gallery in March 1904 prior to being sent up to the Academy, this was described in the *Cornish Telegraph* as being '...as usual, a Newlyn scene of great human interest', while the *Cornishman* reported it 'rich in colour and character study and felicitous in composition'. There is a watercolour of the same subject (1904, 26 x 31cm).

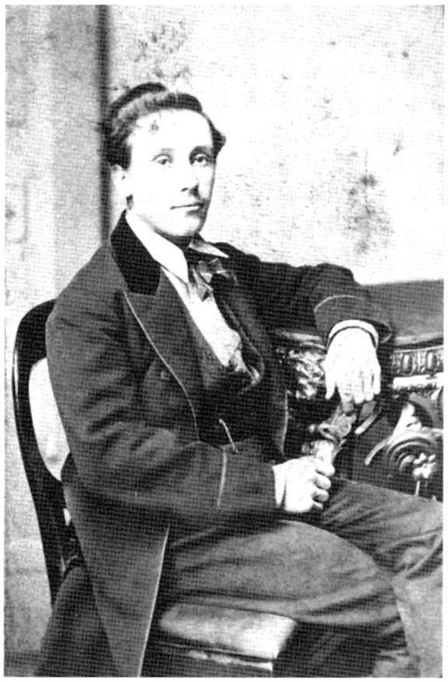

Walter Langley at fifteen
photograph by Sherrell of Birmingham

producing tin-plate, fancy leather, weighing machines, gas fittings and cabinets.

The children were put to work at an early age to supplement William's earnings as a journeyman-tailor which, though above the working-class average, were hopelessly outpaced by the growth of his family. The girls found employment in the local workshops and Alfred signed on at the nearby brass foundry. Walter might have followed his brother into the foundry in due course but for his good fortune in having been enrolled at the age of five at Hurst Street Unitarian Mission School, ten minutes' walk away, rather than at one of the two schools that were literally 'over the road'. Perhaps the school's reputation for teaching practical, job-related subjects carried the day but equally possibly the family supported Unitarian principles.[2]

Under a gifted headmaster, W Wade, three professional teachers aided by monitors taught the school's five hundred pupils in two large, open rooms. It was not the most promising environment in which to learn and Langley admitted later to having been a dull boy in most subjects. Hurst Street School, however, opened his eyes to drawing and design and in those subjects he was invariably top of the class, prompting the headmaster to suggest he should enrol in evening classes at the Birmingham School of Design. When Wade's suggestion was turned down by Langley's father, who was unwilling, or unable, to add to the tuppence a week his son's education was already costing, his mother intervened. Determined that he should receive every encouragement to study further, she took in laundry to pay his Design School fees.

Langley's schooling and evening classes proceeded uneventfully until February 1865 when Alfred, at eighteen one of the family's principal breadwinners, fell victim to pulmonary phthisis, contracted at the brass foundry. It was now incumbent upon Langley to earn a living. But how? The answer, he said in later years, came via a consultation on March 25, 1865 with G P Hemming, a 'Practical Phrenologist'. This may seem now to have been an odd way to resolve the issue but it is clear from Hemming's analysis, which included a warning to young Langley about his too frank and co-operative nature, that phrenology was akin to present-day counselling and not just a fanciful interpretation of bumps on the cranium. That, and the fact that the consultation would have been an expensive present for a boy who still had some months to go before his thirteenth birthday, gives some credence to Langley's later claim.

Confronted by a slight and rather weedy-looking youth, and probably made aware of Alfred's recent and untimely death from a wasting disease, Hemming began his analysis by advocating improving exercise, proper attention to diet and the avoidance of over-working. Then, his hands doubtless passing meaningfully over Langley's head as he casually asked his probing questions, Hemming delved further, his analysis eventually running to several pages.

The 'bumps' revealed Langley to be an ambitious, energetic, persevering and forceful young man, of an independent and self-reliant cast of mind — although tinged with a susceptibility to the good opinion of others. Hemming also detected a sharp temper, a disturbingly restless nature and an inability to complete the matter in hand. But what led to his discovery that Langley had a disconcerting talent for mimicry?

Hemming found Langley was warm and loyal towards his friends and ever ready to defend the interests of others, having a scrupulous regard for right and justice. On matters of conscience he concluded:

> You possess strong sympathy and will take a deep interest in the general welfare of others, but are influenced more by a feeling of kindness and justice, rather than reverence or veneration, and in religious matters will take the direction of reform.

It appears that when Langley went for his consultation with Hemming it was in the knowledge that an apprenticeship awaited him with one of the town's lithographers, provided the phrenologist gave a satisfactory report. Only then would the family accept the financial sacrifices entailed. Hemming's words on Langley's suitability for such a career were, therefore, crucial:

> You are very fond of the sublime, the magnificent and the grand, both in nature and art, and manifest good taste and skill where

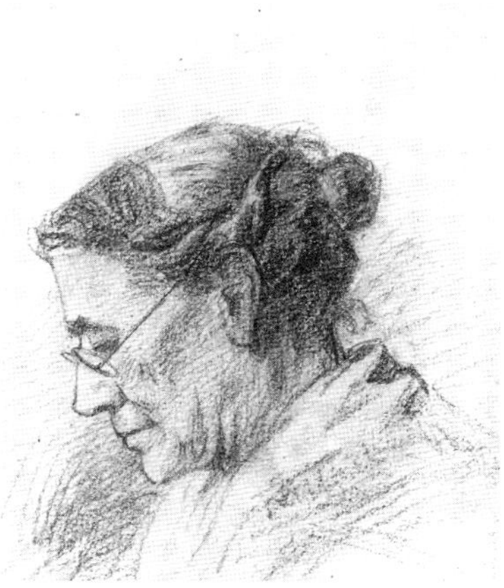

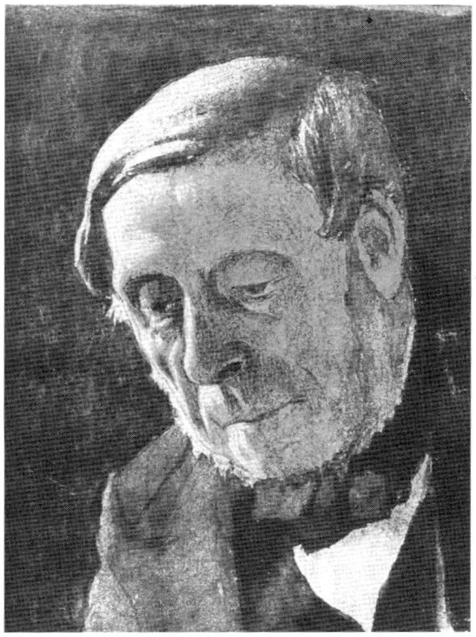

William Langley 1871
watercolour, 15.5 x 11.3cm

Walter's father

TOP
Mary Ann Langley c1877
pencil, 15 x 11.5cm

Walter's mother

PAGE 35
Fisherman c1887-92
watercolour, 26.7 x 17.8cm

> finish and nicety of touch are required. You possess good ability to imitate and to work from a pattern, united with good judgement of form and proportion and ability to plan and are well qualified for a Draftsman, Designer or an Engraver.
>
> You are naturally of a quick disposition, and will be known for your powers of observation. Your judgement of colours is only fair, yet you will manifest good taste in this respect, but will be more skilful in drawing and where expression and taste are required, than in the colouring department.

All doubts were overcome by Hemming's report and that summer Langley was bound for seven years to August Heinrich Biermann, of 106 Newhall Street. Biermann was the son of a forester from Hesse, near Frankfurt, but how he came to be in England and where he trained as a lithographer is not known. He set up in business in Birmingham in the early 1860s and in July 1864 married Amelia Wood. Amelia had lived until then with her parents in Little Hill Street. Not only was that a continuation of Irving Street but Amelia's father, like William Langley, was a tailor. It takes little imagination to envisage the train of events leading to Biermann's offer of an apprenticeship.

Typical of the small businesses that abounded in Birmingham, Biermann employed only two staff, both apprentices. The bread-and-butter output of his workshop was commercial stationery, bill-heads and the like, but Biermann also undertook rather more speculative ventures, such as his 'Monumental Plans' of Birmingham, which he published in 1870 and 1871. Langley and his fellow apprentice probably helped draw those plans, each of which included miniatures of some 200 buildings.

Commercial lithographers seldom revealed their identities in their work but Langley's name can be associated with an entry in the Birmingham and Midland Counties Exhibition held in August 1865, at the very beginning of his apprenticeship. Biermann entered under his own name 'A pen and ink drawing of a theodolite, a Lord's prayer, and same lithographed and printed in colours' but Langley also received a Bronze Exhibitor's Medal from the organisers.[3] No identifiable relics remain of Langley's daily work in lithography,

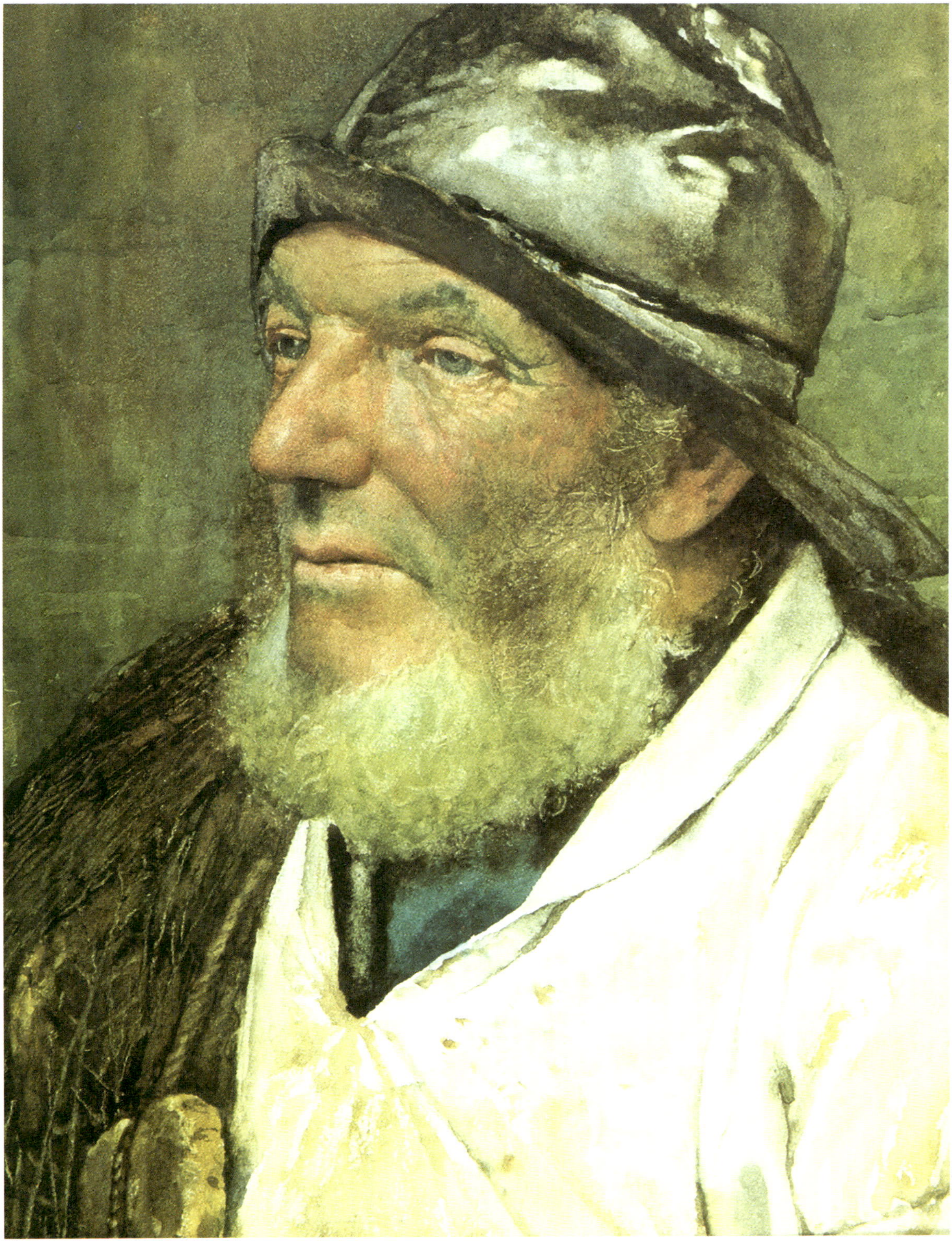

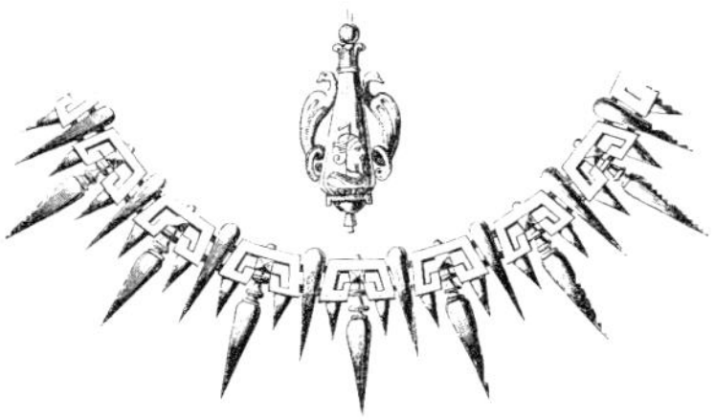

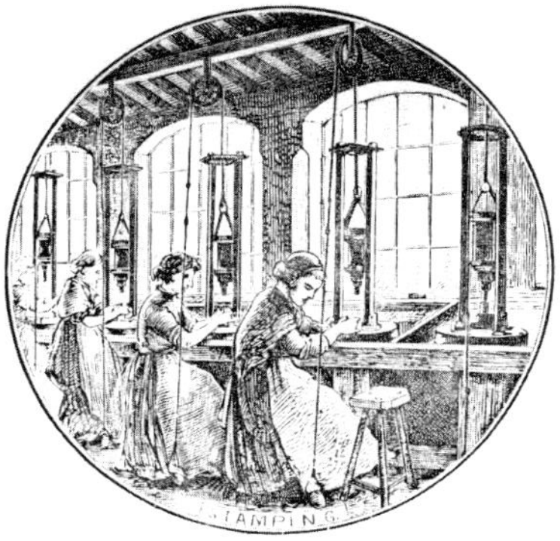

Illustration from a book on the manufacture of steel pens

Though it was published in 1890, this engraving is from a drawing by Langley which is likely to have been commissioned, with others, by Perry's of Birmingham in the 1870s for a booklet on their steel pens. They were stated to have been drawn with a Perry's no.25 pen.

TOP
Two designs for jewellery for Messrs T and J Bragg, as illustrated in the *Art Journal* catalogue of the International Exhibition of 1872.

however, and he said and recorded nothing concerning his years in the trade. Maybe he thought that his work as a lithographer had no significance in relation to his artistic career. If so, that would seem a harsh judgement on a craft where even mundane work demanded a direct, sure touch in drawing and a good eye for line, composition and detail. William Wainwright, who at one time shared a studio with Langley, suggested the latter's early preference for water-colours could also be traced to the training he received in lithography.

Langley continued his studies at the School of Design and won many prizes there but only two scraps of drawings have survived from his class work, a pencil study of a bunch of grapes surrounded by leaves, dated June 29, 1866, and a sepia and wash study of a squirrel amid foliage, dated 1867. A pointer to the direction his study and work was taking was his submission of designs for an 'Egyptian-style' suite of jewellery to the London International Exhibition of 1872, the last full year of his apprenticeship. These were illustrated in the *Art Journal* exhibition catalogue, wherein Langley was described, somewhat misleadingly, as a 'young student of the Birmingham School of Art'. As the designs were submitted by the Birmingham jewellers Messrs T and J Bragg and formed part of their 1872 range it can fairly be assumed they had been commissioned via Biermann.

Two works of art also date from Langley's apprenticeship years, an unfinished watercolour sketch of his father and an etching, *The Dog and Duck Inn, Birmingham*, both of which date from 1871. There were undoubtedly other artworks from this period that have been lost or are not recognised.

Langley's progress at the School of Design was marked by an impressive annual haul of prizes, culminating in 1873 with awards for jewellery and silverware design, figure studies ('free and spirited', according to the *Birmingham Post*), and botanical and costume drawings. In the same year he was awarded a two-year scholarship to study at the South Kensington Schools, an achievement that drew somewhat grudging recognition from the Birmingham School:

> Two more of our pupils, John Watkin and Walter Langley, have each had scholarships of £52 per annum awarded to them,

> making altogether twelve since the School's foundation seven years ago. This success, by taking the recipients to South Kensington, removes the principal material on which the School relies for the higher prizes and it is found that these gentlemen hardly ever return to take a position in their native town.

Though less than wholehearted in their valediction, the School of Design purchased the scholarship drawings of both students as 'specimens of decoration and design', Langley receiving three guineas for his.[4]

South Kensington not only awarded prizes to the local schools, it also prescribed their courses and teaching methods. Their grip on the whole structure of education in design led to one of Langley's few later references to his early days, made in his presidential address to students of the Sutton Coldfield Art Class, in 1891:

> ... as an instance of misdirected energy there are those here who will no doubt remember the time when elaborate stippled drawings had to be made — generally of the antique — and it is painful to think of the valuable time wasted over these productions, which in many instances must have resulted in wearying and, ultimately, alienating the student from further effort. How was he to learn to appreciate breadth and character when many nights were spent over a few inches of stipple ... one is constrained to wonder how intelligent teachers could have enforced such a system ...

Langley completed his apprenticeship in the summer of 1873 and took up the scholarship at South Kensington in September of the same year. His studies in Birmingham prepared him well for the move south and the portfolio of his London work shows he spent much of his time in the museums, copying from classical works in silver and gold. The leavening to this solid fare came from the life classes of Dr Moody. The doctor's unorthodox methods endeared him to his students but were not much appreciated by the South Kensington authorities, as Langley explained at Sutton Coldfield:

> Dr Moody would pose a living model in the centre of the class and then allow the students half an hour in which to make a

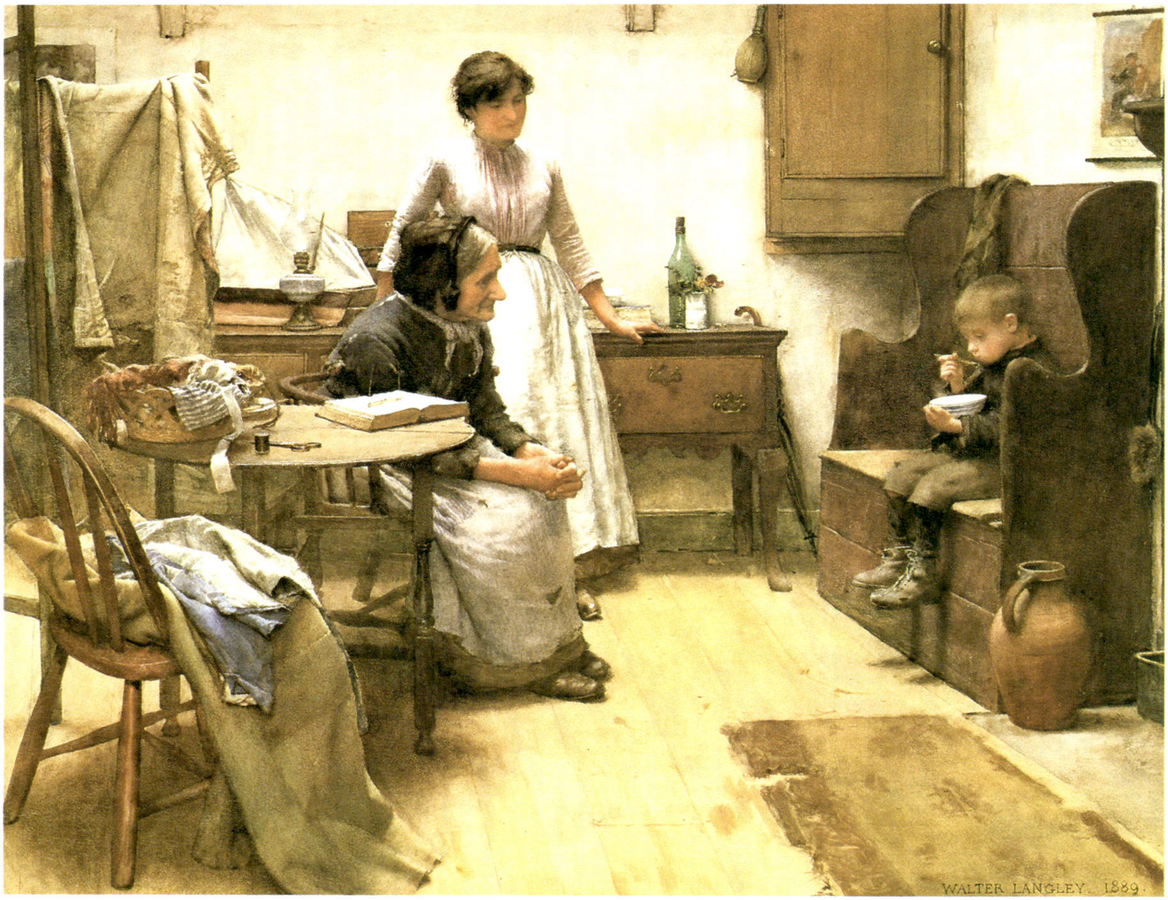

The Orphan 1889
watercolour, 66 x 87.5cm

The settle, the clothes horse, the Windsor chair, the gate-leg table and the large earthenware pot all appear several times in paintings from the 1880s onwards. The fine Welsh dresser may have been brought in specially, however. The heavy drapery (including the old quilt also frequently used) effectively isolates the boy on the right, underlining the subject as, in a similar vein, the woman and the little girl in ... *Charity* are set to isolate the boy.

study of, say, an arm or a leg. Then, each student would exchange places with his neighbour and so on, all round, thus making the acquaintance of the whole figure. Alas for Dr Moody! When the department reviewed the work performed in this manner, which looked like scraps of drawings, rather than the completed works they preferred, they ordered him to discontinue teaching the figure.

Langley lodged at Godfrey Street, a thoroughfare of shops and houses in Chelsea, convenient both for South Kensington and London at large. He revelled in the freedom to explore the city's museums and art galleries but above all London's concert halls and theatres made this one of the happiest periods in his life.

It was not only in London that Langley was spreading his wings.

Shortly before leaving for South Kensington he had reached an important stage in his artistic career, the first submission of work to a public exhibition. This was a momentous step for an entirely self-taught artist, building only on his experience as a lithographer and the results of constant practice, and it was probably with some trepidation that he sent his three watercolours in to the Royal Birmingham Society of Artists Spring Exhibition of 1873. The prices he asked for *The Tired Gleaner*, *Composure* and *La Pensiera*, were £3, £5 and £7 respectively.

There is no record of sales for this period but presumably the returns from the exhibition were encouraging for that summer Langley, and a fellow amateur artist named Holyoake, went on a sketching holiday to the picturesque Lyn Valley in Devon,[5] where he found sufficient material for three further watercolours.

In the spring of 1875 Langley, eighteen months into his two-year

The quay, Newlyn c1887
watercolour, 25.4 x 35.5cm

This is a wider version of *The Last Gleam* (1888, 31 x 22.5cm), a watercolour in which the western sun is just catching the tops of the chimneys and roofs above the level of the top of this painting. The view is of the beach at Newlyn immediately below the Fradgan, where Langley's studio was, and with what may be the beginning of the long North Pier showing on the far right.

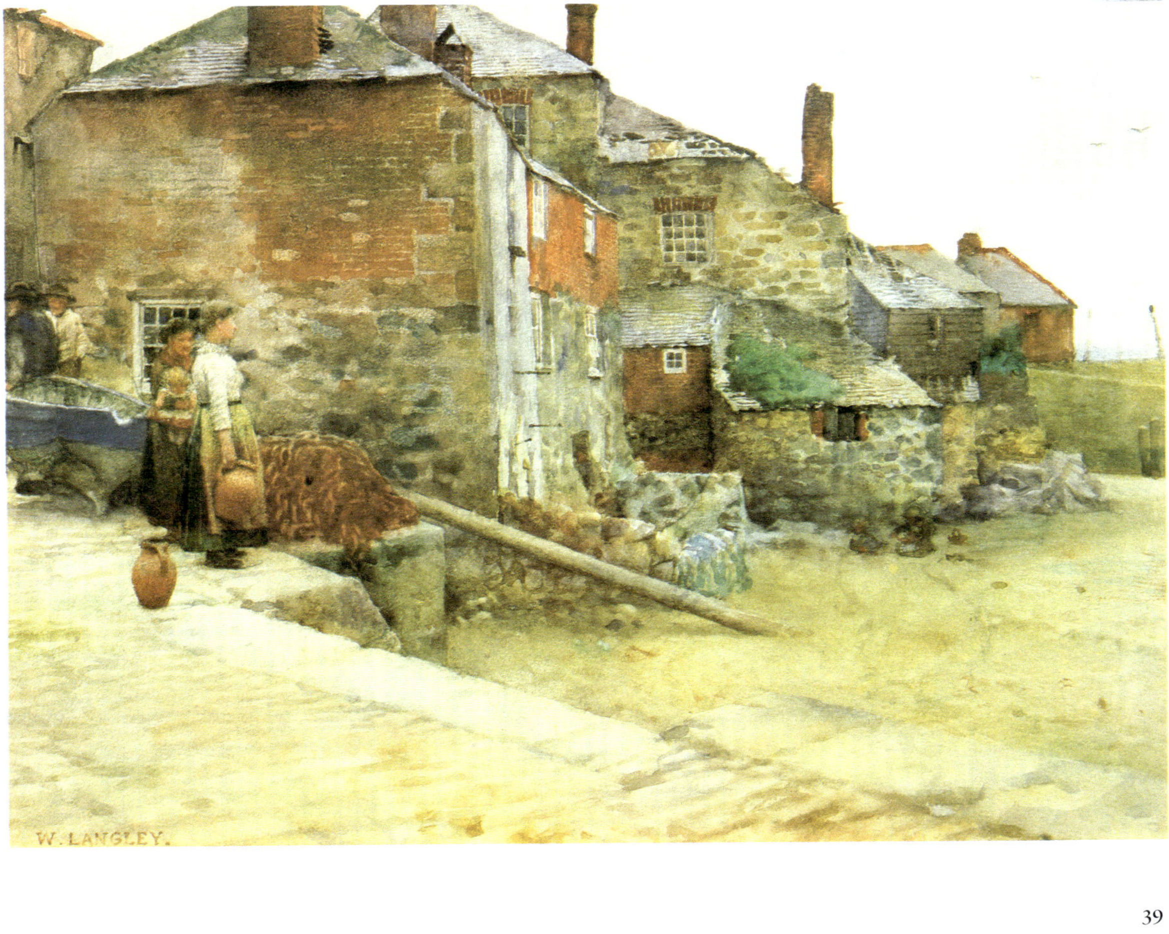

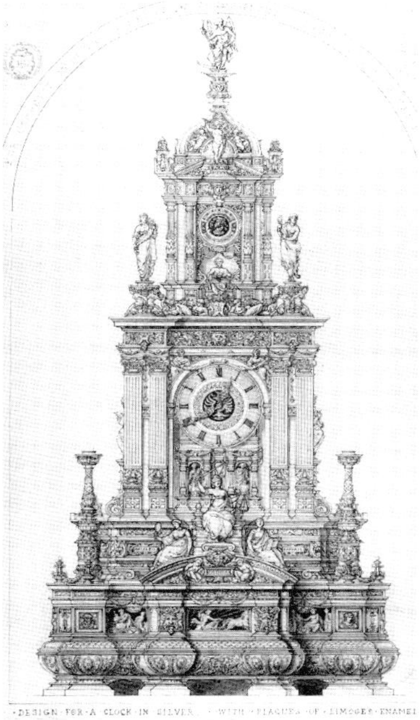

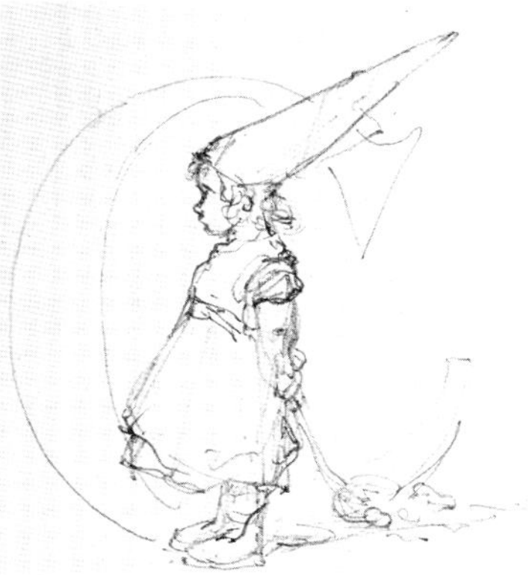

Study for a decorated letter mid-1870s
pencil, 16 x 9.5cm

TOP
Design for a clock 1876
watercolour and pencil, 73 x 44cm

scholarship, received an offer of partnership from Biermann. This promised much-needed financial security and the opportunity to devote more time to painting. Langley accepted the offer with alacrity, declaring he had nothing further to gain by staying on in London for the remainder of his scholarship.

Teaching himself, Langley had developed his watercolour painting to a point that might have satisfied many but he wished to go further. Recognising that progress would depend on professional art tuition, he enrolled in classes on his return to Birmingham. At first he joined those given by the Midland Art Guild at Queen's College but they turned out to be of a poor standard and he promptly decamped to the Birmingham Society's figure and costume classes, given by Jonathan Pratt and H T Munns. His lead was followed by many of the Queen's College students, causing that body to make a rapid overhaul of its teaching — which it did to such good effect that the students returned there in later years.

The next three years, to the end of 1878, were a time of frantic endeavour. Besides his daily lithographic work and evening art classes, Langley studied on alternate evenings at the Birmingham School of Design, under David Raimbach, and still found time in which to paint. Stanhope Forbes was later to comment that 'Langley was a fast worker'[6] and doubtless lithography's need for a swift, sure hand worked to his advantage, but it was not 'all work and no play' at this time. A fellow student later recalled that Langley used to entertain his colleagues with a display of tap-dancing on the pavement, as they awaited admission to the classes, and would still be first up the stairs when the doors to the Art School were opened. Also, the seven studios Langley rented or shared in the three years up to 1878 hosted many convivial meetings of Birmingham's young artists and perhaps his frequent changes of address owed as much to his banjo playing and tap-dancing as to the invasive smell of artists' colours.

At work, Langley continued to concentrate on design commissions. One of these, a 'Drawing of oblong border enclosing arch with allegorical figures and Masonic Emblems', was registered at Stationers' Hall in 1877 and led to the identification of his lithographic master and partner from among the many practitioners in Birmingham.

On Langley's own later admission the years after South Kensington were a time in which he was 'beating about between lithography and painting' and undecided about which profession to pursue. It was also, though, a time of crucial developments in his artistic career, according to William Wainwright:

> At the time Langley joined the classes at the Society of Artists and the Art Guild there was an artist of marked personality named Francis Hinckley, who conducted remarkable studies in watercolour which were often of masterly character. Hinckley, who painted figures and still-life, followed very closely the tradition of old William Hunt [and] exerted a considerable influence on Langley's work at this time, a period in which there were remarkable exponents of the watercolour art; to name but a few figure painters, Sir John Gilbert, E J Gregory, Herkomer, Walker, Pinwell and Sir James Linton, all of whom exhibited regularly at the Royal Birmingham Society of Artists and none of whose works escaped the observant eye of Langley. Of these, from conversations with him and observations of his work, I am inclined to think he was drawn more strongly to the work of Herkomer and Walker.[7]

Wainwright suggested that the grandeur, toil and pathos evident in the work of Michelangelo, Millet and Israels also inspired Langley in this critical period of his artistic career and he named two tutors to whom Langley owed a considerable debt. They were Edward Taylor, of whom Langley himself was to say 'a better and kinder teacher it would be impossible to find', and Frank Jackson.

It was not only in his painting that developments took place on Langley's return to Birmingham for he was also able to resume his friendship with Clara Perkins, the daughter of near neighbours of his parents. Clara's background was as modest as his, though the recent marriage of an elder sister to a man shortly to become the editor of a London newspaper suggests the Perkins family was somewhat livelier than average.

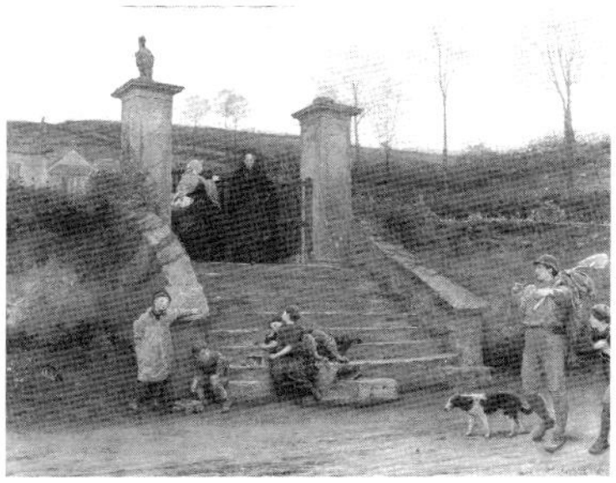

Frederick Walker
The Old Gate exh.1869
(Tate Gallery)

PAGE 42
The seas are quiet when the wind gives o'er, So calm are we when passions are no more. 1884
watercolour, 37 x 27cm

PAGE 43
Woman by a cottage door c1889
watercolour, 40 x 27cm

Not positively identified but has been known as *The Return of the Fishing Fleet*.

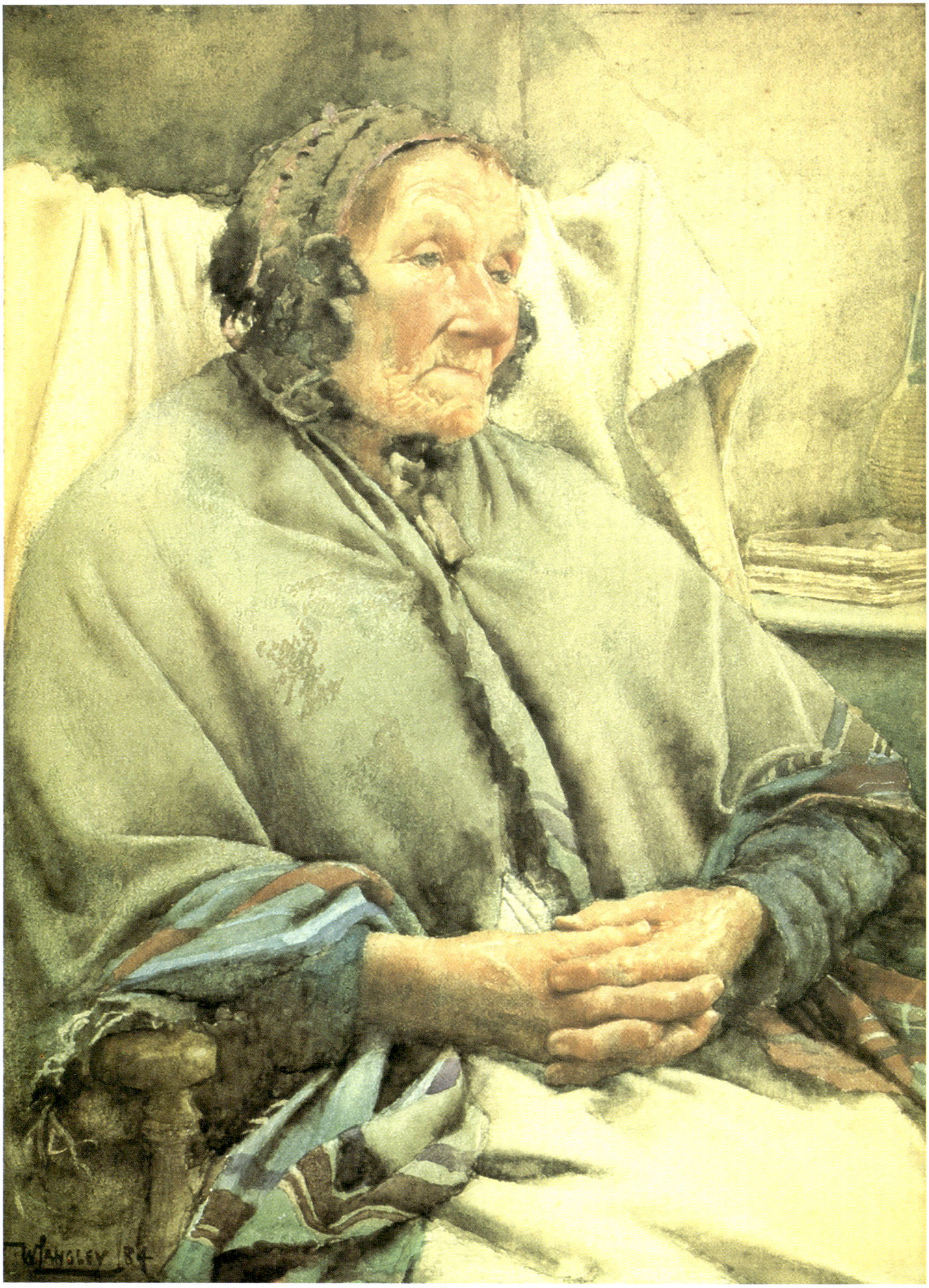
W LANGLEY '84

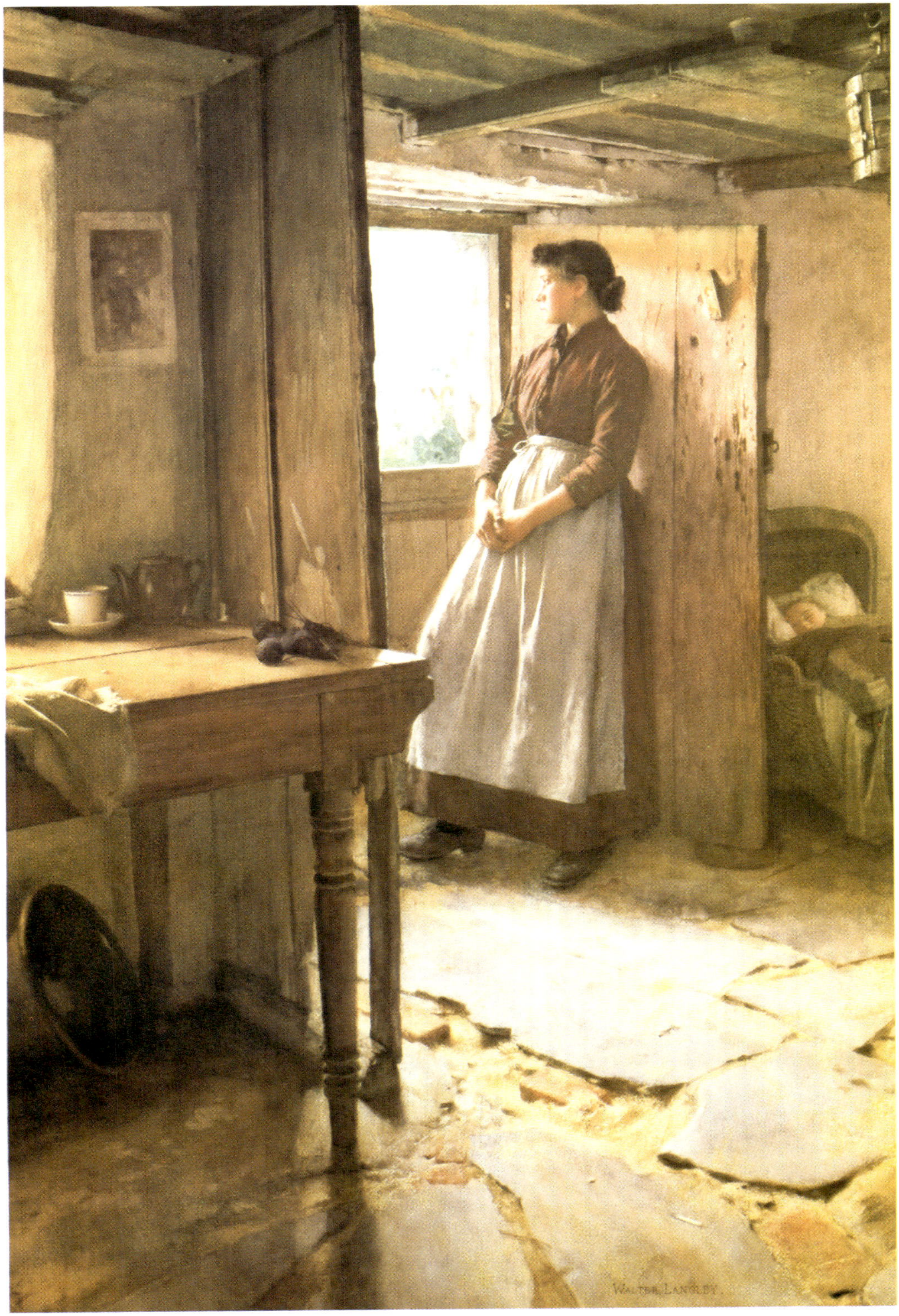
WALTER LANGLEY

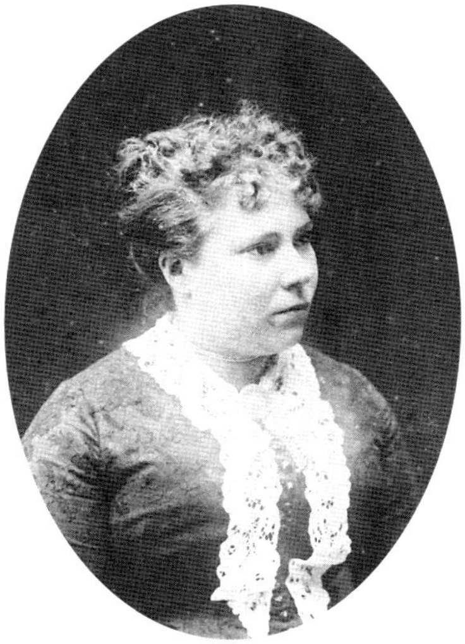

Clara 1888
photograph by John Collier of Birmingham

The friendship between Clara and Langley blossomed and they were married in Birmingham on August 26, 1876, at the Unitarian Church of the Messiah. The couple honeymooned in the Yorkshire village of Whitby, a favourite haunt of Victorian artists. This was probably Langley's first encounter with a working fishing-village, but the experience seems not to have inspired any paintings by him at the time. On returning to Birmingham the newly-weds took up residence just three doors away from her parents and a stone's-throw from his, for both came from close-knit families.

No sooner had they begun married life than a slump in demand cut down Langley's lithographic commissions to three days' work a week. The financial situation was serious and when he sought to broaden the scope of his work through further study at the School of Design he applied for free admission to the classes. This was at first refused but Edward Taylor then intervened and the application was granted, in November 1876, on condition Langley 'would undertake to attend the classes on at least three nights a week during the session and conform to regulations laid down by the committee for the maintenance of discipline'.

With more daytime at his disposal Langley was released from the confines of a studio and took the opportunity to stay from time to time with a married elder sister, Charlotte, at her home in Grafton Flyford. There he was conveniently near the picturesque Avon valley villages of Welford, Evesham, Elmley Castle, Bredon and Pershore, all of which he featured in rural scenes that found a ready market in Birmingham, particularly among rising families such as the Cadburys.

The birth of his first son, Lorraine, on September 8, 1877, was followed by a dramatic increase in Langley's output of paintings and he began to keep a record of his work. This was in the form of a *liber veritatis* of pen and ink copies of each painting (another homage to Claude Lorraine, perhaps) and spanned a period of about fifteen months, to the end of 1878. His output for that period is shown to have included numerous studies of rural folk, village scenes and some narrative works.

In 1878, Langley illustrated a book of poems, *Imaginary Loves*, written by a friend, John Harrison, and published in Birmingham by Cornish Brothers. Langley greatly admired the book illustrators of the day and may have seen Harrison's commission as a promising opportunity to diversify. If so, he was doomed to be disappointed for the poems were decidedly poor, the literary correspondent of the *Birmingham Post* being moved to write to Langley 'if my brother had written them I should exercise all my powers of persuasion to induce him to give up writing verse'. Langley's only reward was to see in print a poetic tribute to his son, 'To Lorry on his first birthday'.

The comparatively high output of paintings in 1878 suggests Langley was now professional artist in all but name, but he had not given up lithography. Then came the news that Clara was expecting twins, in March 1879, and he realised he could no longer delay a decision as to where his future best lay. Late in 1878 the die was cast and lithography abandoned as a major source of income. Langley's financial record of picture sales commences in 1879 — when he also ceased to keep a *liber veritatis* — and that year his name and studio address were listed for the first time in the artists' section of the Birmingham directory. Time would tell whether he had taken the right decision.

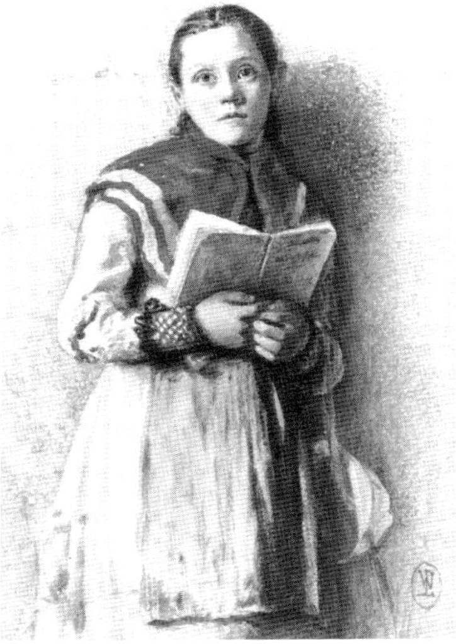

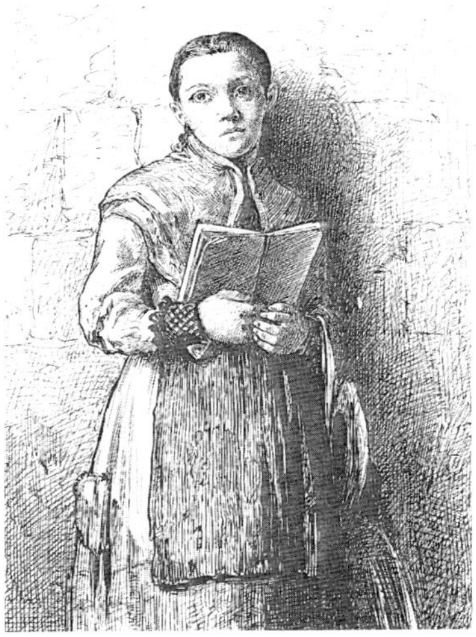

Girl with a book c1877
ink, 17 x 12cm

from the *liber veritatis* Langley kept from about 1877 to the end of 1878.

TOP
Girl with a book c1877
watercolour, 24 x 16.5cm

Known as *The Lesson*; though he kept a pen and ink *liber veritatis* of his works at this time, it was not until 1879 that he recorded the titles of his paintings.

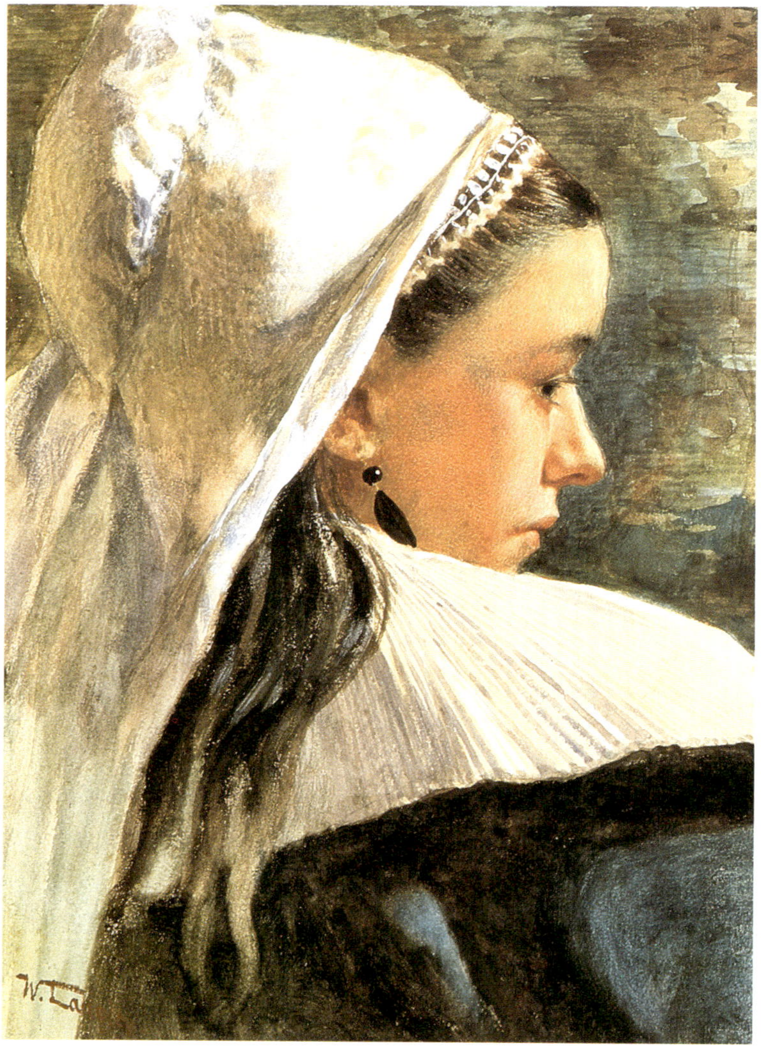

1879-1881 Birmingham, Newlyn & Brittany

CHAPTER TWO

When his painting was an occupation for his spare time, Langley could be content to record steady progress in his art and achieve a useful additional income on top of his earnings from lithography. Such a relaxed approach could not be adopted by a professional artist. Technical skill assumed, the first priority for the professional was to establish his distinctive artistic identity for without that he would be forever competing with his peers on the treadmill of high output and low prices.

In his first professional year Langley struggled without success to achieve the breakthrough he needed, his records showing he had to sell 66 paintings to earn £288. This was more than a skilled factory worker might earn but was by no means an ample reward, even if augmented by the occasional unrecorded lithographic commission. It was not a good year and had begun on a disastrous personal note when Clara lost at birth one of the expected twins. The survivor was the Langleys' only daughter, Eleanore.

The highest price Langley could achieve in 1879 was only £19, for a work he described in his records as the 'Head of an Eastern Girl' but in exhibition as *She gazed upon the golden gift, Absorbed in pleasant reveries*. More worrying even than the low ceiling price, another work, *An Old Resort for Young Gossips*, failed to sell at the Society's Spring Exhibition and when moved on to the Liverpool Water Colour Society's Autumn Exhibition again failed to sell. The painting then returned to Birmingham, where it was eventually bought at a discounted price by a dealer. This disappointing pattern of events was to be repeated for many paintings over the years to come.

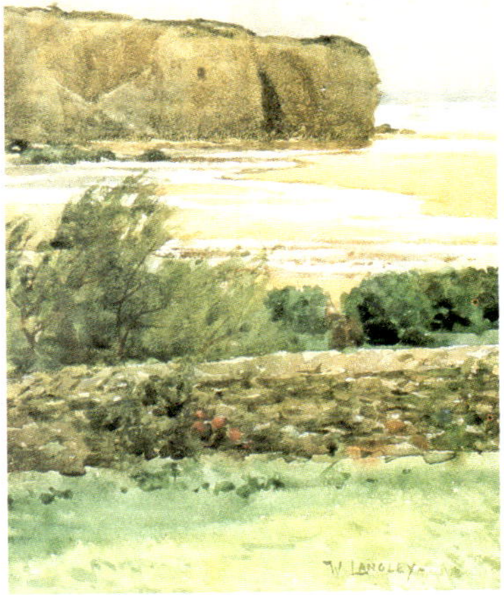

At Beer, Devon 1910
watercolour, 25.5 x 13cm

PAGE 46
A Breton Peasant Girl 1881
watercolour, 40.6 x 28cm

The exhibition, and sometimes re-exhibition, of so large an output of paintings was an administrative burden for which the only remedy, short of a major commission, was to place greater reliance on dealers to find purchasers. This was a costly route but one which Langley decided to take, feeling on balance that the dealer's deduction of a 35 to 45 per cent commission was a necessary exchange for access to his contacts in the art buying market.

A further problem faced by Langley and by other artists of his generation was that their work tended to be swamped by that of the established men, at the huge exhibitions mounted by the Society. A solution proposed a few years earlier was to exhibit outside the Society but it was not until a group of six young artists, including Langley, got together to thrash out the problem that any action was taken. The result of their deliberations was the creation of the Birmingham Art Circle. At the Circle's exhibitions their work would stand alone and only marginal rates of commission would be deducted from any sales proceeds, sufficient to cover the Circle's modest expenses. The Circle held its first exhibition in 1879, in a member's studio. Admission was by invitation and, the venture being deemed a success by the members, a public exhibition was planned for the following year.

As 1879 closed, Langley could reflect upon a year of mixed fortunes in which perhaps the most promising feature was the launch of the Circle. There was, however, one further consolation when a painting he submitted to the Society's Spring Exhibition, *Musing on the roaring ocean, Which divides my love and me*, the first for which he drew inspiration and title from a poem, was also the first work to catch the eye of the press:

> ... the excellent lighting of the work lifts it out of the commonplace and invests it with some of the qualities which redeemed and vivified the merely technical excellence of the late W[illiam] Hunt's works.

When 1880 got off to a poor start, with sales to June amounting to barely £100, the outlook must have seemed depressing indeed but an important landmark in his life was about to be reached, his first visit to Cornwall. He had no doubt seen from paintings exhibited

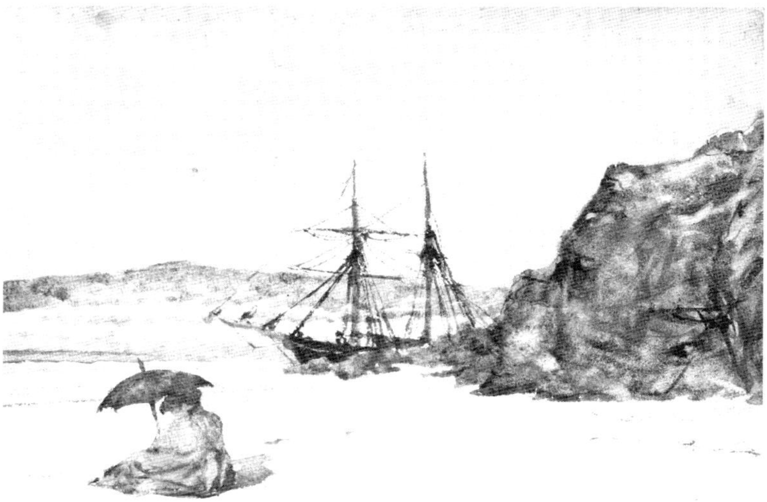

Sketchbook study of a beach, early-1880s
watercolour, 12.5 x 17.5cm

Though it may be argued this shows a shipwreck, it is more likely to be the sand-banked inlet where the Hayle estuary emerges and boats follow the narrow navigation channel through into the harbour.

BELOW
Sketchbook study of a Newlyn alley, early-1880s
pencil, 17 x 8.2cm

at the Society that the county had a great deal to offer the artist and decided to make the long journey down there. His choice of Newlyn as a destination rather than, say, St Ives may have been fortuitous.

Newlyn has changed considerably since 1880 and though photographs can convey an idea of the appearance of the village as Langley first saw it, a more rounded impression is given by a near-contemporary description, written by 'A Perambulating Contributor' for the *Cornishman* newspaper. The writer approached Newlyn over the beach from Penzance, as there was no coast road in those days:

> On the landward side were a couple of fishing boats on the stocks, in the course of construction, with men busy in hammering and planing at their great hulks ... fishermen on the banks were spreading out their nets to dry and close by the ropemakers, with bent backs and shuffling gait were hanging out the slender yarns, which shone in the sunlight like gossamer threads. Just beyond were the irregular, straggling houses coming down close to the margin of the sea ... green fields and waving corn and, nestling amongst some trees, whitewashed cottages and villas. Newlyn, it cannot be denied, is picturesquely placed and certainly healthily situated, but the poor fishermen who form the bulk of the inhabitants have hitherto been much neglected. The

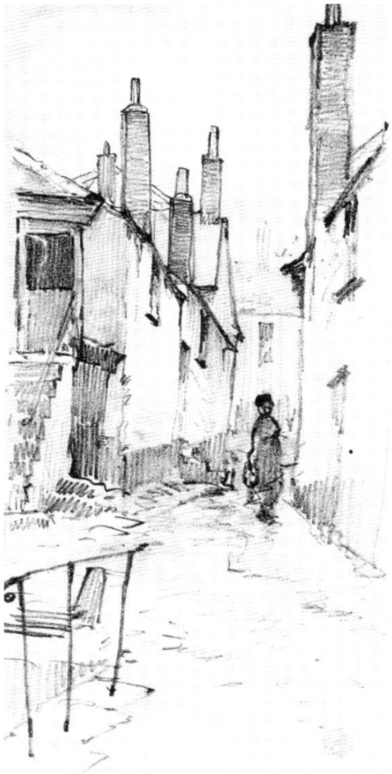

Simple in structure but in bounty great 1879
watercolour, 38.7 x 48.2cm

There is an ink drawing of this in the *liber veritatis.*

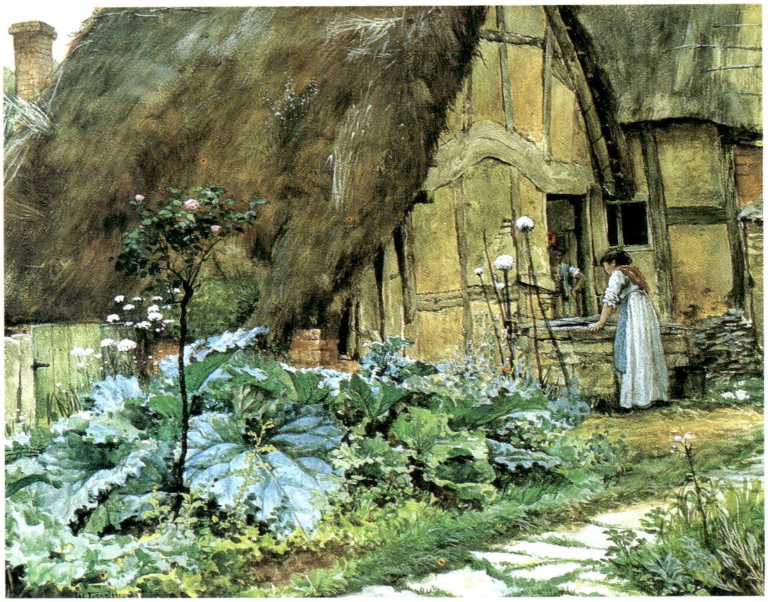

> town is hopelessly irregular in the construction of its houses and the arrangements of its streets and, indeed, this feature is what principally contributes to its picturesqueness. There is a maze of tortuous lanes, crooked streets and blind alleys and the buildings have grown up in a very independent and uncared-for fashion and assumed most queer and original forms of architecture ... it certainly has, from some aspects, a forlorn and ragged air ...

The detailed description of Newlyn begins at the bridge spanning the Coomb River, which divides the village into Street-an-Nowan, nearest to Penzance, and Newlyn Town:

> Here are to be seen, or were to be seen on the occasion of which I speak, all the paraphernalia of a fishing port. A large pile of mackerel boxes stood to one side and several men, up to their knees in the river, were busy cleaning them; nets and fishing gear of all sorts lay about on the pebbles. Against the walls of the houses were hung rows of dried and salted fish; on an old upturned boat a couple of worn out old fishermen ... a group of strong, lusty young fellows reclining against the low wall, with pipes in their mouths and hands in their pockets ... little blue-jerkined youngsters improvising a raft on the river from a

number of disabled fish boxes ... a youngster driving by with a load of freshly barked nets and two blowsy old fishwomen with cowals [baskets] at their backs, trudging heavily along. To get from Street-an-Nowan to Newlyn Town you have to go through a strange medley of courts and byways, over slippery and uneven stones. Several times I have been shocked and disgusted with the state of the thoroughfares, mud and filth and rotten fish lying about and trampled underfoot. And then the smells! In certain conditions of the atmosphere the effluvia are something appalling and anyone with a delicate olfactory apparatus would barely survive the stinks and stenches which rise at such times and pollute the live air. But the inhabitants go about their business or their pleasure with a stoic indifference for such trifles and might be furnished with wooden noses for all it affects them.

The sanitary condition of Newlyn is truly woeful and alarming and offers a grave attraction for any germs or disease floating in the air and must prove, until the existing drainage and water supply is corrected, a continual menace to the well-being of the district.

Another grievance of which the Newlyn folk sorely complain is the nil accommodation for their splendid fleet of boats. The time before last that I was in town the tide was up and a large number of these boats were moored close in to shore. They were crowded with busy hands, some cleaning the masts and spars, others putting a few touches of paint in here and there, some stowing away nets and coiling ropes and making the little craft as smart and taut as possible. The boats were preparing for the North Sea herring fishery and would set sail from port within the following week. The 'Cliff', a dangerous promenade of pitfalls and slippery places ... was crowded with friends and acquaintances of those on board, watching the work proceed below and passing occasional criticisms thereon.

The little bit of harbour was also full of boats, exhibiting the same scene of activity. The existing harbour will not hold more than a score of drift boats, and Newlyn owns two hundred boats of one sort or another ... [and the fleet] can get no accommodation at all unless it comes to Penzance and in

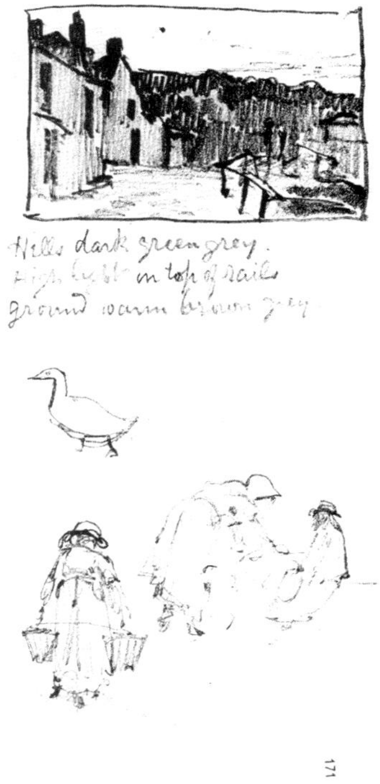

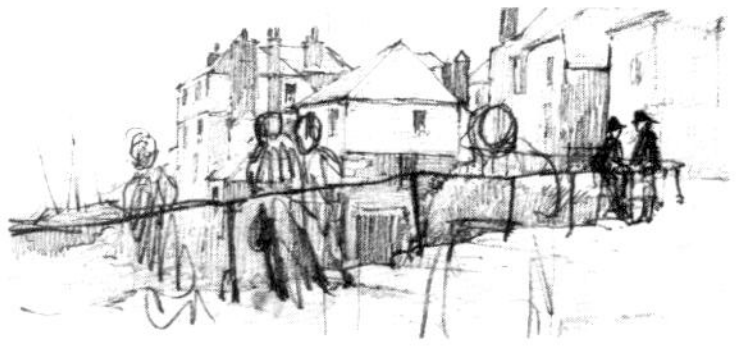

Sketchbook study of a harbour rail,
early-1880s
pencil, 8.2 x 17cm

TOP
Sketchbook page, Newlyn,
early-1880s
pencil, 17 x 8.2cm

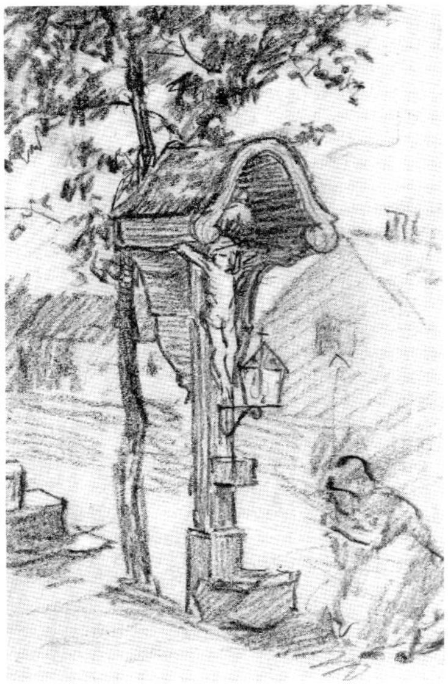

Study of a wayside crucifix,
Brittany 1881
chalk on tone paper, 19 x 12cm

boisterous weather this is not infrequently difficult of accomplishment.

'A Perambulating Contributor' was not alone in drawing attention to Newlyn's sanitary state and smells, for the same phenomena had been remarked upon by the *Daily Telegraph.*

Newlyn's picturesque appearance was of little consolation to most villagers. Fishing was an ill-rewarded and erratic industry and at best a family might expect an income of £1 a week when work was to hand. It is hardly surprising that frequent demands were made by the fishing community on the Penzance Board of Guardians and local charities. This was never more so than in the winter preceding Langley's visit, when the Board made weekly payments to over eleven hundred of the local destitute, while four hundred Newlyners also received distributions of flour from the County Distress Fund. When death or incapacity of the breadwinner was the cause of distress not even the Board could do much to help. Their maximum distribution was seven shillings a week for a sick man and his family.

Shortly after Langley returned to Birmingham, in the autumn of 1880, the vulnerability of the fishing community was cruelly highlighted when storms caused havoc around the Cornish coast and brought about the loss of the lugger 'Jane' and its crew, only a few yards from the safety of Penzance harbour and in full view of the townspeople. This tragedy became the focal point for a national collection in aid of the fishermen. Langley doubtless knew of the loss of the boat and the damage and distress caused generally by the gales, but his paintings that year were of Newlyn in its calmer, sunnier moments. Later, his art would reflect a deep-felt sympathy for the cares and hardships faced by the fishing community.

The visit to Cornwall did not prove financially rewarding, the result for 1880 being marginally worse than that of the previous year, but subsequent events show that Langley had been impressed by the painting opportunities there. The visit also gave him a taste for travel and when Edwin Harris set off on a continental painting tour, early in 1881, Langley resolved to follow him once more. Harris was single and sponsored by the dealer Edwin Chamberlain but Langley, a family man having to pay his own way, could afford to take only a short break away from home and headed direct for Pont Aven in Brittany, where an art colony was already well established. Harris later described the scene in the journal, *Edgbastonia*:

> ... in those days there was hardly a village in Brittany which was not occupied by one or two painters, but at Pont Aven they simply swarmed — English, French, Americans and representatives of almost all nationalities.
>
> The little village, shut in on all sides by the wooded hills, was then, and probably still is, a most unhealthy spot in which to make a lengthy habitation. It can boast none of the picturesque wooden architecture, which is so attractive in so many of the Breton towns, but the costume of the natives, who are popularly supposed to gain their living by washing one another's clothes in the intervals of posing as models, is probably the most picturesque in the whole of Finisterre ... Crowding its small hotel and few inns, and overflowing into one or two narrow streets, some seventy or eighty painters, mostly quite young, were spending a happy life of hard work, intermingled with joyous recreation. Within the walls of the Hotel des Voyageurs, familiarly known as 'Julia's', after the landlady, a buxom dame whose reputation extended to every place where art jargon flourished in France, were to be found representatives of all the 'schools' and movements of the day.

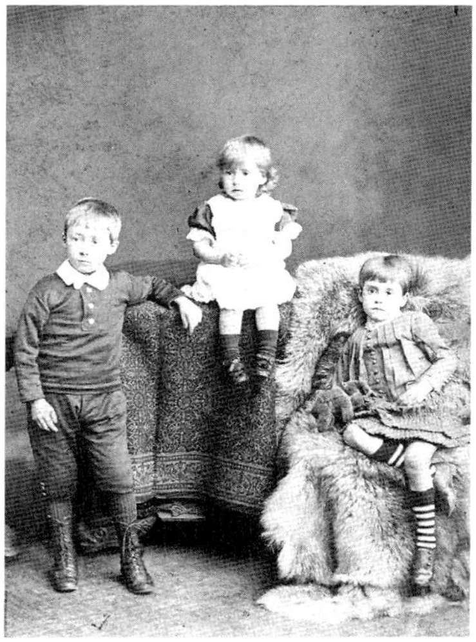

Lorraine, Gabriel and Eleanore, in about 1881-82
photograph by Preston of Penzance

Langley visited Quimperlé and Rennes during his brief stay in Brittany but his base was at Pont Aven. His name is recorded in a transcript of 'Julia's register alongside that of Jonathan Pratt, suggesting that master and former pupil may have travelled together. Several group photographs exist of the Pont Aven artists but a common uniform of beard, corduroy jacket and wide-brimmed stetson makes identification of individual artists somewhat uncertain. The banjo also appears to have been a regular accompaniment to an artist's life, judging by the photographs.

In the fly-leaf of one of his Brittany sketchbooks, Langley jotted down some of the costs he incurred on his visit, including seventy francs for three outfits of traditional Breton clothing. These, along

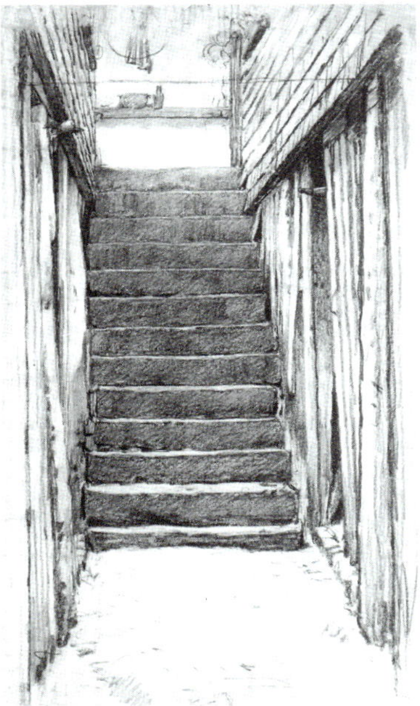

Study of steps c1881-82
chalk on tone paper, 54.7 x 31cm

RIGHT
Wandering Thoughts 1882
watercolour, 104 x 56cm

One of Langley's watercolours for the Alldays' commission, carefully composed from studies of steps in an alley and of models for the figures. The contrast of the young girl with the soft fall of the quilt was an effective device at this date and later. This is related to a smaller Brittany work, *The Jackdaw of Rheims*, 1882, and a number of others of c1881 of steep perspectives up cobbled streets and steps in Newlyn.

The location of this scene has been identified as Vaccination Court, recalling the not too distant days of cholera epidemics, but swept away now by re-development.

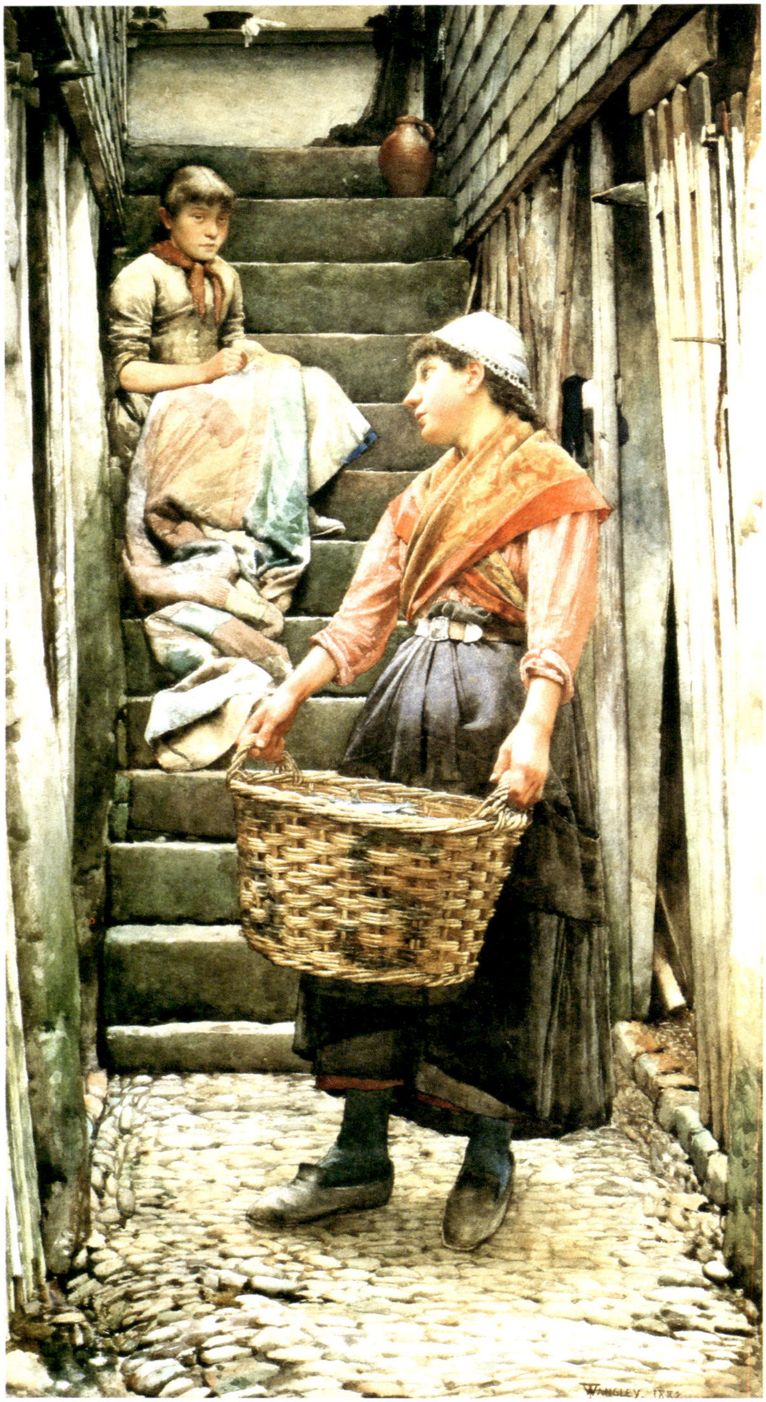

with other props purchased locally, were to be invaluable to him when he returned to Birmingham and give a clue as to the nature of his Breton works, which were heavily weighted towards costume studies. Models in Brittany, he noted, cost two francs a session for a man, one and a half francs for a woman and seventy-five centimes for a child and seem not over-expensive by today's standards. However, five pounds for the return fare from Southampton to St Malo, equivalent to over £200 in 1997, was no bargain.

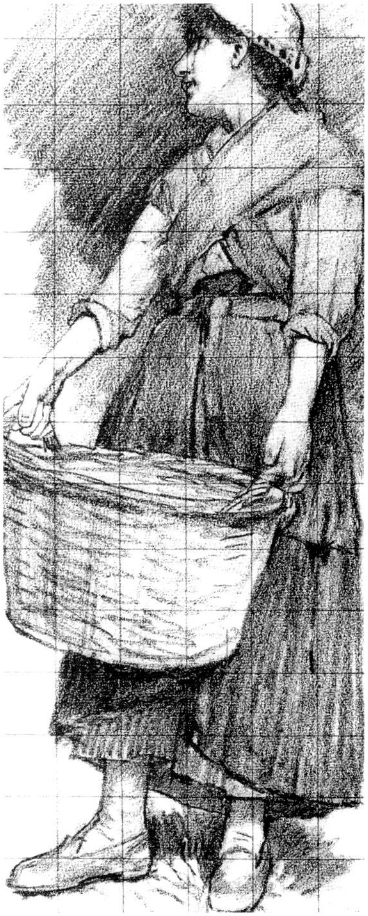

Study of a girl with a basket
c1881-82
crayon, 38.2 x 15.2cm
A study for *Wandering Thoughts*, opposite.

Langley sold no paintings in May, when he was in Brittany, or in June, which he spent in frenzied activity in his Birmingham studio translating his Brittany sketches into finished works of art. His efforts were amply rewarded from July onwards by a burst of sales to the two dealers, Clarke and Keeley. It was Clara, though, who had to handle the sales, for by July 2 her husband was once more in Cornwall, on the first of two visits he would make that year. He had received a commission from Edwin Chamberlain for twenty paintings and planned to spend some time in Newlyn, sketching in preparation.

The first visit was only brief as Langley returned home again on July 17 to be with Clara, who was expecting an addition to the family in November and was apprehensive following the loss of one of the twins, and to help prepare for the Birmingham Art Circle's second exhibition. This was also to be in November, at Edwin Chamberlain's gallery, and Langley, the Art Circle's first secretary, was anxious that it should be a success. When he was satisfied that all was well, Langley returned to Newlyn early in September for a month's sketching.

On November 21 the Langleys' second son, Gabriel, was born and three days later the eighteen members of the Art Circle opened their exhibition at Chamberlain's gallery.[8] The catalogue for this exhibition opens with a list of patrons which even the best-established artists of the day might have envied, and which was headed by the Mayor of Birmingham. The Chamberlain family was prominent among the patrons, led by Edwin's uncle Joseph, the Liberal MP for Birmingham, but perhaps it was the inclusion in the list of two of the town's most notable industrialists and cultural benefactors, the Cornishmen George and Richard Tangye, that set

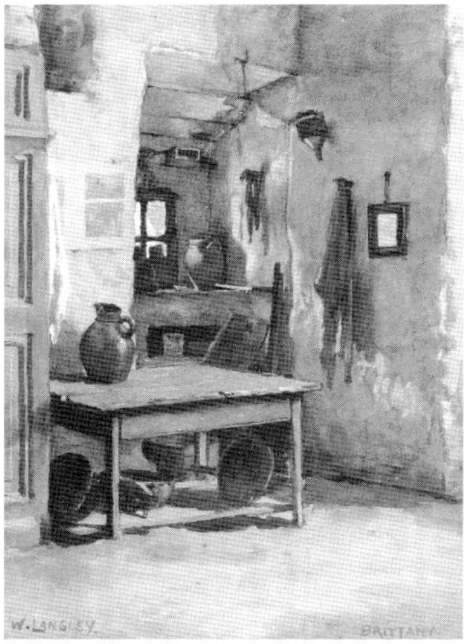

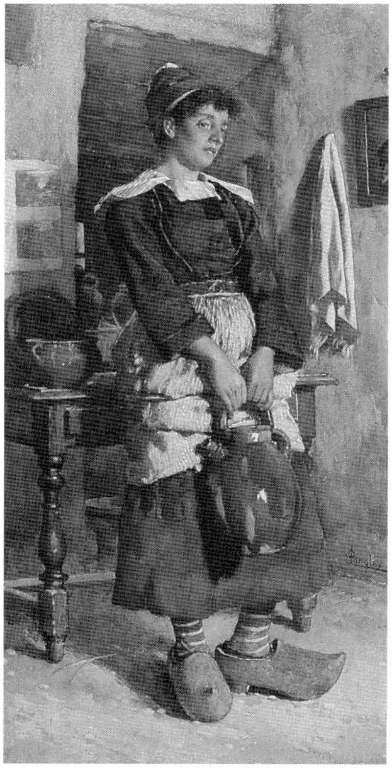

A Breton girl 1881
watercolour, 54.5 x 27.3cm

The jar the girl is holding belonged to Langley and the figure stands in front of the recessed window that appears in *A Corner of the Kitchen, Brittany,* above.

the seal on a venture that would become a part of the Birmingham art scene for some years to come. Langley's visible contribution to the public launch of the Circle was to outline its brief history in the exhibition catalogue. He also sent in to the exhibition two Midlands scenes and one Brittany study, all of which sold.

Towards the end of the year Langley received, apparently out of the blue, an astounding offer of a year's Newlyn work for £500. This commission came from J W Thrupp, a Birmingham photographer and art dealer, acting as agent for a person or persons later identified in Langley's sales records as 'Alldays'. 'Allday' and 'Alldays' were not uncommon names in Birmingham and, earlier in the year, Langley had sold two Newlyn views direct to 'Alldays of Warstone Lane'. It seems likely that those sales prompted both the commission and its emphasis on Newlyn subject matter, but there were four Alldays in Warstone Lane at the time so the exact identity of the patron may never be known.

Langley was now in a considerable predicament. The Edwin Chamberlain commission was of lesser value than Thrupp's, but would enable him to return more quickly to work for other clients. Moreover, his sales for 1881 seemed likely to far exceed £500, which suggested he would be better off in 1882 without Thrupp's offer. After some hesitation, and only when Chamberlain offered to defer his commission, Langley came to an agreement with Thrupp whereby he would undertake work to the value of £500, which would require less than a year to complete.

Langley had made only brief visits to Newlyn in 1881 and barely a handful of Newlyn works can be dated to that year. The emergence of the two commissions, however, indicates that Newlyn was seen to offer promising subject matter and the account Langley opened in Penzance at Bolitho's Mount's Bay Bank on July 2 was left open when he returned to Birmingham after his last sketching trip. He may well have planned to return to Newlyn early in 1882, to complete the Chamberlain commission, but now he would take his family with him.

A busy year, 1881 had its reward in sales of 102 paintings yielding £723, over £30,000 in 1997 terms and three times as much as Langley might have expected to earn from lithography alone.

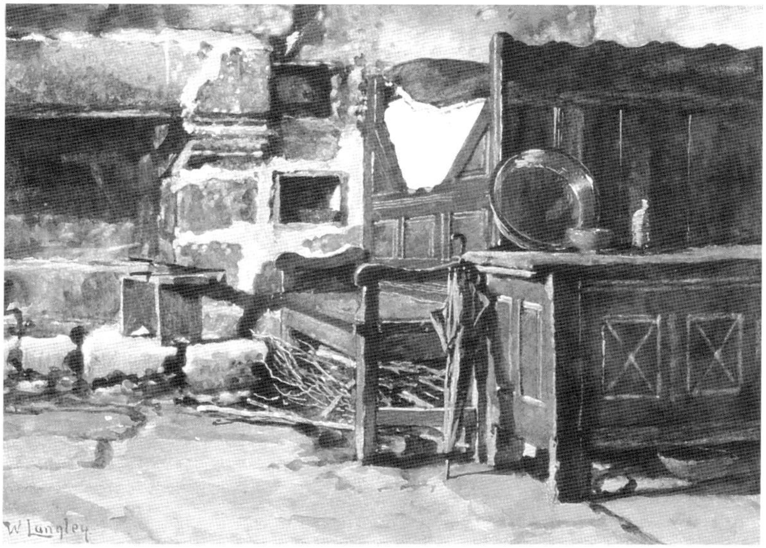

A Brittany Interior 1881
watercolour, 22.5 x 31cm

There is another watercolour with two figures in Breton costume in this same interior with its high box bed.

PAGE 56, TOP
A Corner of the Kitchen, Brittany 1881
watercolour, 30.5 x 22cm

This deeply recessed window appears in at least two much later works, *Motherlove*, 1913 (oil, 137 x 101.5cm) and *A Reverie* of 1908 or 1909. (oil, 58.5 x 34.5cm).

While most of his work was sold through dealers, Langley also exhibited widely, showing six paintings at the Society, three at the Art Circle and one each at Liverpool, Bristol, the Dudley Gallery and the Royal Society in London, and Southport. These were essentially selling exhibitions and though sales did not always materialise the exposure given to Langley's work was of value. That he could maintain such a high level of activity was a tribute not only to his energy but also to the support he received from Clara. The crowning achievement of the year was his election as an Associate Member of the Royal Birmingham Society of Artists. Langley had sent in his best work to the Society's exhibitions from 1873 on and the recognition of his skills in 1881, the first year in which Associates were admitted, was a pleasing indication that he was becoming an established Birmingham artist.

In his first two years as a professional artist Langley may have harboured doubts about having abandoned lithography but the events of 1881 had been a triumphant vindication of his choice. If there were any doubts at all on the horizon they probably stemmed from the varied nature of his output which, though amply demonstrating his considerable technical skill, gave no indication of any particular style or treatment that would distinguish his work from that of other artists.

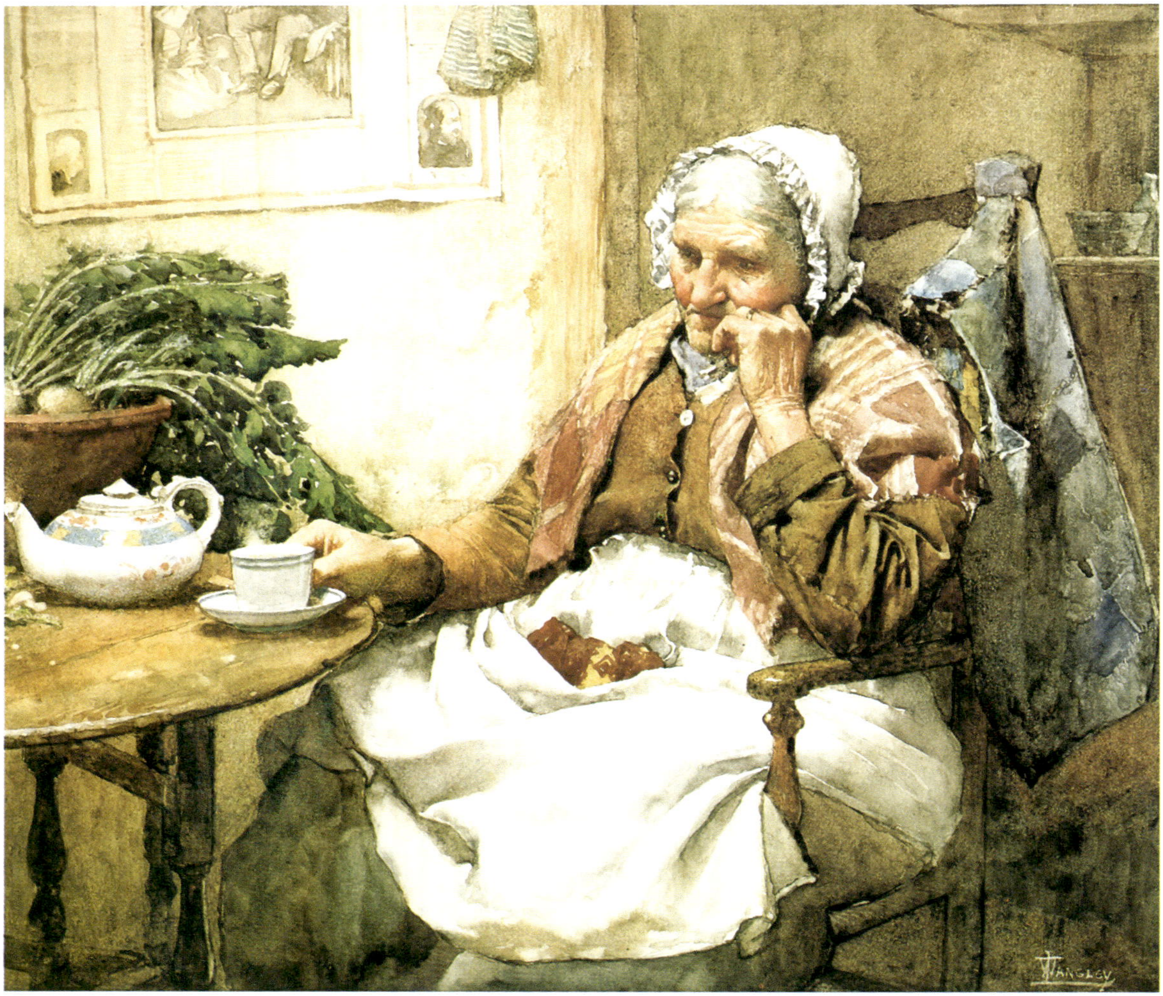

1882-1885 Newlyn

CHAPTER THREE

Late in March, 1882, the Langleys took up residence at Pembroke Lodge, a house overlooking Mount's Bay and set amid orchards and market gardens, a few hundred yards west of Newlyn's tiny harbour. A ropewalk lay just beyond their new home and close by, at Cliff Castle Cottage, lived Henry Martin, an artist who had started life as a midshipman, sailing round the Cape of Good Hope to India, before discovering Newlyn in 1870. The financial cost of the Langleys' translation to this idyllic environment was a year's rent in advance, £62, and £58 spent on furniture.

The clear light of west Cornwall held out the prospect of painting en plein air but it owed much of its quality to the peninsula's frequent and heavy rainfall, which had driven the previous tenant of Pembroke Lodge, the Irish artist Charles Durdin, to build a studio in the garden. For the convenience of his sitters, Langley rented a second studio down in the village and, thus

PAGE 58
A Quiet Afternoon 1882
watercolour, 26.5 x 30.5cm

Like *Time moveth not* and *But men must work*, this shows the tenderness with which Langley depicted the old women he used as models. Together these works mark the maturity of Langley's technique in watercolours painted from life.

BELOW
Waiting for the Boats 1885
watercolour, approx. 16.5 x 48cm

Probably a study for the large watercolour of this title shown at the RI in 1885. It seems to be related to *Departure of the Fleet for the North* of 1886 in style, in the girl with pink blouse and woollen headscarf, and in the poses of the old lady and young girl at the far right in both compositions.

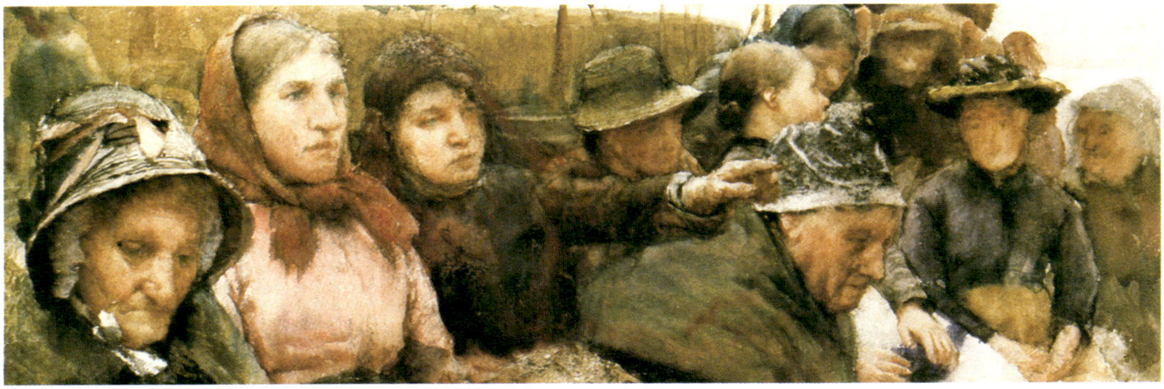

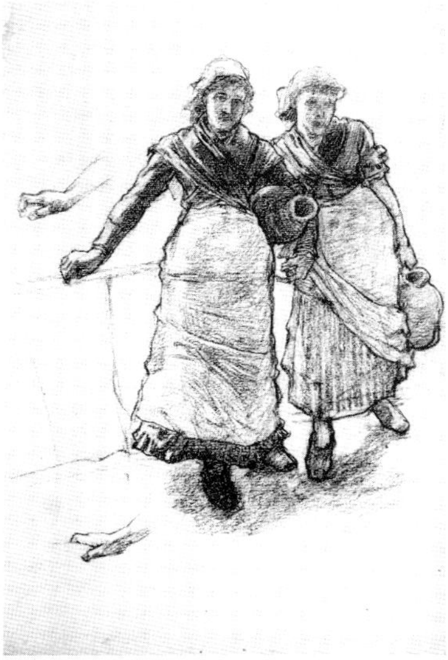

Study of two girls early-1880s
chalk, 38 x 24.7cm

RIGHT
Time moveth not, our being 'tis that moves 1882
watercolour, 55 x 21cm
(whereabouts unknown, reproduced from a contemporary Burlington print)

This was Langley's first success in London, in January 1883, and led to his election to the Royal Institute of Painters in Water Colours later that year. The *Birmingham Post* reported that 'it created some little sensation and attracted general admiration' and asks, is it of 'the distant days when that tanned cheek was as the rose, and that rugged forehead was smooth and white, when she first embraced the joys and cares and heartaches of a fisherman's wife that she is thinking?...'

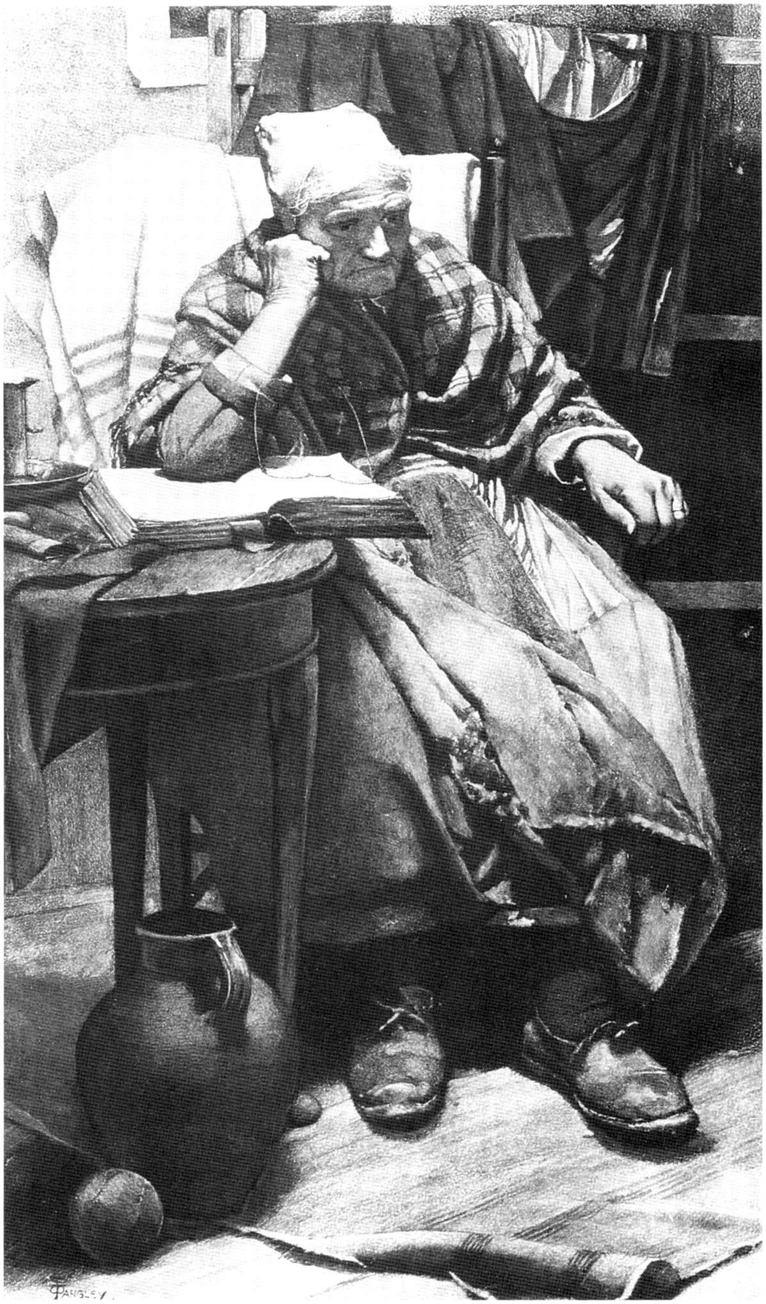

equipped, soon had the Alldays commission under way. By the end of November the work was done, 43 paintings that cost Alldays £607. Thrupp, who had arbitrated on the paintings' values as they were received in Birmingham, deducted his charges and sent the balance of £500 in instalments to Langley.

While the commission was in progress and accounting for all his Newlyn work, Langley was able to exhibit only Midlands studies. These were particularly well received and, with Clara once again pregnant, Langley might have been tempted to return home at the end of 1882, but he had not yet exhausted the artistic potential of Newlyn. The commission paintings had followed the pattern set in previous years — well-observed scenes and studies of local people — but in the latter days of 1882 Langley's empathy with the fisherfolk of Newlyn, whose hard life so echoed his own early struggles, found expression in a radical change in subject matter towards what might now be described as social realism.

Langley decided to test out his new theme in London and, in December, sent some watercolours up to the London artist and dealer W Ayerst Ingram, whom he had met in Newlyn in 1881. Ingram, in turn, arranged for the study of an old Newlyn fishwife, entitled *Time moveth not, our being 'tis that moves*, to be exhibited at London's Dudley Gallery. This was a highly significant course of action as the Institute of Painters in Water Colours (later the 'Royal' Institute) had recently recruited 21 new members from exhibitors at the Dudley and had further vacancies.[9] Furthermore, Edmund Wimperis was on the Institute's governing body and Edwin Hayes on its Admissions Committee, two artists who, coincidentally, had also been in Newlyn in 1881.

Any doubts Langley may have had about how his new work might be received were quickly dispelled. *Time moveth not* proved the outstanding painting at the Dudley Gallery exhibition and, in February 1883, Langley received a request from Hayes for the loan of further examples of his work for the Institute's Admissions Committee to consider. He had every reason to be pleased with the course of events but then a complication arose, with an invitation from Alfred Newton, secretary of the Royal Society of Painters in Water Colours, to put himself up for membership of that body. Here was a first-rate dilemma. The 'Old Society' was as prestigious a body as the Institute and to join either was a great honour. To join both, however, was not feasible while to reject one and then be rejected by the other was too appalling even to contemplate.

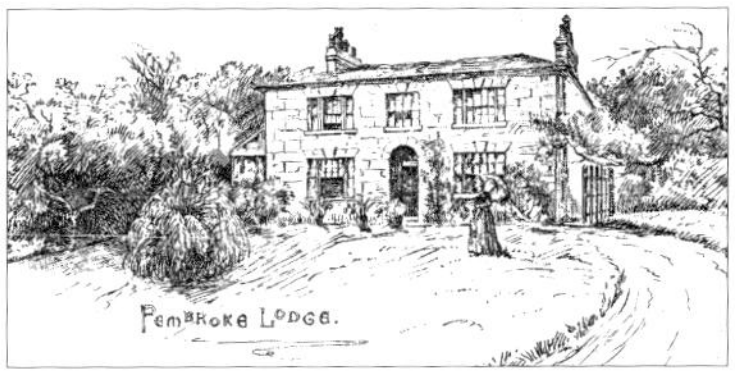

Illustration of Pembroke Lodge from the *Edgbastonia* magazine, July 1890

Langley may have supplied a drawing for the engraver of this, the house he rented in Newlyn.

The Sunny South 1885
oil, 122 x 61 cm

The Sunny South was painted at a time when Langley was seeking to emulate in oils the success of his watercolours of 1883 and 1884. He had already completed one major oil in 1883 *(Memories,* now in the Birmingham Art Gallery collection) and wished to paint more.

In *The Sunny South* the artist's viewpoint is from the garden of Pembroke Lodge, Newlyn, where he lived at the time, looking towards the old harbour and across Mounts Bay.

PAGE 63, TOP
The Sunny South, a Study 1885
watercolour, 22.6 x 11.1cm

Painted looking down from Pembroke Lodge.

PAGE 63, BOTTOM
Study for *The Sunny South,* c1885
watercolour, 34.3 x 22.9cm

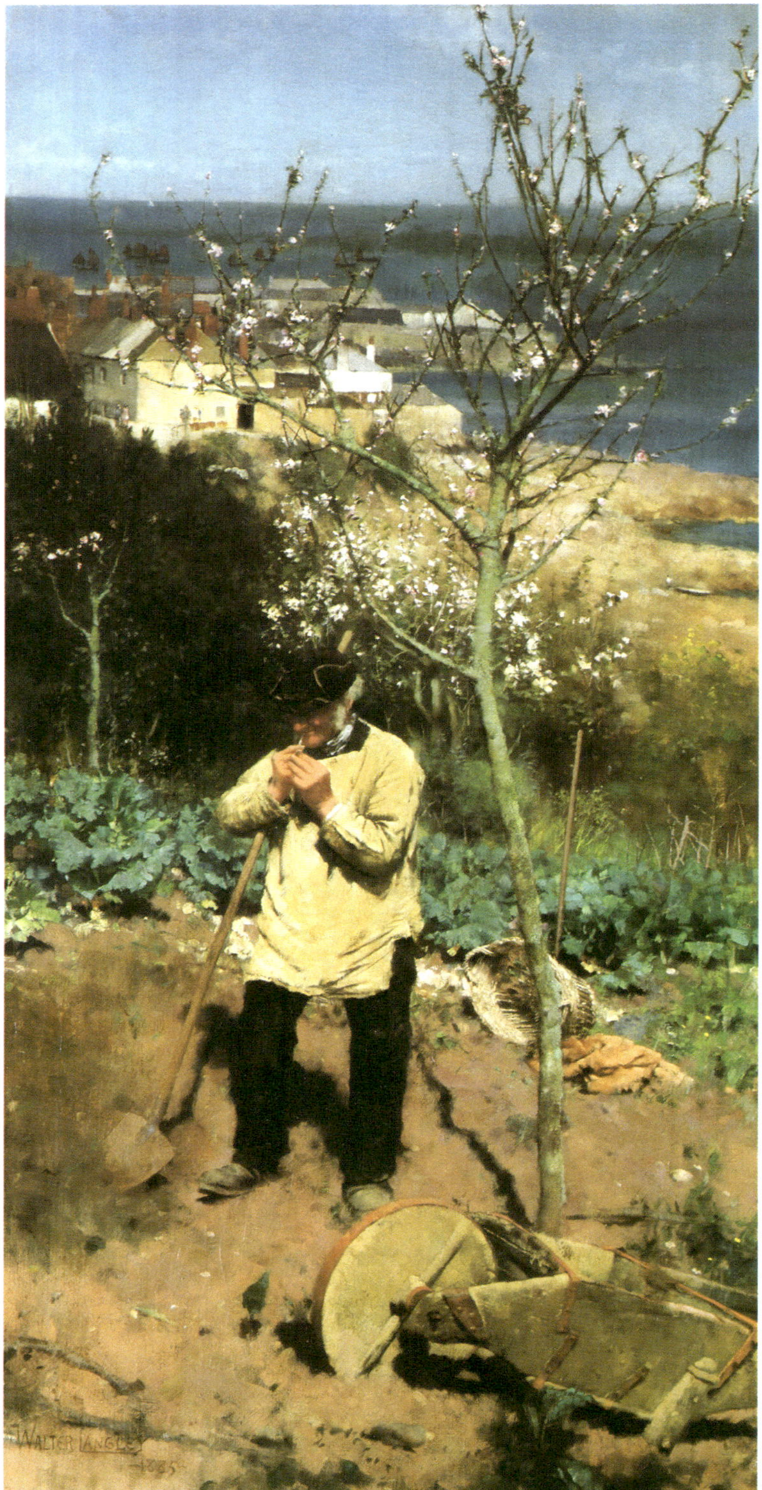

Being so far from the scene of action, Langley enlisted Ingram's help to see how the land lay. A few days later, Hayes wrote to both Langley and Ingram. The letter to Ingram has survived:

> I have written as you requested and told him [Langley] that I am as certain as anyone can be that he will be elected. The meeting is on Monday night. I have seen the Committee and am sure it is alright. Thanks for your interest in the matter.

Was 'as certain as anyone can be' certain enough? Langley had to curb his impatience until the Committee finished its deliberations. A letter from Wimperis, dated March 13, completes the story:

> You will have heard by telegram this morning from your friend Mr Ingram of the election last night. You were elected unanimously on the nomination of the Selecting Committee. After the meeting was over I went to the Hogarth Club and there saw Mr Ingram and he begged to be allowed to telegraph you. As he has been very kind in his efforts to help us I consented to him doing so, though I ought to have done it. But I content myself with writing my congratulations ...

Langley wrote to Alfred Newton to explain the position, and in reply was told: 'I am very much disappointed ... as you would have been sure of success, but I suppose it cannot be helped.'

Amidst the turmoil of his election to the Institute, Langley's diary entry for February 17 reads — with a fine sense of priorities — 'Received £20 from Keeley. Baby born 11.30am.' The baby was Cecil, the fourth and last of his and Clara's children.

The launch of Langley's career in London did not go unnoticed in his home town where E Barran Brightwell, art correspondent of the *Birmingham Weekly Post*, penned an enthusiastic report:

> I am sure that I am by no means singular in the great satisfaction I feel in knowing that one of the band of gifted artists whose work has been both flower and fruit of the 'Birmingham School' makes his mark this year in the London exhibitions.
> Mr Walter Langley has hitherto sent little, or nothing, to London. This year, at the Dudley Gallery, the post of honour is

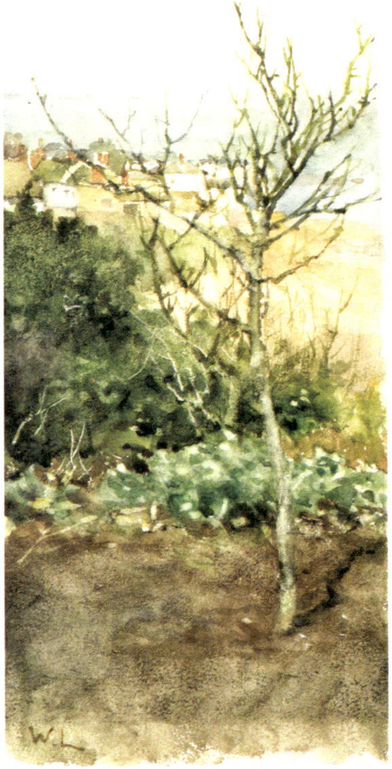

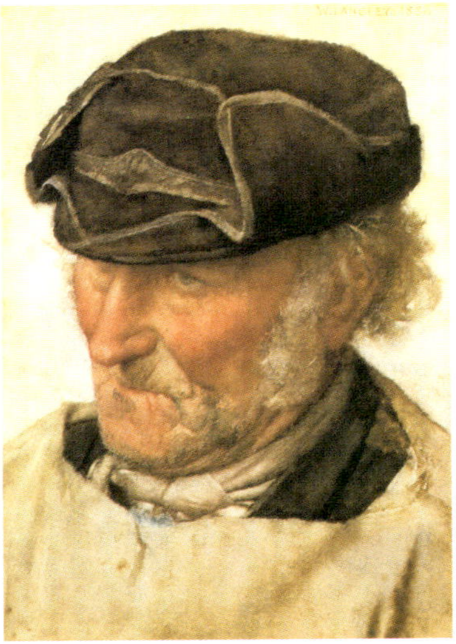

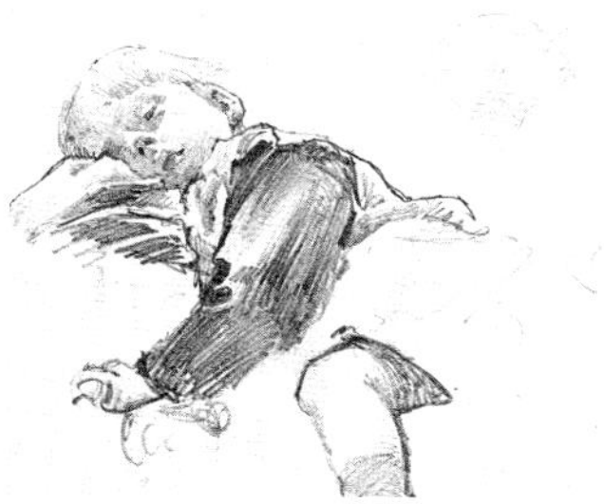

Sketchbook study of a child asleep,
c1879-82
pencil, 9.5 x 16cm

assigned to him, and his work has been warmly praised by several of the journals which, if they do not form, at all events indicate the current of a cultivated taste. One of these describes Mr Langley's work as an imitation of Mr Herkomer's earlier style. Whoever knows anything of Mr Langley and of his work knows that whatever he may or may not be he is no imitator of any other artist, living or dead. He is thoroughly independent and original, working out the conceptions of his own mind in his own way. What of likeness there is between Mr Langley's work and Mr Herkomer's is due to the fact that both are earnest, thoughtful men, going direct to nature, and that both are moved by a large and tender sympathy with the deeper emotions of the human heart.

The change in Langley's status was startling. Only two days after the news of his admission to the Institute his diary records the receipt of a Birmingham School of Art prize for still life, indicating he was a student there at least up to the close of 1881. A further consequence of the swiftness of events was that he had no work on hand for the Institute's 1883 Spring Exhibition, the first at which he was eligible to exhibit, and Ingram had to loan paintings from the selection Langley had previously sent him. These works included a telling demonstration of his heartfelt rapport with the Newlyn fisherfolk. Although by now familiar, his words are well worth repeating:

> One night, in the winter of 1882, as I was reading 'The Three Fishers', I heard the gun go off as a signal of distress. I went out into the black night — an awful storm was howling — and saw the blue rockets being fired from Penzance as a signal to those who were at sea. The scene was in the last degree impressive — a fearful contrast to my cosy fireside — and the idea of the painting at once suggested itself.

Langley always took great care when choosing titles for his work to make clear the intended theme of each painting and from Charles Kingsley's poem he chose the following lines:[10]

> But men must work, and women must weep

Though storms be sudden, and waters deep
And the harbour bar be moaning

Langley set the scene for his painting in the bare comfort of a cottage parlour. There, an old fisherwoman, seated at a window from which she can see the storm raging outside, comforts a young mother on whose lap a baby sleeps peacefully — three generations that may be deprived at the storm's whim of son, husband and father.

In both *Time moveth not* and *But men must work*, Langley demonstrated his deep understanding of the role of women in the Newlyn community. As in the home in which he spent his childhood, so in Newlyn women faced a lifetime of hard work and patient reconciliation to a portion in life that promised, and often gave, nothing. These paintings established Langley's distinct artistic style and choice of subject matter in the mind of the art viewing and purchasing public and, coupled with his admission to the Institute, drew attractive offers of commissions, ensuring he would stay on in Newlyn.

Recognition for his work was particularly important for Langley. Though he had not been alone in Newlyn in 1882, the colony of artists there may truly be said to have been born in 1883 when no fewer than nine painters, including William Wainwright and Edwin Harris, made their home in Cliff Castle Cottage. The newcomers added greatly to the social life of the colony — the elder Langley children particularly enjoyed picnicking with the artists — and the attractions of life in Cornwall increased. With the stimulus of other artists around him, Langley embarked on a period of intense work, peaking in July with twenty-six painting sessions in eighteen days. The names of the models he used in 1883 are recorded in his diary but not, unfortunately, the paintings in which they featured.[11] Mrs Lanyon, 77 years of age, was Langley's favourite 'old lady', closely followed by Annie Warren, a 58-year-old widow from Mount View, Newlyn. Jack Cotton, 34 years old, was the fisherman he painted most often.

Several of the Newlyn artists moved on as winter approached and the departure of Wainwright for an atelier in Paris gave Langley a good enough reason to spend a week there in October. There is little doubt he went as a sightseer only, the working opportunities in Newlyn being more to his taste. It was a very much diminished

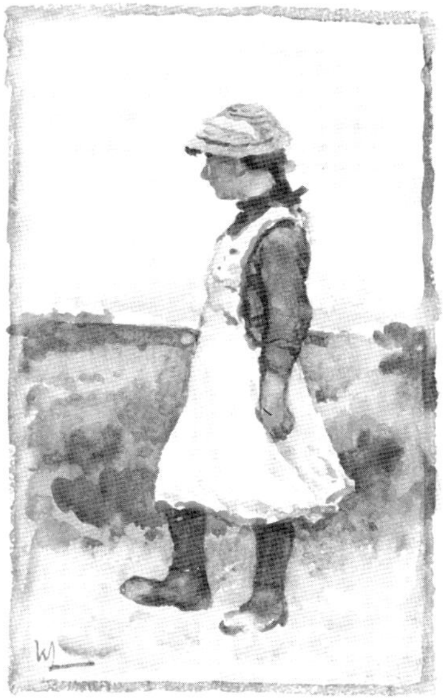

ABOVE
On the Moors c1882
watercolour, 19 x 12.3cm

PAGE 66
A Reverie 1883
watercolour, 17 x 12.5cm

PAGE 67
The Way to School 1892
watercolour, 38 x 26.7cm

Shown in the Fine Art Society one-man exhibition in 1893. The unprecedentedly large number of watercolours brought together for this exhibition made it a landmark in Langley's career.

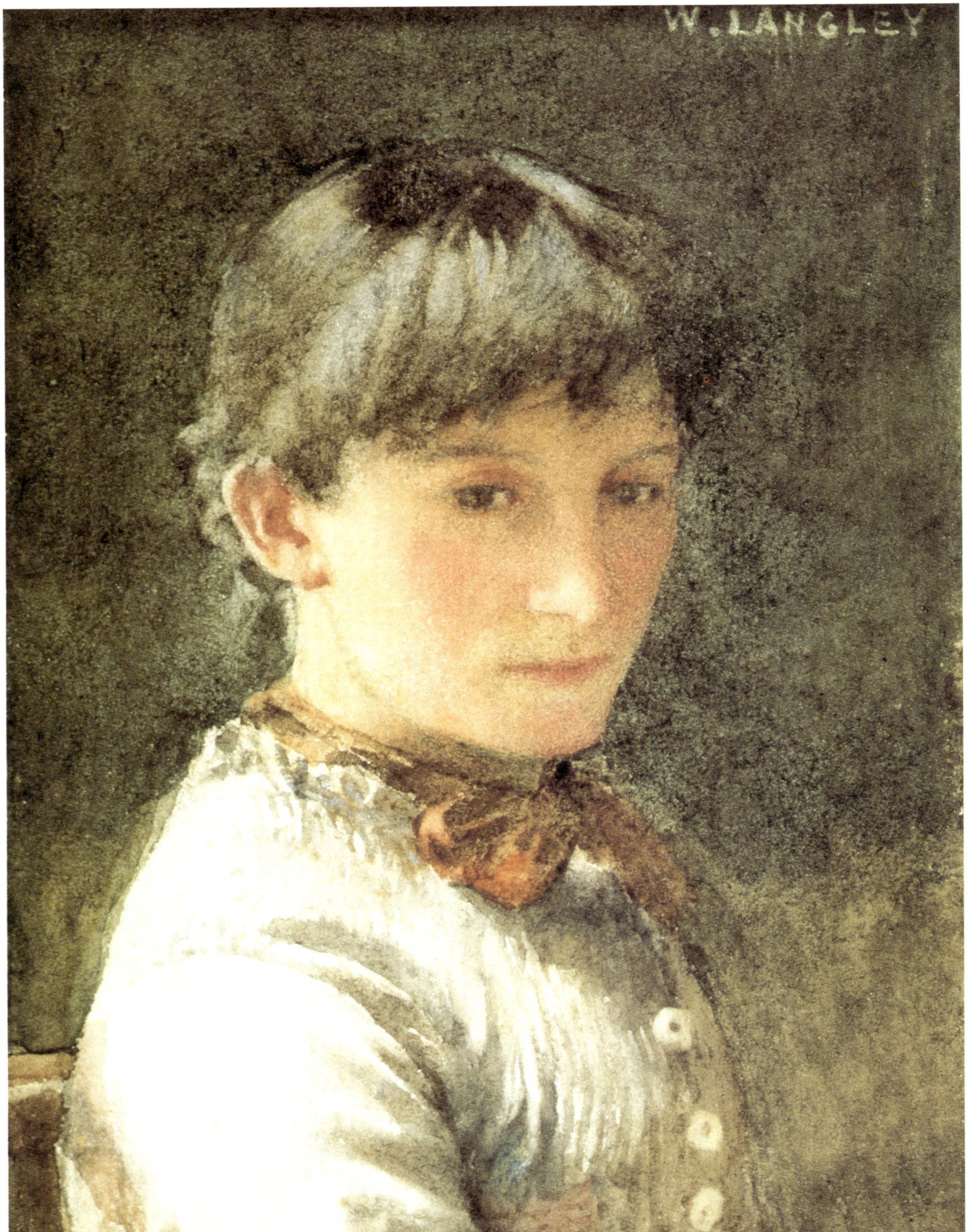
W. LANGLEY

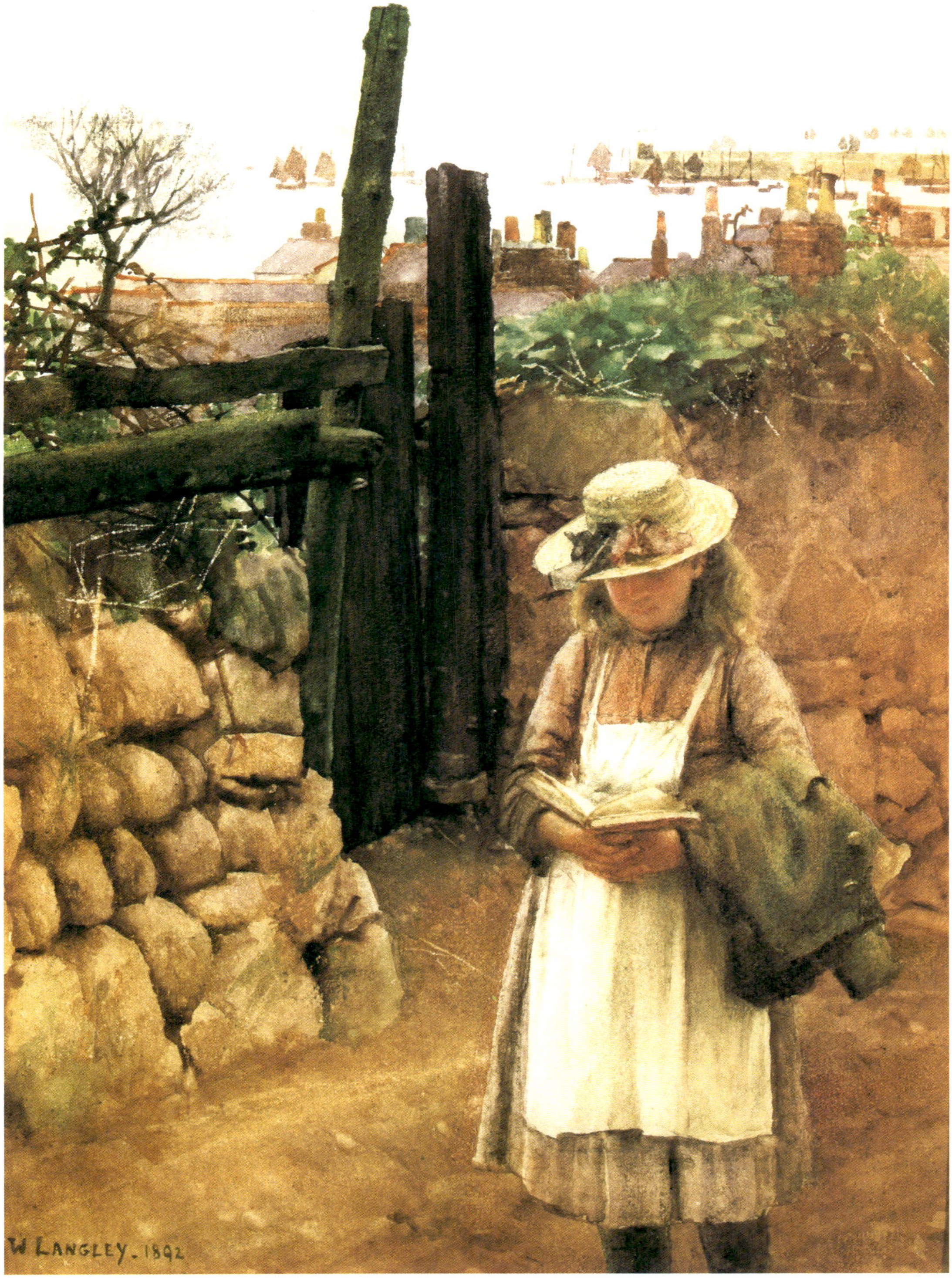
W LANGLEY . 1892

RIGHT
A Fisherman's Son 1884
watercolour, 34.3 x 24.1cm

PAGE 69, MAIN PICTURE
A Daydream 1884
watercolour, 34.3 x 24.1cm
Besides the study, the head shown on page 139 may also be the same girl. This and *A Fisherman's Son* were both bought by the Midlands dealer, Franks.

PAGE 69, FAR RIGHT
Study for *A Daydream* 1884
chalk, 30 x 20.3cm

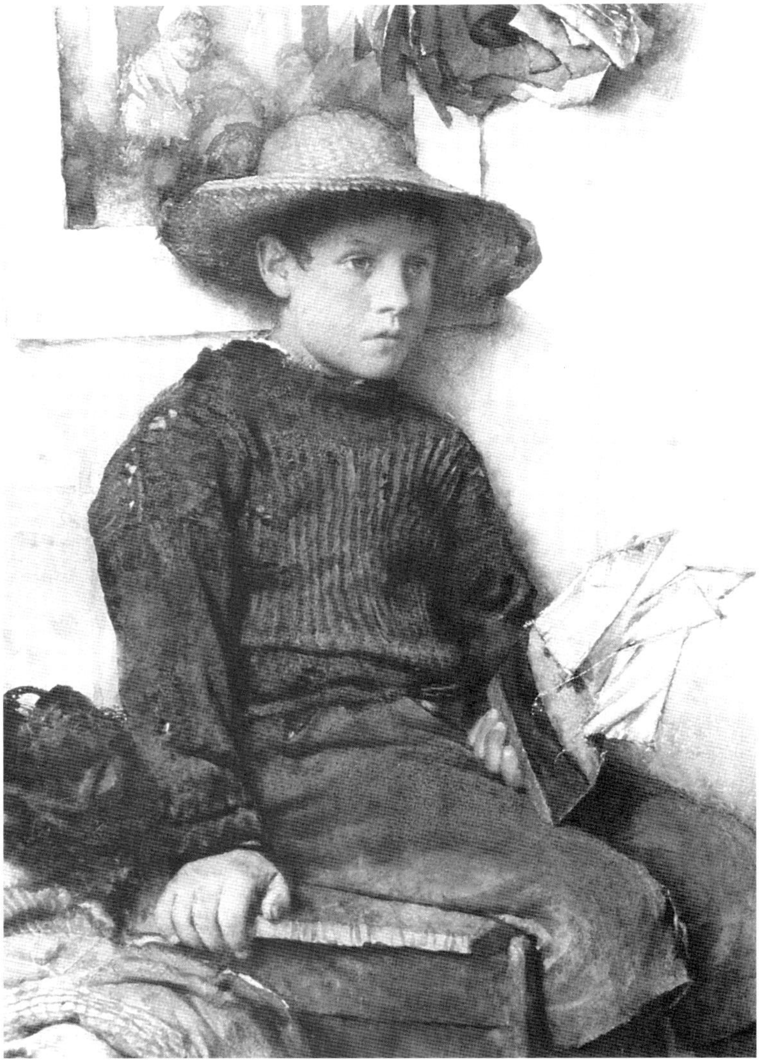

colony to which he returned but the fall in numbers proved only a temporary setback. The few pioneers who wintered in Newlyn were joined in 1884 by an impressive group of newcomers, Leghe Suthers, Fred Hall, Frank Bramley, Percy Craft, Chevallier Tayler and Stanhope Forbes. Henry Scott Tuke, like Langley a Rationalist by conviction, called in briefly, before departing for Falmouth.

Of the new generation of Newlyn artists, the most important was Forbes and although, from a more mellow perspective, he revealed in the *Cornish Telegraph* of January 12, 1905, that he had been drawn to Newlyn from Brittany by the enthusiastic reports he

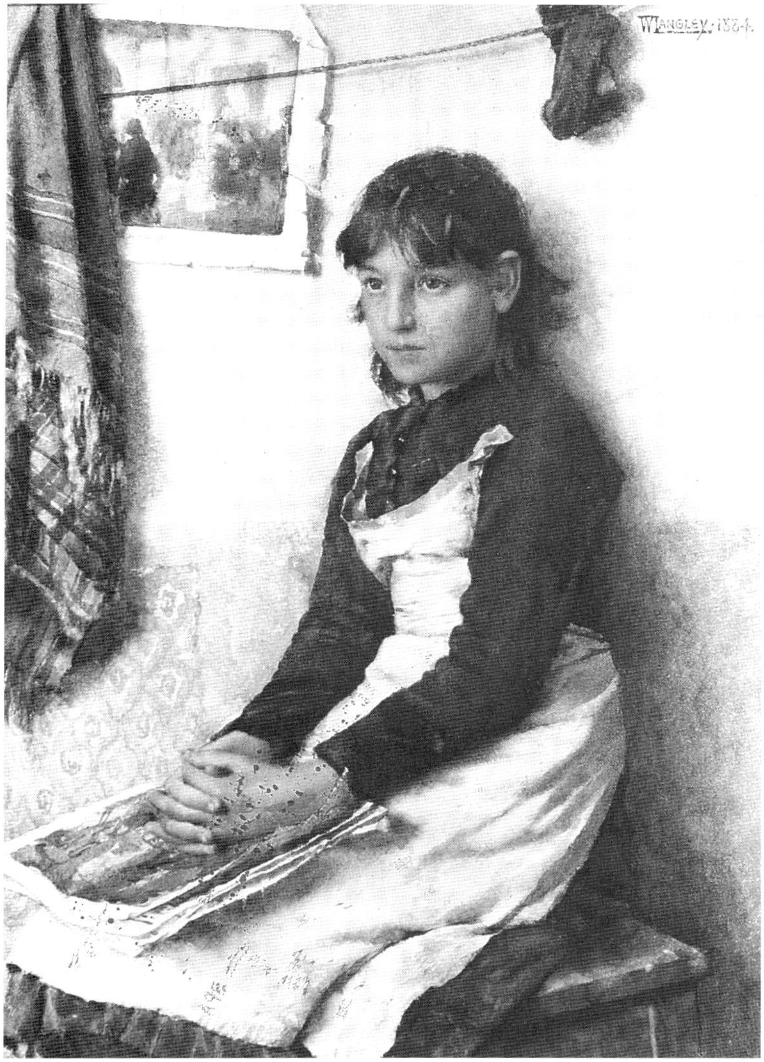

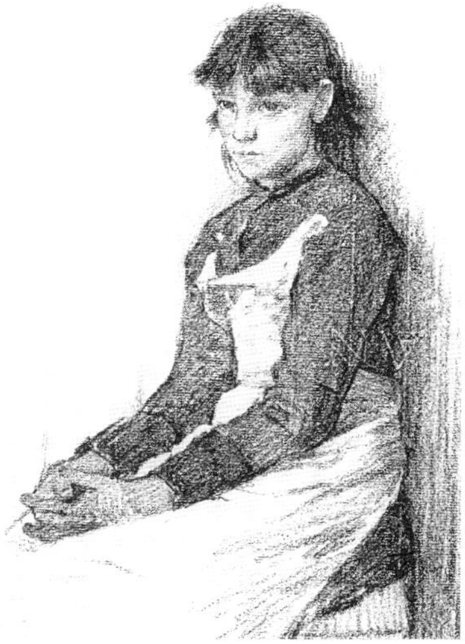

had received from Langley and Wainwright, he wrote at the time to his mother that the Newlyn artists were 'an unsympathetic set'. He described his relationship with Langley as 'coldly friendly'. Langley, dependent on art for a living, was doubtless more concerned to see whether any of the new arrivals would follow his line in subject matter, than to worry about disharmony on a social level. As events transpired, he had no cause for alarm.

A major difference between Langley and his fellow artists at that time was that he painted only occasionally in oils and had never exhibited in the medium while they, in the main, gave watercolours

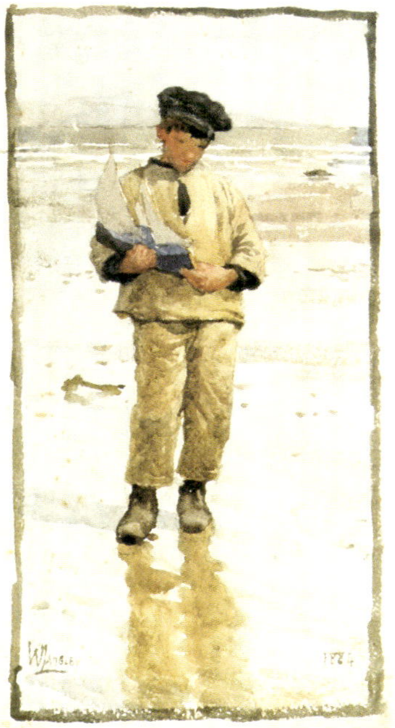

a wide berth. In 1883, however, he had submitted an oil painting, *In Memoriam*, to the spring exhibition of the Institute of Painters in Oils. Even Wainwright, who had once shared a studio with Langley, was surprised to see a Langley oil painting when he visited the London galleries. Was it, he asked, 'a picture upon which the magic of a French brush has operated?'

Langley's preference for watercolours may seem to have placed him at some disadvantage when the pre-eminent artistic body of his day, the Royal Academy, made little secret of its disdain for the medium. This did not deter Langley from a conscious choice of watercolours over oils, as Wainwright explained in 1923, in a valedictory Clarendon Art Fellowship Lecture:

> Why on his emergence from lithography and industrial design, did Langley choose watercolour as his means of artistic expression, in preference to oil? It is a useful and pertinent

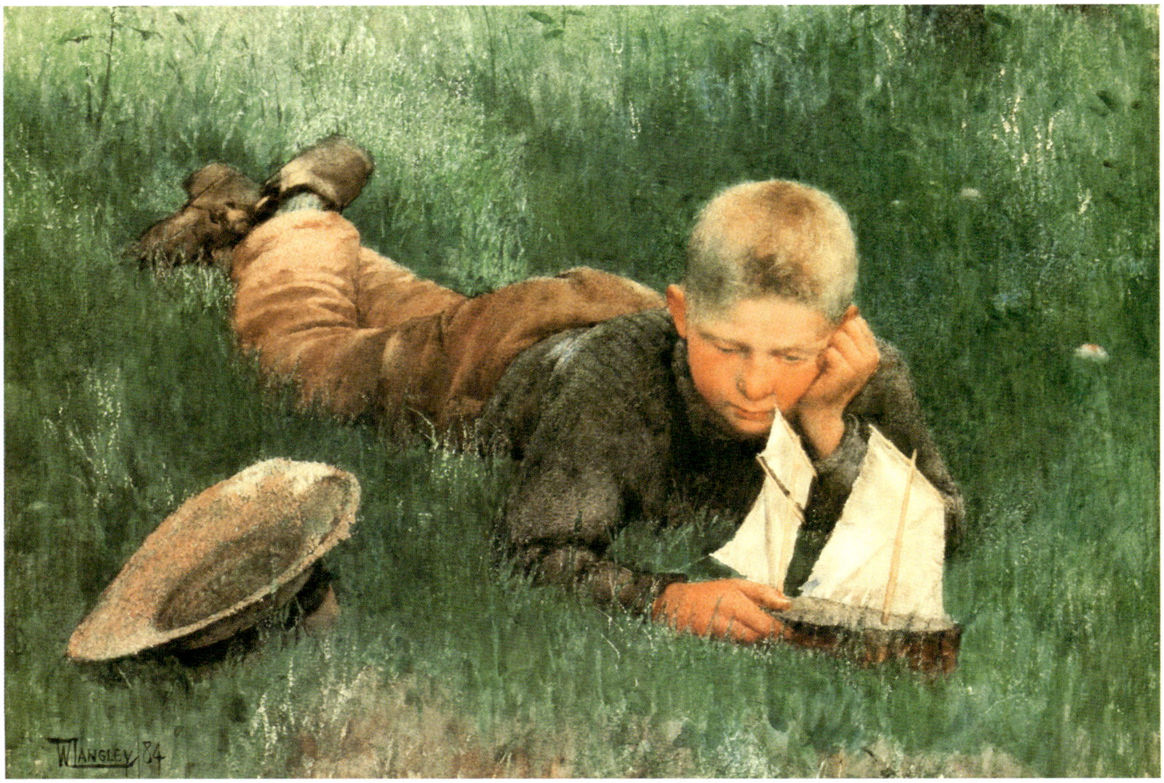

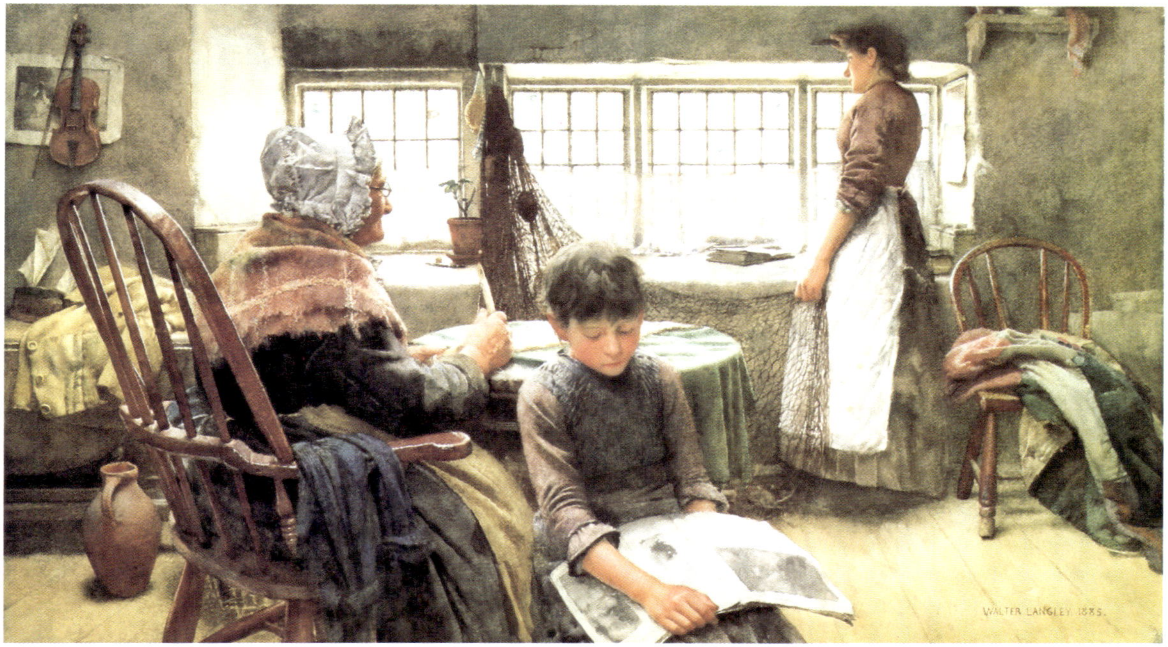

question. To a person of Langley's sensibility this could not be a matter of indifference and I am inclined to see in that decision a distinct choice formed by personal preference and artistic conviction that for him it was the medium in which he could reach his highest expression.

Possibly Langley would have devoted more time to oils had not his 1884 Institute watercolour, *Among the Missing*, proved a great success:

> *Among the Missing* is ... one of the most striking drawings in the present exhibition ... and decidedly the most important of the artist's works hitherto. It has attracted much attention by its excellent technical quality and by the facile power and breadth with which a familiar scene is presented; the interest it creates, though so spontaneously evoked, is not of the kind that is quickly exhausted. Freshly and even vividly felt as its pathos and power are at first sight, the appeal to our sympathy and understanding is made with such simplicity of method, and is so broadly based on a sentiment common to humanity, that the impression is deep and lasting.

Memories 1885
watercolour, 45.8 x 79cm
(Birmingham Museums and Art Gallery)

Presented to the Gallery by Cllr Michael Davies in the year it was painted and following its first showing at the Birmingham Art Circle, for whose catalogue Langley drew a pen and ink version. The wide horizontal format is used here, possibly for the first time, to great effect for a major exhibition painting. The width of the cottage window upon which the painting is centred may well have been extended for the purpose of composition. In other works similar windows of one or two casements appear, and one of three in at least one other painting, *Once Upon a Time* 1896.

PAGE 70, TOP
The Fisherman's Son 1884
watercolour, 25.3 x 13.2cm

PAGE 70, BOTTOM
Wonderland 1884
watercolour, 25.4 x 35.6cm

Has been known as *I think I'll be a Sailor*.

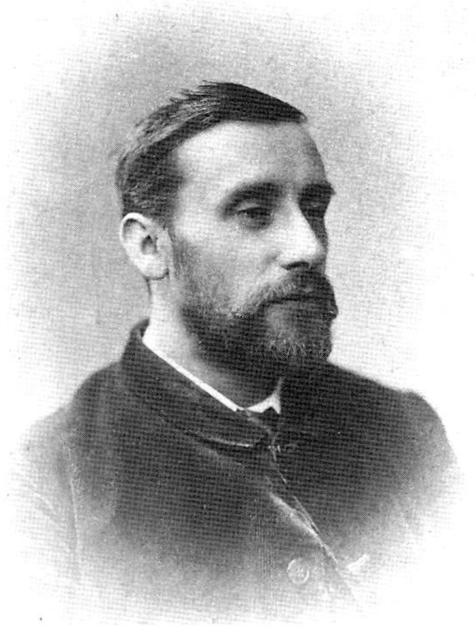

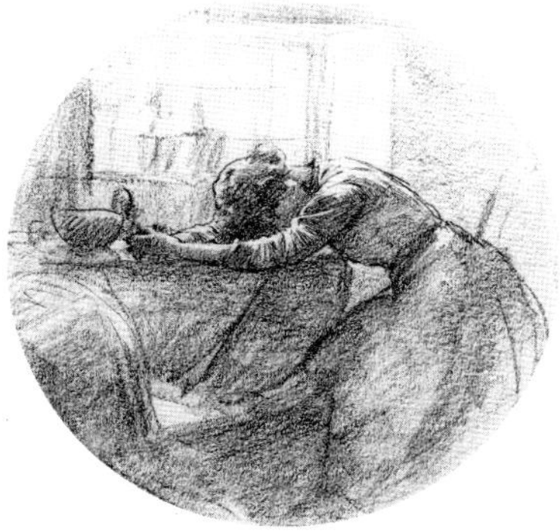

Study of a woman grieving mid-1880s
crayon, diam. 23cm

The format suggests this may have been a study for an illustration.

TOP
Walter Langley, about 1885-86, photograph by Baker of Birmingham

The *Magazine of Art* reviewer concluded his panegyric by discussing the execution of the work:

> There remains for notice the scheme of colour and the admirable skill with which it is worked out and harmonised; the dramatic force of the incident derives considerable value from the breadth of the atmospheric medium and the truth of the local colour. The wild windy weather of the burdened sky, the happy tumult of the surging trees beyond the grey shingled roof, the suggestion of verdure so finely harmonised with the tone of the grey wall and door-coping, all combine to quicken the sense of calamity.

Among the Missing was sold to a Manchester businessman for £420, four times greater than the highest price Langley had achieved up till then. The success of this painting prompted the Penzance newspapers to take notice for the first time of the art colony on its doorstep, though with mixed results. In four lines, the *Cornishman* gave the painting the wrong title, said it had been exhibited at the Academy rather than the Institute, attributed the wrong gender to the purchaser and mis-stated the price it fetched by a wide margin. Not surprisingly, this effort drew a somewhat acerbic correction from the aggrieved artist. The *Cornish Telegraph* did better, however, declaring 'Mr Langley's Newlyn picture is a hit, a palpable hit' adding, for good measure, that 'an artist of established reputation writing to a relative in Penzance declares it is the picture of the year'.

In 1884, his sixth year as a professional artist, Langley was elevated from 'Associate' to 'Responsible Member' of the Royal Birmingham Society of Artists. The lithographer of 1878 had every reason to be pleased with the way things were going.

Not least among the benefits arising from the sale of *Among the Missing* was that it paved the way for a welcome reduction in output over the coming year. His next Institute painting, *Waiting for the Boats*, sold well in April 1885 and all seemed set fair but sales for the next five months amounted to only £60. Bad times became worse when Langley discovered that one of his Alldays commission paintings had been sent in to the Institute without his knowledge and at double the price he had received, making him realise he had

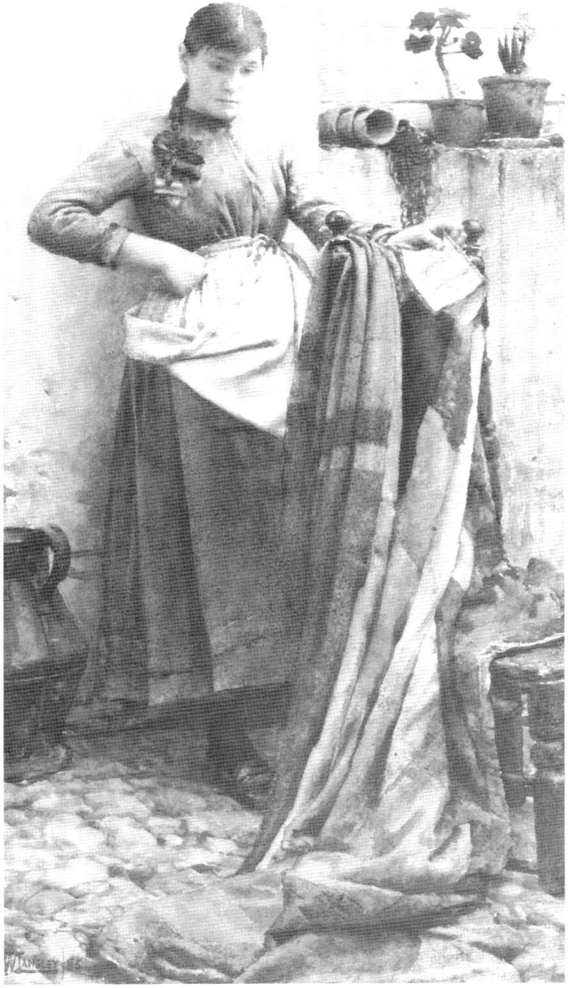

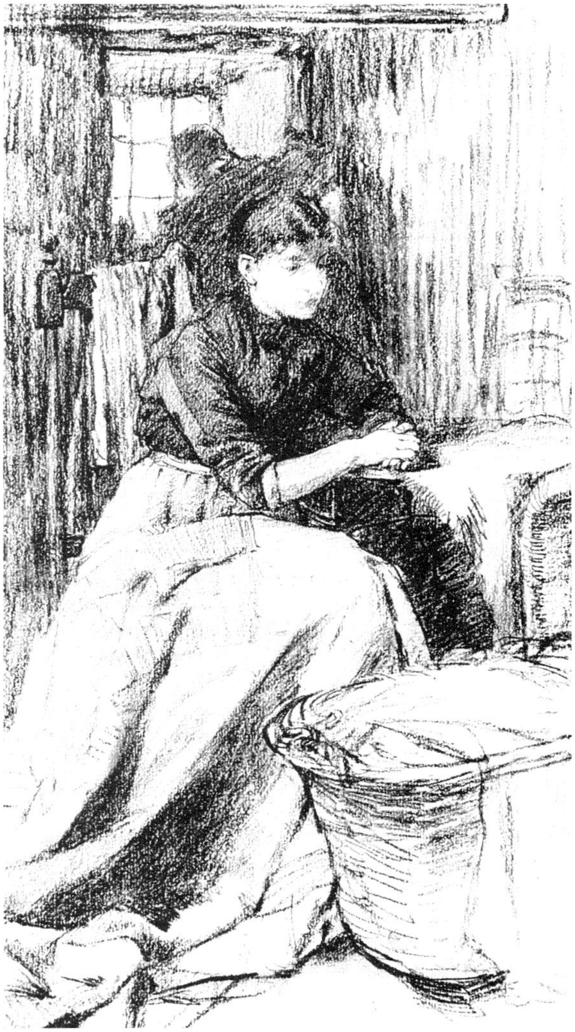

seriously underpriced his earlier Newlyn work.

With a wife and four children to support, Langley could not afford to sit idly by hoping things would get better and, concluding that Newlyn had yielded him all it had to offer, he decided to move back to Birmingham. Being near family and old friends would make the move home the more agreeable, besides which he had some positive ideas for the future.

ABOVE LEFT
Sad News 1885
watercolour, 32 x 17cm

ABOVE RIGHT
The Gathering Storm 1883
crayon, 38 x 21cm

A study for the watercolour of this title 1883 (76 x 44cm).

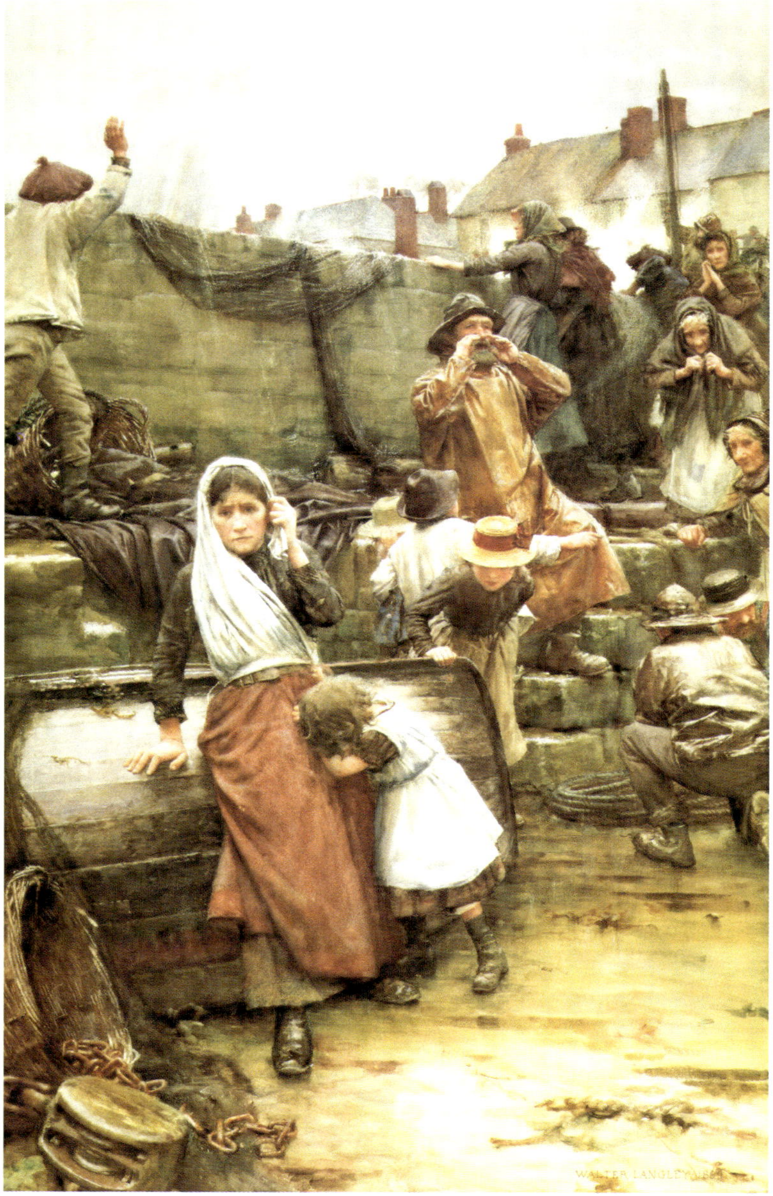
WALTER LANGLEY

1886-1893 Birmingham & Newlyn

CHAPTER FOUR

With Clara and the children settled into a home in Birmingham's fashionable Bristol Road, Langley returned to Newlyn to complete his watercolour for the Institute's 1886 spring exhibition. The peaceful afternoon scene depicted in this painting — *In a Cornish Fishing Village: Departure of the Fleet for the North* — was in sharp contrast to Langley's own frantic activity, as he shuttled between his lodgings overlooking Penzance harbour, Ralph Todd's studio, where he was working, and Birmingham. Todd's offer to share his studio was a generous gesture that proved of mutual benefit, Langley gaining companionship at a trying time and Todd making 'astounding progress' in his watercolours, according to a letter from Stanhope Forbes to his mother. Not until April did Langley finally leave Newlyn for Birmingham:

> Mr Langley has some notion of entering upon a comparatively little traversed range of subjects quite close to home. In some of

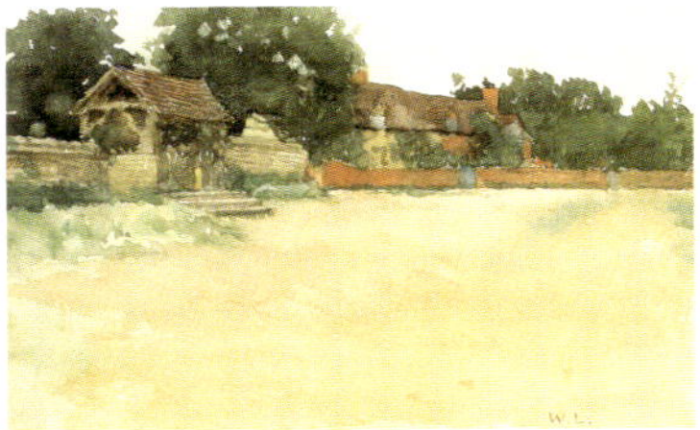

The Lych Gate, Welford-on-Avon
c1886
watercolour, 12.9 x 19.9cm

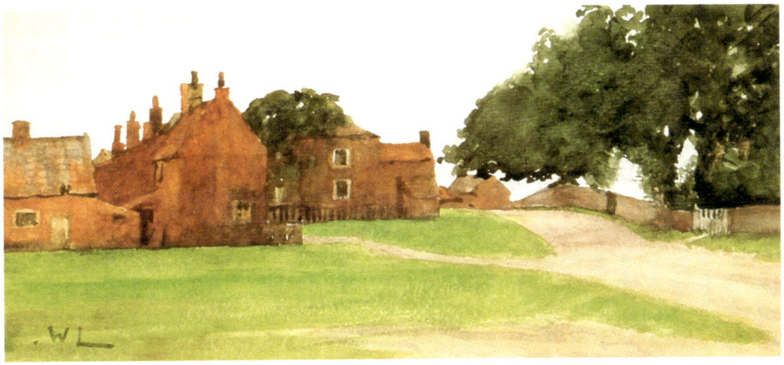

BELOW LEFT
A Worcestershire Village c1886
watercolour, 11 x 23.2cm

PAGE 74
Disaster! Scene in a Cornish Fishing Village 1889
watercolour, 122 x 76.5cm
(Birmingham Museums and Art Gallery)

There is a full size crayon drawing for this dated 1888, and a small pen and ink done for the engravers for the RI catalogue in 1889. There were also numerous studies for the component parts of the composition. This was exhibited nine times between its first appearance at the RI in 1889 and 1911 and must have been one of Langley's best known paintings. There were in fact only three such complex and dramatic paintings of a disaster's aftermath, *Among the Missing* 1884, see page 16, this and *After the Storm* 1894, see page 99.

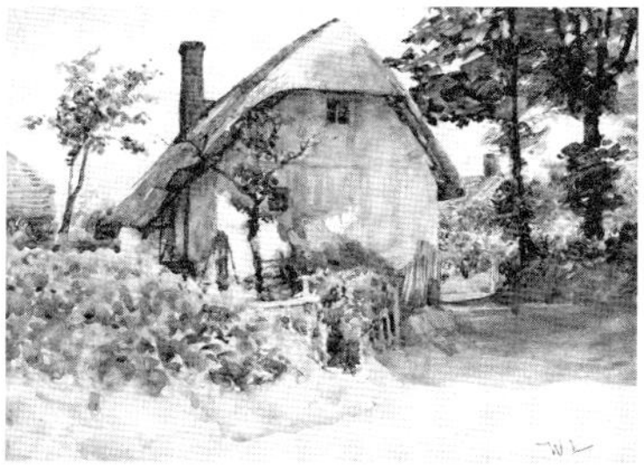

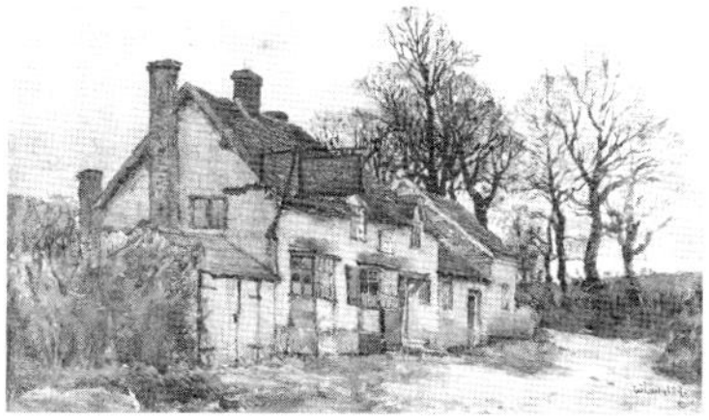

A Country Inn c1886
watercolour, 14 x 22.9cm
Probably in Warwickshire.

TOP
The Thatched Cottage c1886
watercolour, 19.3 x 26cm

PAGE 77, BOTTOM
My Youngest Son, Cecil 1886
watercolour, 25 x 38cm

A portrait of Cecil Langley at the dining table in the house in Bristol Road, Edgbaston where the family lived for a time in 1886-87. This provides one of the few insights into their life and style of living.

our factories and nail forges, where women and young girls have to work to keep the wolf of poverty from the door, it is not improbable that Mr Langley will find situations as full of pathos and sympathy as in the more picturesque Cornish interiors he has so beautifully depicted. As in the past so may it safely be predicted he will render high service, not only to Art but to humanity, by broadening our sympathies and awakening in the hearts of all who view his pictures, responsive echoes to the calls and needs of brothers and sisters in the humbler walks of life.

The tenor of the article in the *Birmingham Post* suggests Langley leant towards the left politically and there is little doubt of this, given the feelings expressed in his major paintings. In his younger days in Birmingham it was the Liberal Party that espoused progressive ideas and because the party gained much of its more active support from the Unitarian community Langley, not surprisingly, championed Liberal politics. He later became a good friend of Charles Bradlaugh, possibly the most radical Liberal politician of the day, and in December 1903 he was a member of Asquith's platform party when the Liberals were drumming up support in Penzance.

Langley's political leanings were no guarantee of acceptance for his new ideas in subject matter, however, and it seems clear he failed to consult his dealers adequately before deserting Newlyn. From them he might have learned that the hardships endured by workers in the 'factories and nail forges' were too close to home for his Midlands patrons, who preferred paintings of Newlyn's more remote and picturesque 'brothers and sisters in the humbler walks of life'. Doubtless the heroic nature of the fishermen's calling added to the appeal of Newlyn scenes. In vain could Langley point to the slump in sales of those very scenes, which had driven him homewards.

The *Birmingham Post* contributor was on firmer ground in closing his remarks with the comment that 'although fond of oil painting, Mr Langley's friends allow him so little release from watercolours that he is unable to follow it as much as he could wish'. However, failure to achieve this ambition was probably of less immediate concern as Langley was elected to membership of the Institute of Painters in Oils in January 1886. At 34, time was still on his side.

The arguments for a return to Newlyn grew more compelling when the recently opened Birmingham Art Gallery held a small exhibition of Langley's work, in September 1886. This was only the second exhibition at the gallery, the first being devoted to the work of G F Watts and Edward Burne-Jones, and was a considerable honour to bestow on a comparatively new artist.

> The ten drawings together exhibit with remarkable force the high quality and the variety of Mr Langley's work, its marvellous execution, admirable drawing, fine colour and powerful, yet tenderly felt sentiment. As a painter of homely pathos the artist stands unrivalled amongst our watercolour men and there is evidence in this collection he has also a keen sense of humorous character. No-one who cares for good art should fail to study the collection.

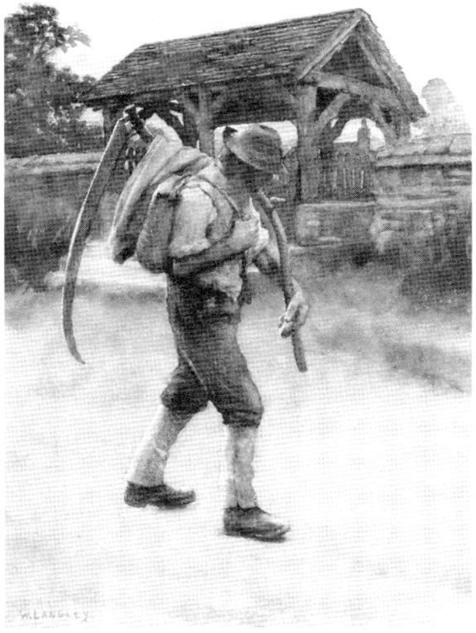

Study of a man with a scythe by Welford-on-Avon lych gate c1887 watercolour, 25.5 x 23cm

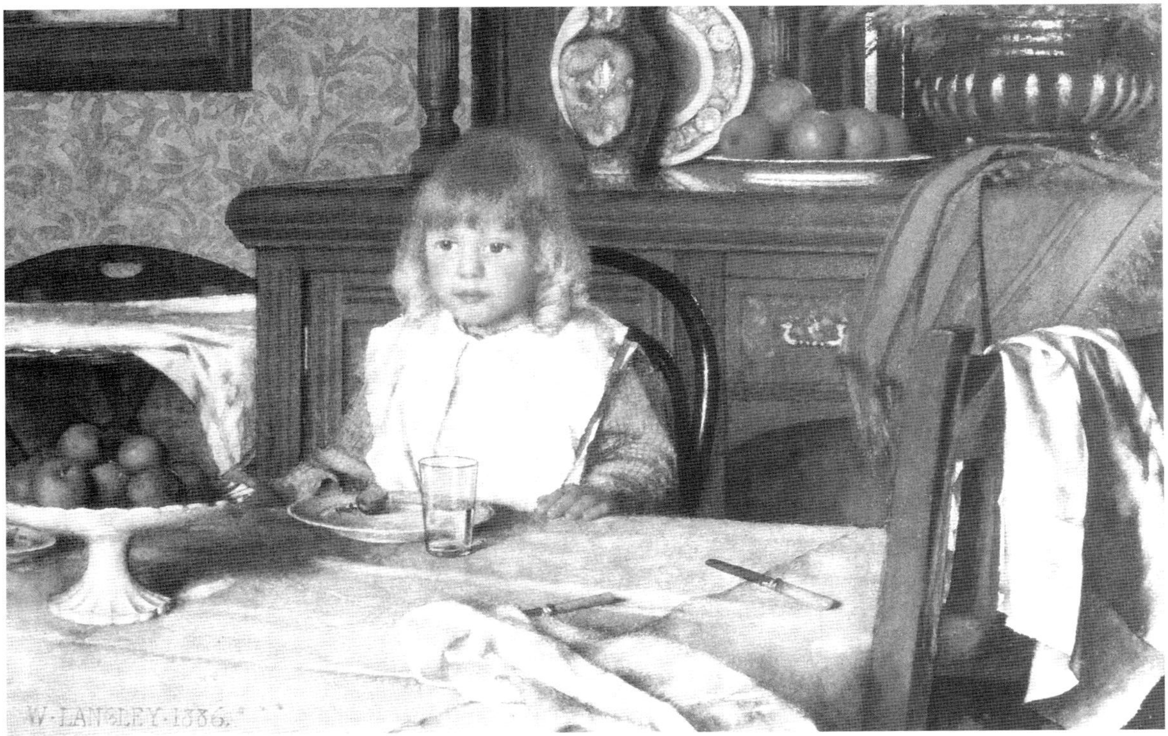

RIGHT
Study of rooftops, late-1880s
watercolour, 15.3 x 19.7cm

BELOW
Whisperings of the Past 1888
watercolour, 48.2 x 66cm

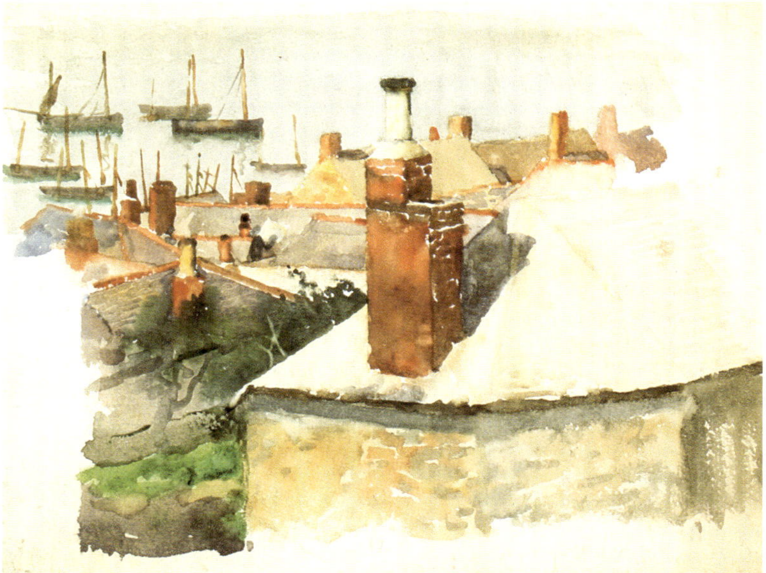

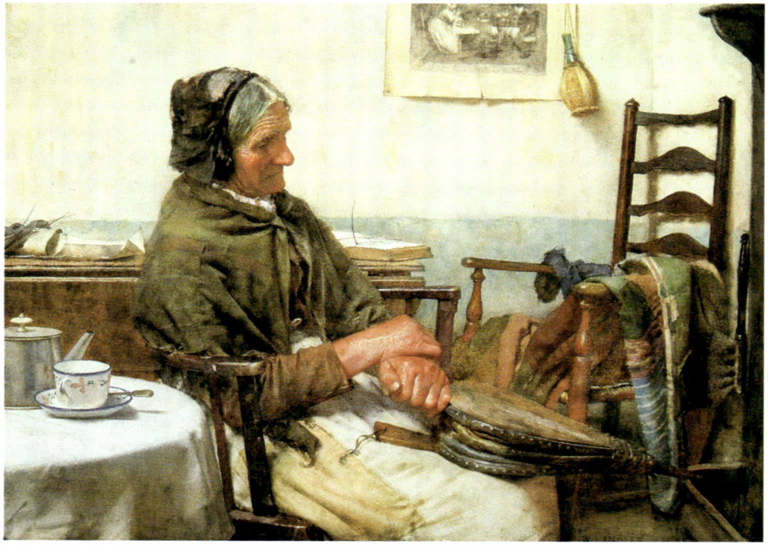

So thought the *Birmingham Post* art critic, who might have observed that there were no Midlands scenes among the ten drawings. Indeed, though Langley was working on a major Midlands painting for the Institute's Spring Exhibition in 1887, for the whole of 1886 virtually all his sales were of Newlyn subjects, from stock.

Perhaps because Langley realised he needed time to regain acceptance as a painter of Midlands scenes, he was happy to be

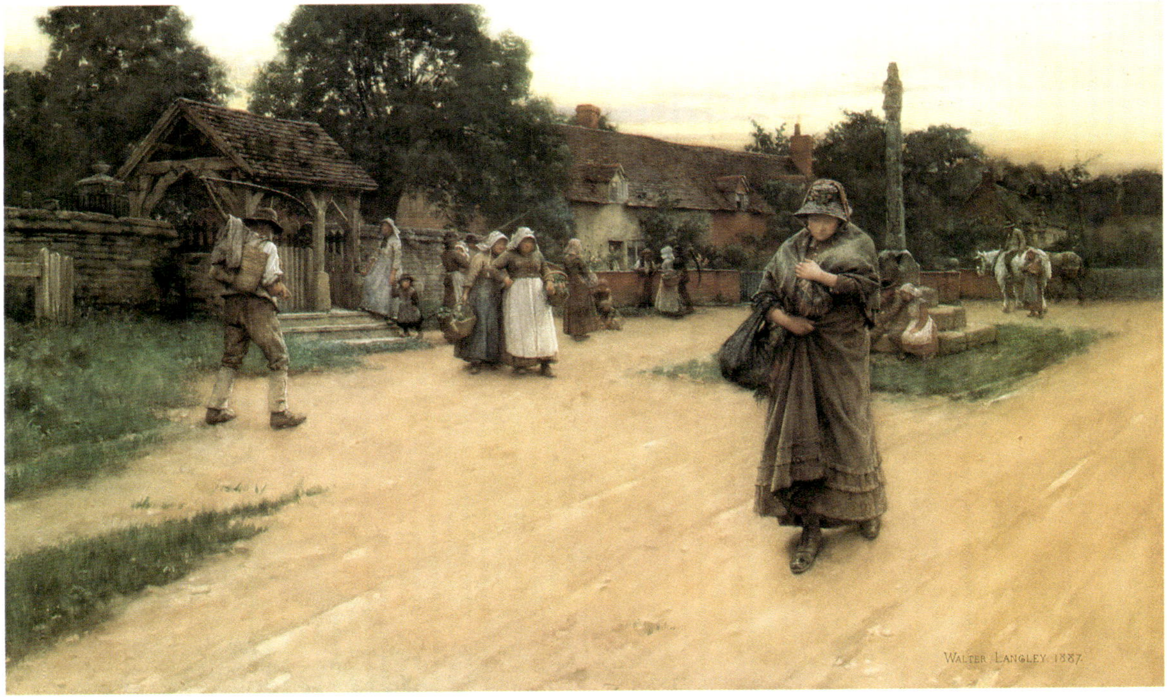

Betrayed 1887
watercolour, 75 x 120cm

The largest of three important watercolours shown at the RI in 1887, and of a subject bound to cause comment. This represents Langley's only major statement on a moral issue though the hardships of women's lives were a central concern.

He made a series of studies of the village, the cottage in the centre, the lych gate and the cross. *Betrayed* was described at length by M H Spielmann who rounded off his review for the *Magazine of Art* by suggesting Langley might be 'the Jozef Israels of Birmingham'.

elected President for 1887 of Birmingham's recently formed Easel Club.[12] The Easel Club had wider, more 'improving' aims than the Art Circle, which was primarily a vehicle for the exhibition of members' work, and Langley is recorded in the Club's minute book as having taken part in a debate on the subject of 'Impressionists v Realists'. Unfortunately the minute book gives no further details and the debate appears not to have been reported in the Birmingham press. The Rules of the Easel Club conjure up visions of an entirely earnest body of artists but one of Langley's first presidential acts was to inaugurate 'Smokes' where 'the fragrant weed was freely indulged in'. Two elaborate smoking caps surviving from those days suggest the 'Smokes' were picturesque as well as fragrant.

Langley's Institute painting for 1887, *Betrayed*, signalled his abandonment of the 'nail forges' idea and return to the familiar villages of the Avon valley. Nonetheless it represented a considerable departure in terms of subject matter and was well received, particularly in the *Magazine of Art* where a full-page etching was accompanied by an appreciation from M H Spielmann:

The Truant 1887
watercolour, 52 x 25cm

Shown at the Birmingham Art Circle exhibition the year it was painted and sold through Chamberlain, the Birmingham dealer, who sold a number of Langley's works between 1880 and 1896.

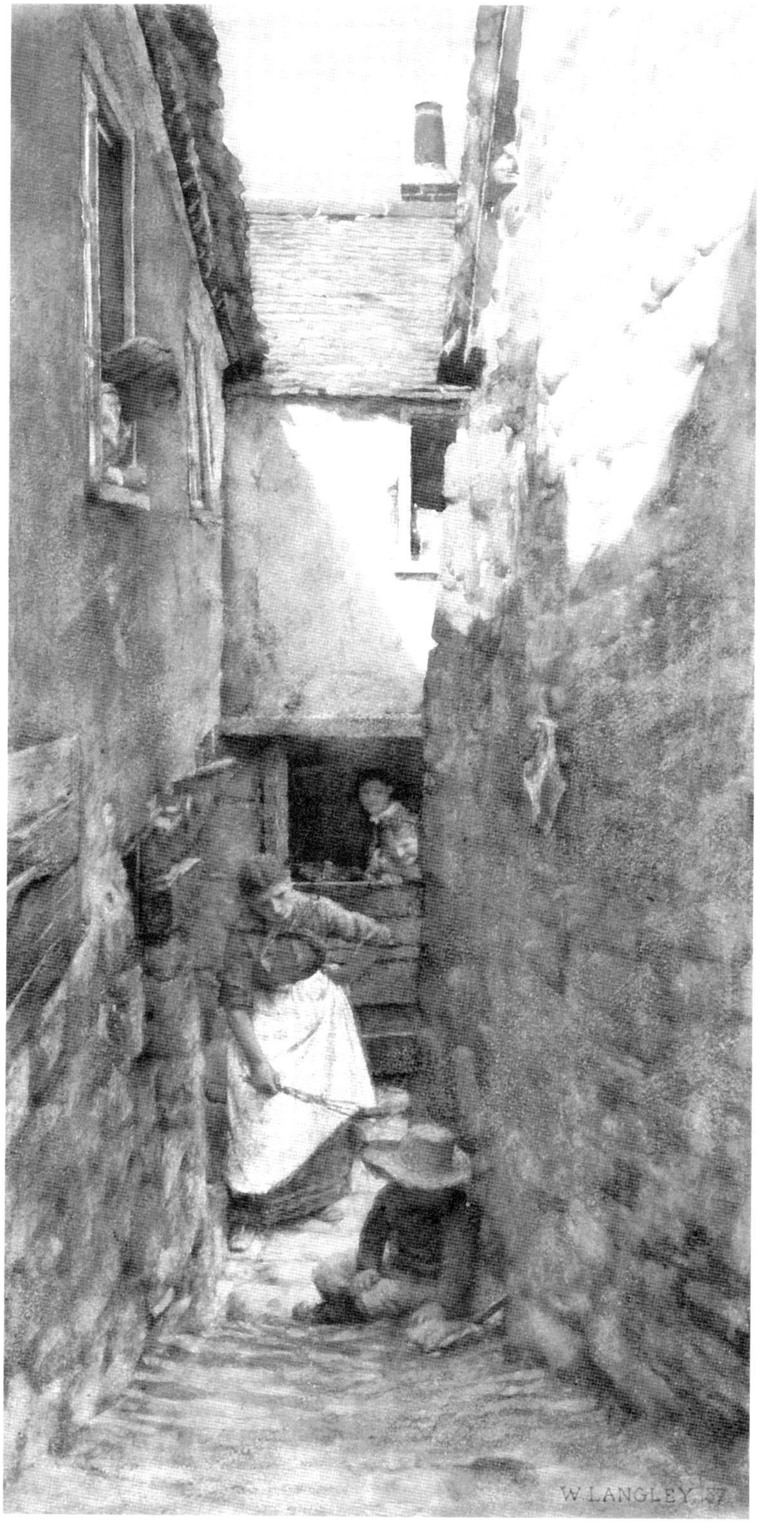

> Mr Walter Langley has certainly reached a high degree of excellence, and he has succeeded just where success was most difficult. In point of fact, no theme has been more be-plastered with paint, or torn to shreds by leading ladies, than the pitiful one of the en-trapped and cast off girl, deserted to bear alone the burden of her mis-doing. The subject is one that needs the utmost care and delicacy of treatment to avoid mawkishness on the one hand or repulsiveness on the other. A middle course is necessary to bring about a poetical result, and this is precisely what Mr Langley has succeeded in doing. The achievement is a picture at once touching and true, tender and, morally speaking, duly forbidding ... he may be considered, in some respects at least, the Jozef Israels of Birmingham.

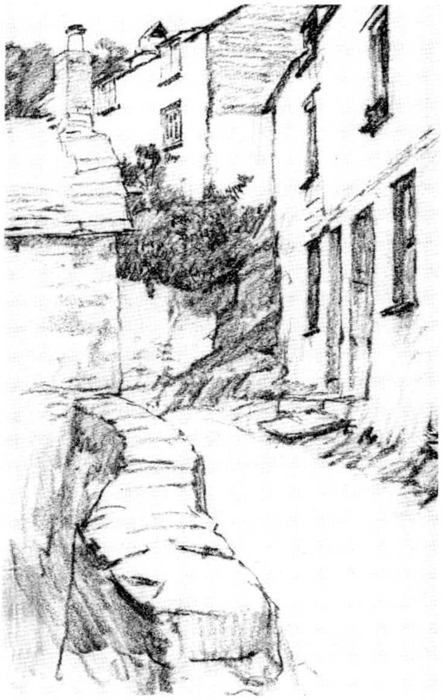

A Newlyn Byway c1883
crayon, 30 x 19.5cm

It is evident from the painting's title and composition where Langley's sympathies lay. He must have hoped that his treatment of the subject would strike a responsive chord in a purchaser but *Betrayed*, though an artistic success, was a commercial failure. The asking price opened at £420, the amount Langley had received for *Among the Missing*, but fell to £157 before the painting found a purchaser, late in 1888. Long before then Langley, with little to show for his return to Birmingham and at least some assurance that there was a fresh demand for his Newlyn work, set off once more for the south west.

The strain of returning to Cornwall, in the spring of 1887, was made worse by the shortage of accommodation there and Langley, forewarned of this, had to leave the two eldest children behind in Birmingham while he and the rest of the family took lodgings in Penzance. Then he was taken ill — 'ominously ill' as Forbes put it in a letter to his mother — and it was not until July that Langley recovered and the autumn before he could reunite his family once more in Cornwall.

Langley's illness coincided with the colony's first theatrical production, the enigmatically entitled *Freezing a Mother-in-Law*. This proved a great success but Langley, with other concerns on his mind and possibly little taste for acting in 'serious' plays, absented himself from the cast list while he searched for a studio.

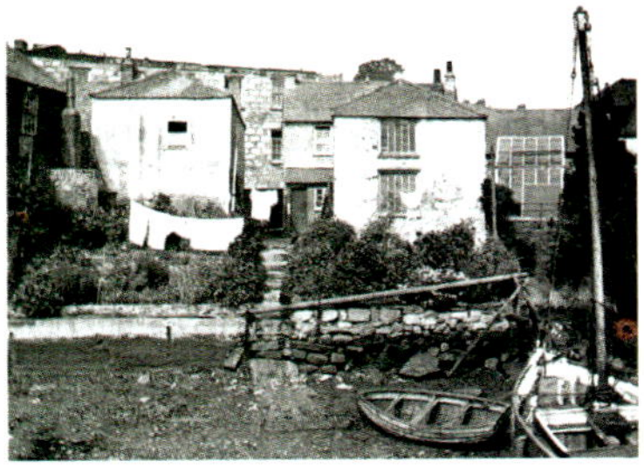

The backs of houses at the Fradgan, by the beach at Newlyn. Langley's studio was the glasshouse on the right, following its conversion from a cottage in 1897.

The need to arrange for the schooling of his four children dictated that the family home should be in Penzance but what was convenient for them was highly inconvenient for Langley's models and a studio in Newlyn was essential. Finding one, however, was proving well-nigh impossible, the influx of artists ensuring that every room which could do service had already been taken. After a long search, Langley had to settle for a diminutive cottage in the Fradgan, overlooking Newlyn harbour. Though far from ideal as a studio, the cottage had an excellent situation and from its window Langley could, as a contemporary writer put it, 'catch not only the scent of the sea but also its spray'. This cottage-studio was the only property he ever owned.

In September 1887 Langley represented the artists at the opening ceremony of the Cornish Art Union exhibition, in Penzance. This was a rare coming together of amateur and professional artists, if the address by H M Geffroi, Head Master of the Art School and Curator of the Art Museum, was anything to go by:

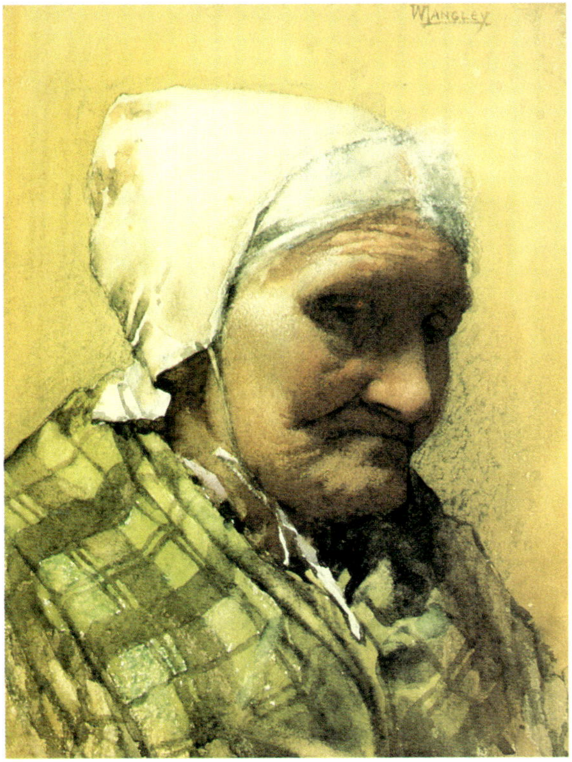

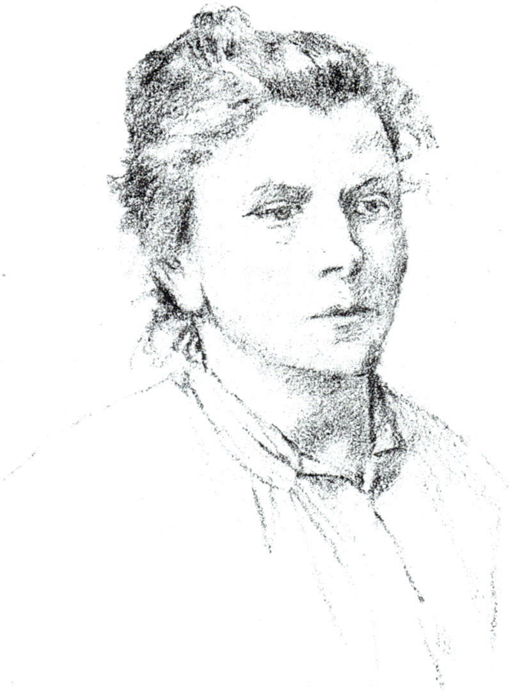

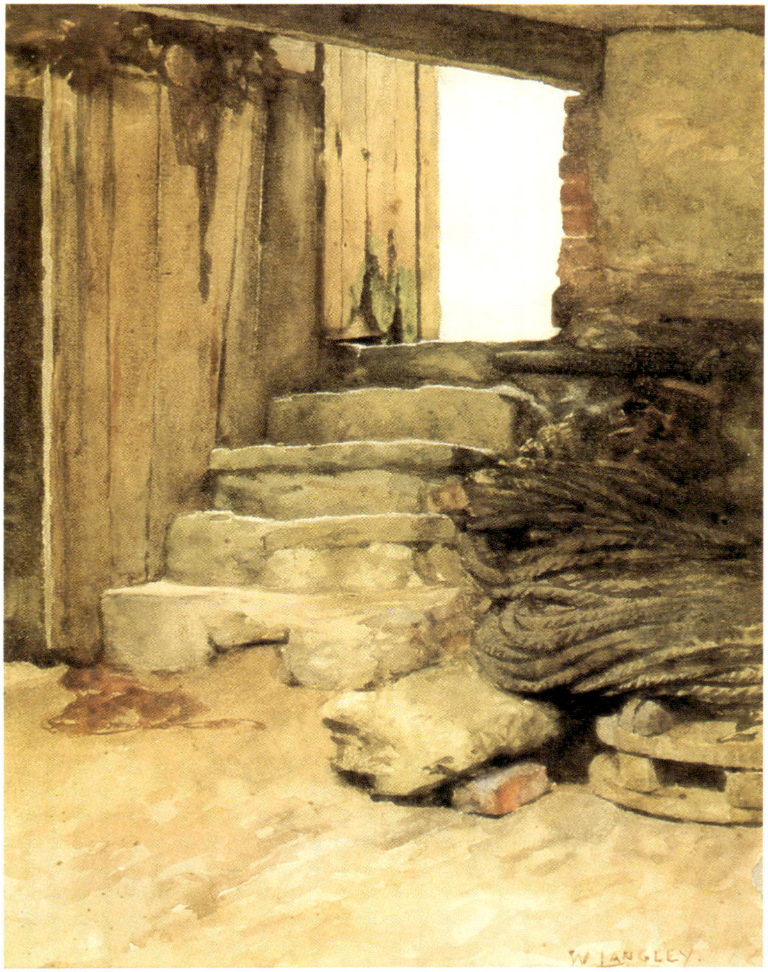

The Fish Cellar c1890
watercolour, 28 x 23cm

Penzance and its neighbourhood are at present the centre of quite a colony of artists of reputation. The people of the town and district are proud to know that so many artists had made their homes here, that they have here found such scenery as they wished to paint. They could not but feel honoured by the presence of so many artists among them, but that very fact made it difficult for outsiders to speak about art ... If some of those artists would explain the principles of their art, if they would endeavour to form and guide the taste of those who were present, there might be considerable advantage ... As it is one feels obliged to hold one's tongue lest one should get out of depth in the presence of so many skilled observers.

PAGE 82, FAR LEFT
Study of an old woman early-1880s
watercolour, 19 x 14cm

Has been known as *The Old Fish Lady*. The figure wears the same kind of cap, and indeed looks like the old lady in *But men must work* (1883, see page 10). This may be a study for *Consolation* 1883, of which a pen and ink version was illustrated in the Birmingham Art Circle catalogue.

PAGE 82, LEFT
Head study c1890
chalk on tone paper, 26.4 x 22.2cm

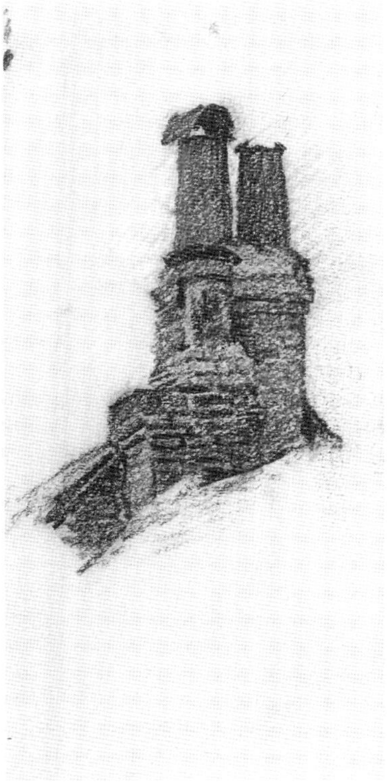

Study of chimney pots, late-1880s
crayon, 16.4 x 7.7cm

BELOW
Interior study, late-1880s
watercolour, 18.3 x 26cm

Geffroi's remarks clearly took Langley by surprise and his response contained no clues as to the 'principles of his art'. Though he had given private lessons in Birmingham, and more recently had made a considerable impact on Todd's work, Langley had no taste for formal teaching. T C Gotch, J C Uren, Stanhope and Elizabeth Forbes, Harold Harvey and Ernest Procter did take up Geffroi's challenge, in due course.

In the two years Langley had been away from Newlyn little had changed there and his paintings, especially his studies of the older folk, continued to reflect the hardships the villagers suffered. In the first major watercolour following his return to Newlyn, *Village Idyll — After the buoyant happy days of youth comes the calm eventide of age*, the key figure is an old fisherwoman. She sits engrossed in recollections of former times while around her other figures give life to her memories. *Village Idyll* was the first painting in which Langley had employed such a device and it proved a successful work, selling for £250.

Still making up for lost time, Langley was once again missing from the cast lists when the artists took to the stage, in February 1888, in a double bill of one-act plays, *Turn Him Out* and *Checkmate*. He was also absent in June when they presented two further plays, *A Scrap of Paper* and *A Crazy Couple*. The artists' productions were now a regular feature of the Penzance year and the

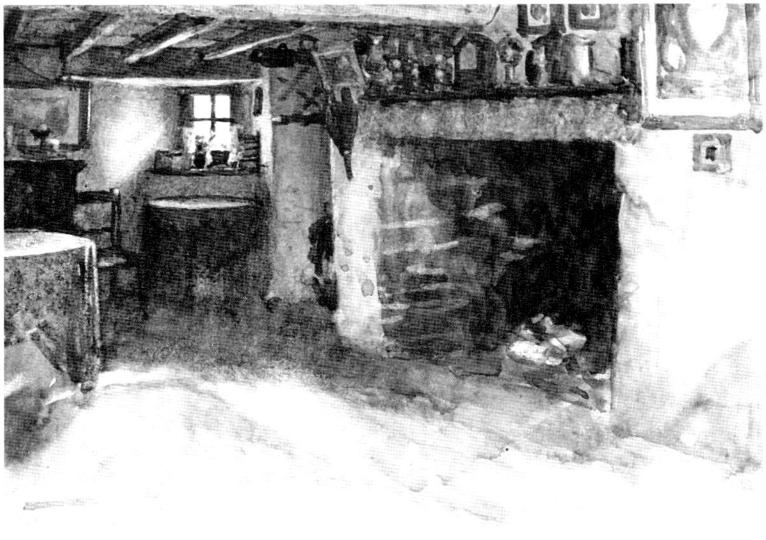

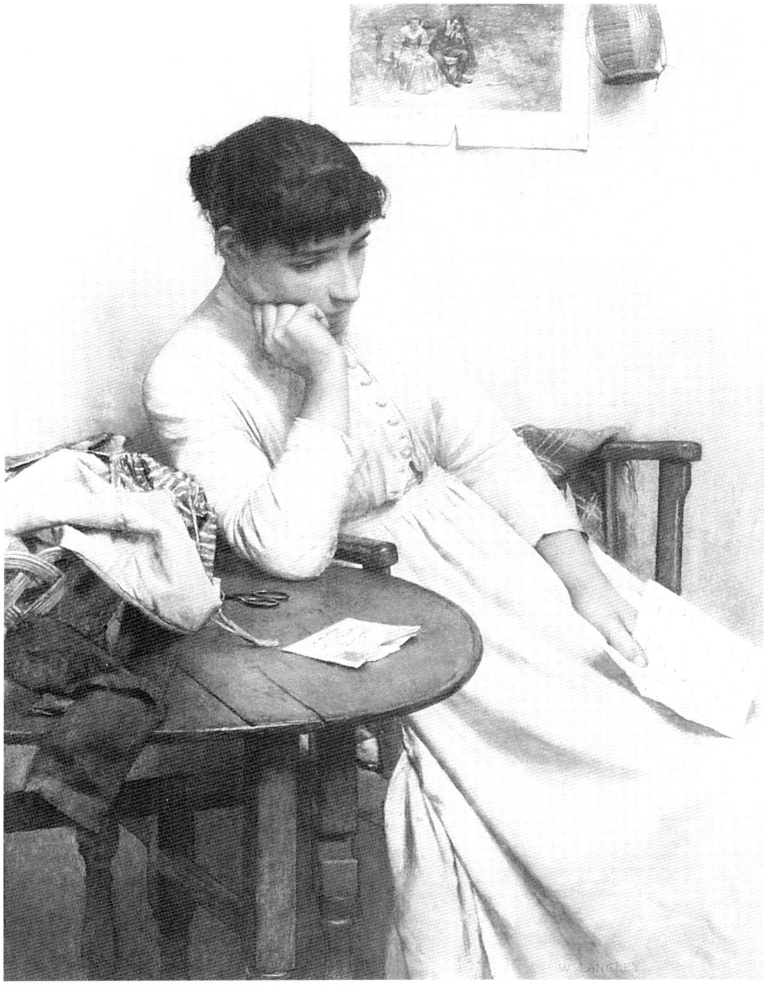

Jilted: The fraud of men was ever so Since summer first was leafy 1889
watercolour, 90 x 67cm

The quotation is from Shakespeare's *Much Ado About Nothing*. The model may be the same as for *O for the touch*, see page 28, and the woman by a cottage door, see page 43.

Cottage Steps, Newlyn c1890
watercolour, 36 x 25cm

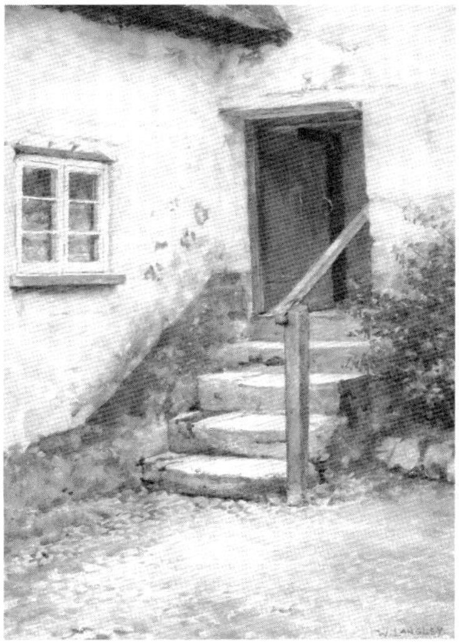

leading players, T C Gotch, Percy Craft, B A Bateman, Elizabeth Armstrong, Stanhope Forbes, Chevallier Tayler and Norman Garstin basked in the general acclaim for their efforts, though the last-named was deemed 'slightly deficient in vigour', in one review.

Not wishing to rest on their thespian laurels, in August the artists turned to the cricket field. Their first match was both serious and ambitious, nothing less than a challenge to Penzance by a combined Newlyn and St Ives team, 'The Artists of West Cornwall'. Maybe the artists hoped the finer points of the game had failed to reach the far south west but, if so, they were soon disabused of the notion. Their team — Tayler, Rheam, Marshall, J and W Titcomb, Norman, Bramley, Stokes, Bourdillon, Deacon and Detmold — was

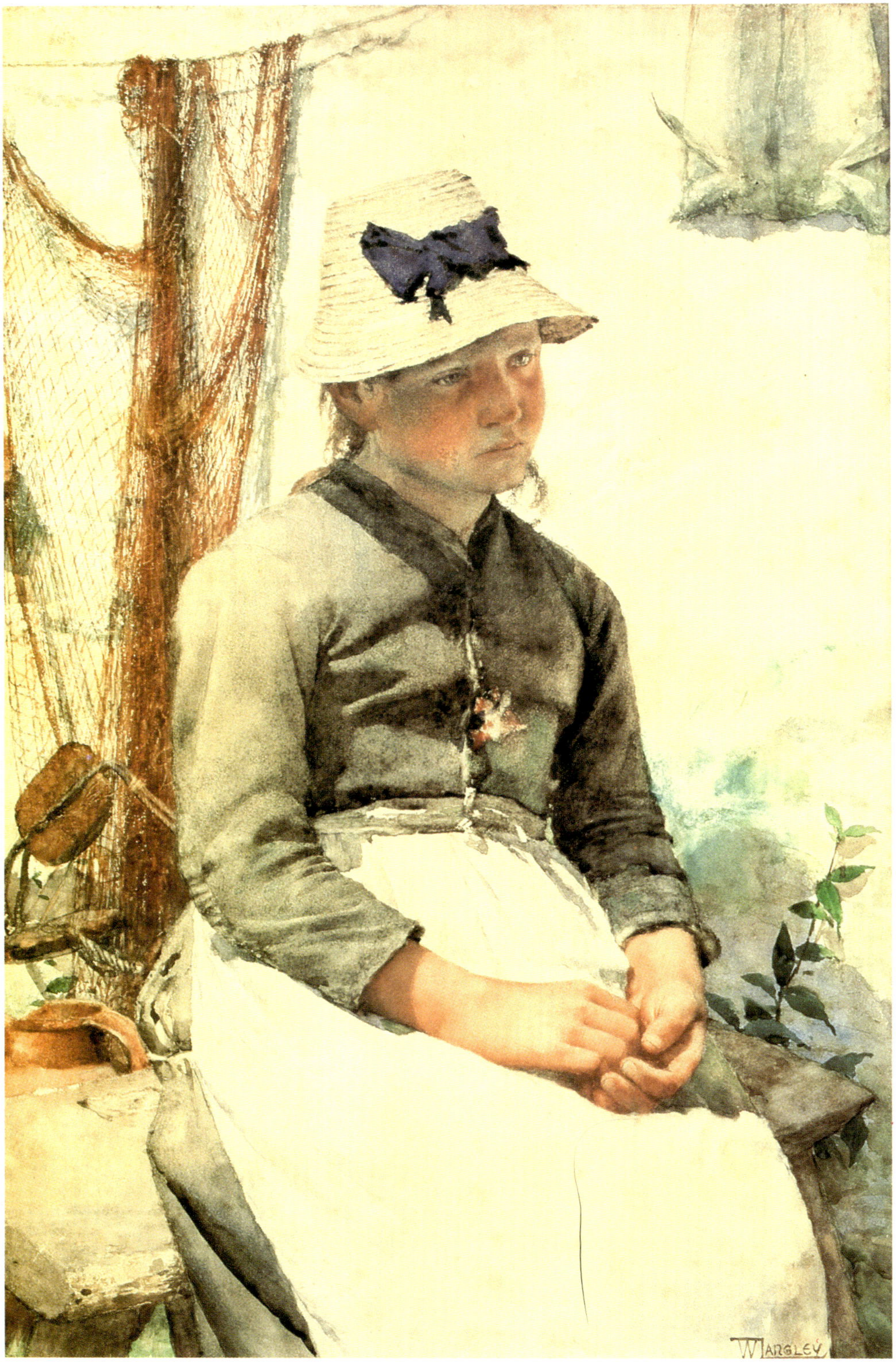
W LANGLEY

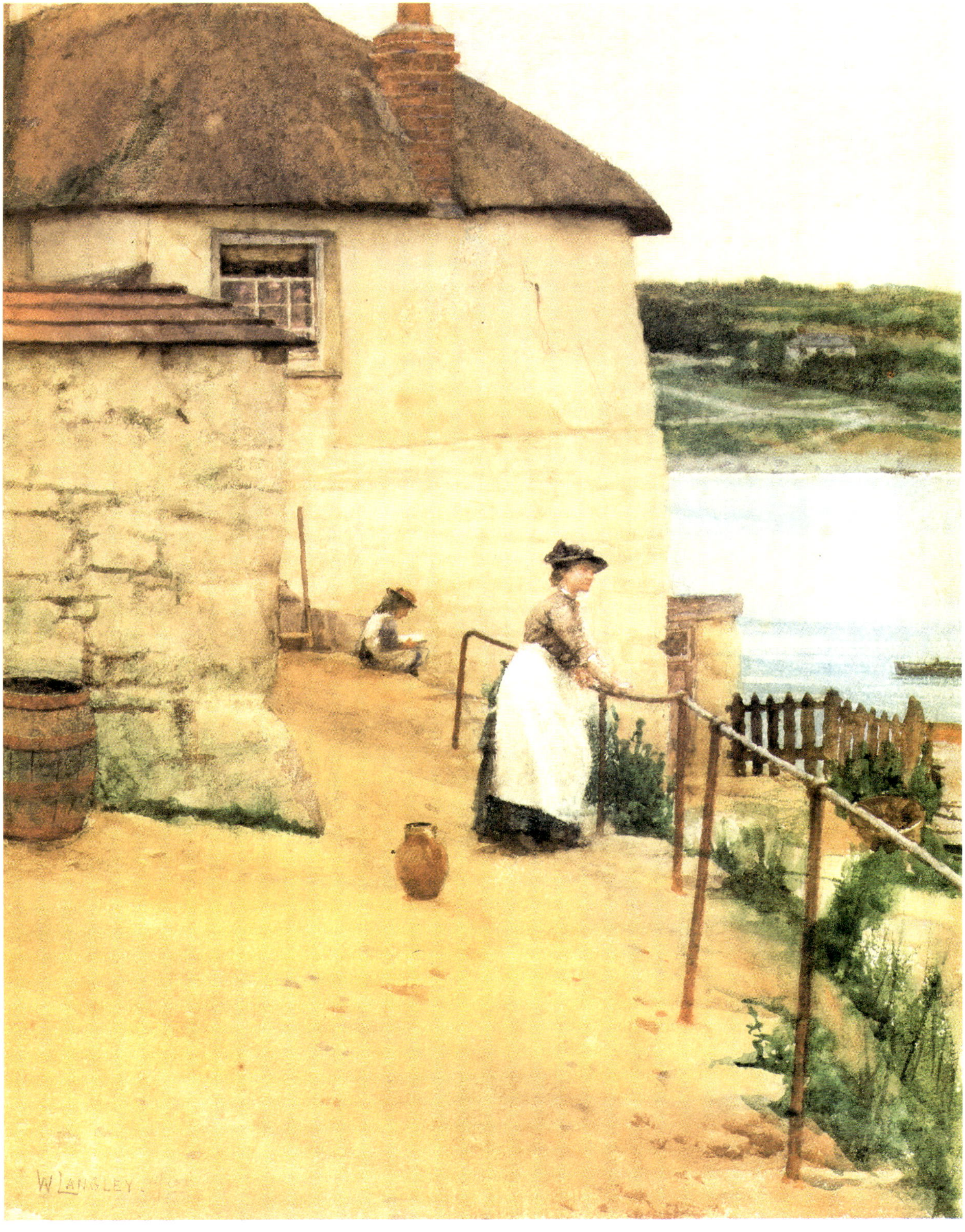
W LANGLEY

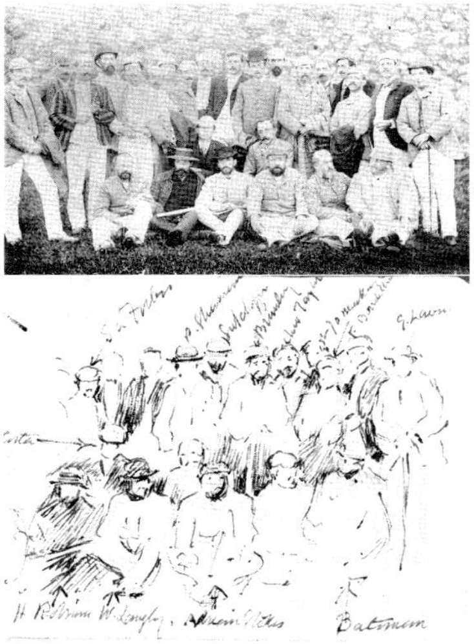

Photograph of the cricket team with a key drawing and annotations by Stanhope Forbes (see also page 185).

soundly beaten by an innings and twelve runs and thereafter the two colonies concentrated on playing each other — and less seriously. Langley, on his own admission no cricketer, nevertheless features in group photographs taken at some of the later games.

The carefree life of the artists was in sharp contrast to the hard times suffered by the villagers of Newlyn who, the *Cornishman* newspaper reported in the summer of 1888, had reached a desperate state:

> There can be no doubt that distress arising from the want of fish is being felt in the place now. It would be worth some person's while to ascertain how the poor live here ... scores of families in Newlyn have not received sufficient to buy bread since June and we may guess the distress they must be in.

The absence of fish was a cause of great hardship to the village generally but to some families a storm at sea brought a far worse fate. In several of Langley's paintings storms are indicated by bent trees or driving rain, glimpsed through cottage windows or doors, or by an apposite title, and it was not until 1889 that he depicted an event taking place in the teeth of a storm. The watercolour, *Disaster: Scene in a Cornish Fishing Village*, became one of his best known and most exhibited paintings.

In *Disaster* a fishing boat is foundering outside the harbour wall while, from within its shelter, spray-drenched fishermen are doing what they can to rescue their companions. The hopeless nature of their task is apparent on the face of the central figure, a young fisherwoman. For her, and for the child whose head is buried in her apron, the prospect is grim.

A letter from Langley to Samuel Keeley, the Birmingham dealer to whom *Disaster* was consigned, seems to confirm the painting was inspired by an actual event: 'I am glad to know you think so much of it as I consider it one of the best I have done. I felt the subject very much, and perhaps that is the reason for it.'

In the winter he completed *Disaster*, Langley painted a work destined to be purchased by the Birmingham Art Gallery. Its title was two lines taken from Tennyson's 'Break, Break, Break':

PAGE 86
Early Cares 1888
watercolour, 63.5 x 40.5cm

PAGE 87
At Coverack, Cornwall 1891
watercolour, 30 x 21.6cm

This is one of two watercolours of this title of 1891.

O! For the touch of a vanish'd hand
And the sound of a voice that is still.

In this painting the title, the haunted face of the solitary figure, the upturned boat and the nets cast aside, tell the whole story.

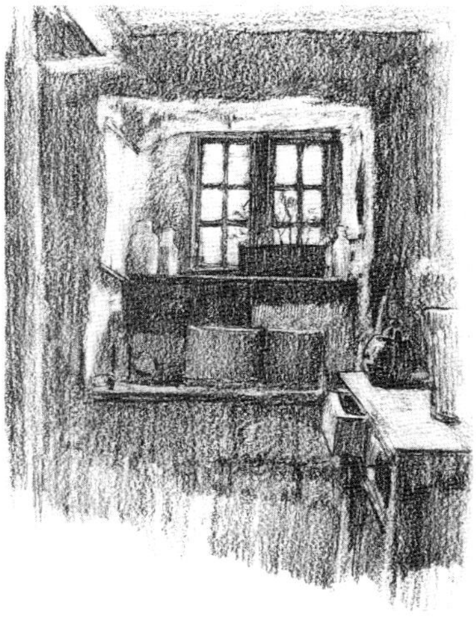

Window study, late-1880s
chalk, 25.7 x 20cm

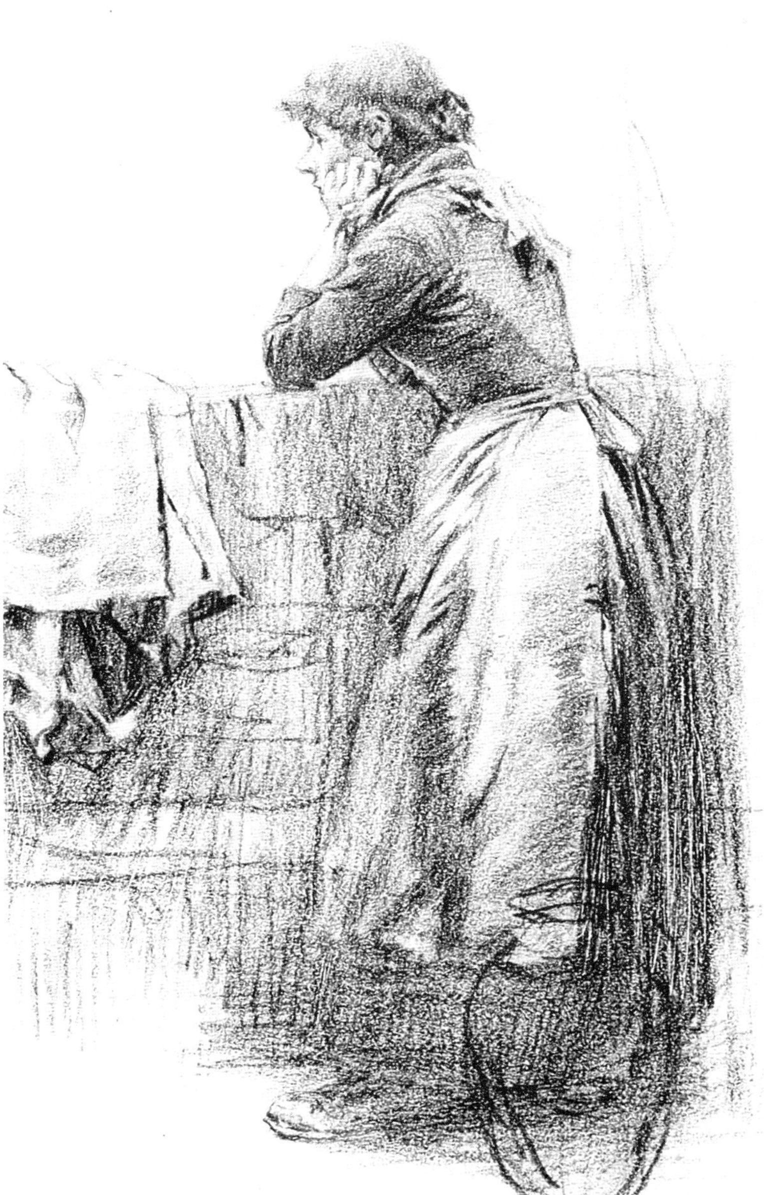

LEFT
Study of a girl at a harbour wall, early-1890s
chalk, 32 x 19.5cm

In a Cornish Fishing Village — Naval Manoeuvres 1891
watercolour, 58.4 x 120cm

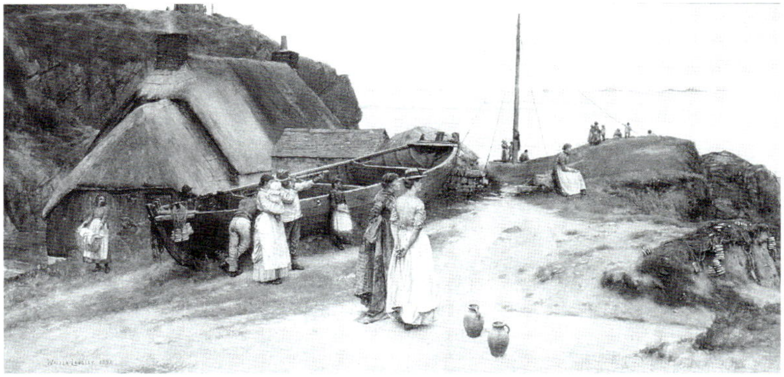

BELOW
Watching for the Fleet, Cadgwith 1891
watercolour, 44.5 x 63cm

This and ... *Naval Manoeuvres* must have been painted after the day in August 1891 when the Home Fleet had assembled in Mount's Bay in preparation for manoeuvres which were cancelled owing to bad weather.

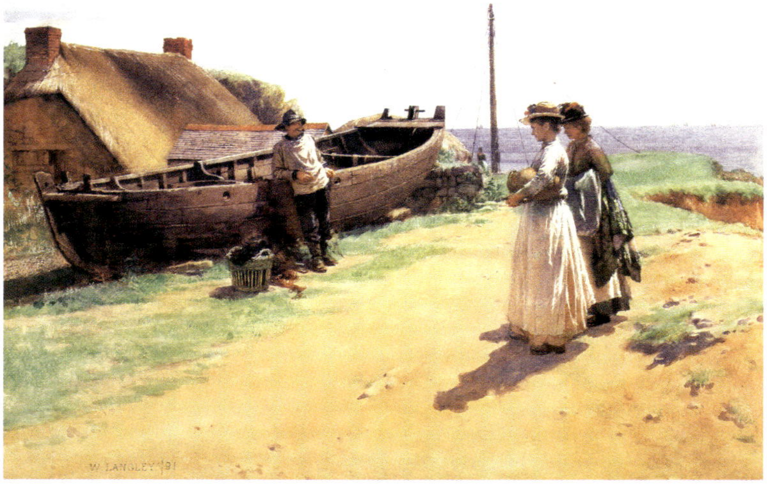

O! For the touch of a vanish'd hand reached a wide public when the Birmingham Art Gallery gave permission for it to be reproduced as a print by the *Penny Magazine*.

Langley's interlude in Birmingham had marked a low point in his career but this was put behind him in Newlyn with sales in 1889 amounting to £905 (about £45,000 in 1997 terms). Most of the paintings sold were watercolours and Langley's pre-eminence in the medium was rewarded that year with a gold medal at the Paris Exhibition for three of his major paintings, *Among the Missing, Departure of the Fleet for the North* and *But men must work*.

A preference for watercolours did not mean Langley had abandoned his hope of painting more in oils but he was able to complete and exhibit only a small number of canvasses each year.

One, shown at the 1889 Cornwall Art Union exhibition, proved he was an accomplished exponent of the medium. The *Cornish Telegraph* commented: '*The Evening of Life* is ... without question the most remarkable work in the exhibition. Its simplicity, its truth, its artistic completeness, its pathos, combine to produce an effect such as is rare in the best contemporary work.'

That Langley painted so rarely in oils was due to the continuing demand for his watercolours which makes brief diversions in his career at about this time all the more difficult to account for. The first was a commission for ten Newlyn drawings to illustrate the poem 'In a Harbour', by George R Sims, which was published by Hildesheimer and Faulkner for the 1889 Christmas season. Shortly afterwards, twelve pen and ink drawings by Langley appeared in a small book, *The Manufacturing Processes of Steel Pens*, written by H Bore for Perry & Co Ltd. The style of these drawings, appropriately executed 'using a Perry's No 25 pen', suggests they date from Langley's lithographic days, the 1870s rather than the late 1880s.

The decade closed on a somewhat sombre note, however, with the death of his father at the age of 73. William Langley remains a shadowy figure of whom little is known beyond his reputed dry sense of humour, and as head and principal breadwinner of a family of thirteen, he probably deserves more by way of an obituary than can be given here.

The buoyant sales of 1889 continued unabated into 1890 and Langley felt sufficiently secure to turn his attention to the fulfilment of two remaining ambitions, to paint more in oils and to hold a one-man show in London. The first ambition necessarily entailed sending in work to the Royal Academy. A rejection there would have been a serious rebuff after so successful a career in watercolours and Langley proceeded cautiously with his first Academy painting, an orchard scene set at Trembath, near Penzance, which was to be submitted in 1892.

The one-man show was to take place in the spring of 1893, at the Fine Art Society gallery in Bond Street, and also needed careful planning. Whether it was on his own initiative or at the suggestion of the gallery is not known, but his Newlyn paintings were to be

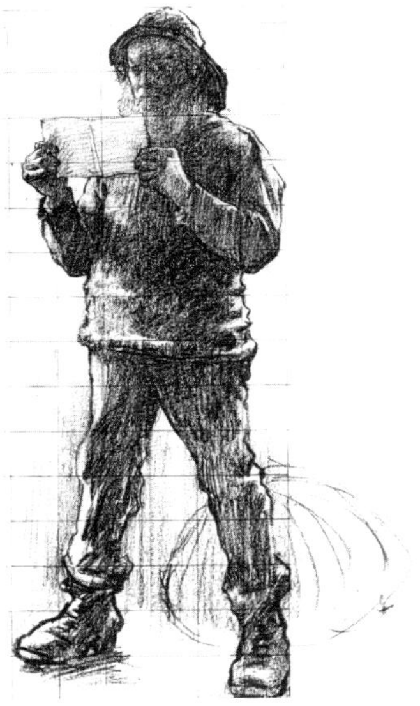

Study of a fisherman, early-1880s
crayon, 30 x 18.8cm

This standing figure has been squared up for translation to a larger scale, possibly for the painting *A Telegram* 1881.

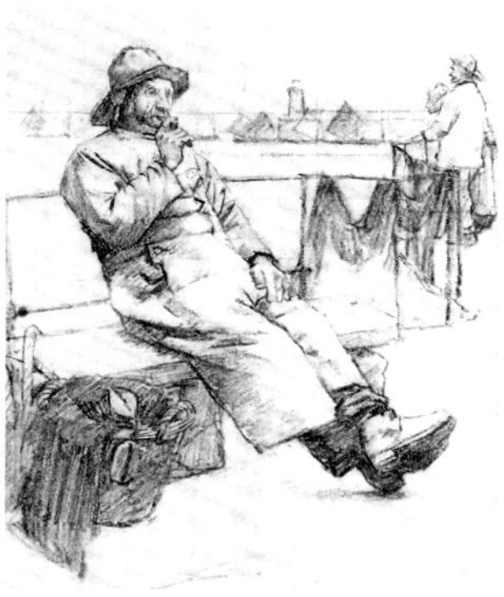

Study of a fisherman, early-1890s
crayon, 22.8 x 18.5cm

augmented by new material drawn from further afield and in 1891 and 1892 Langley visited Walberswick and Southwold in Suffolk, and the villages of Cornwall's Lizard peninsula. To tide the family over, he took out a two-year lease of Pembroke Lodge, in June 1890. This was the family's home in 1883 and had been a veritable hive of industry since then — and not only as a base for numerous artists, as one of Langley's first acts on moving in again was to instruct workmen to remove a quarter of a ton of honey from the roof space.

Late in 1889 Langley accepted the presidency for 1890 of the Art Class of Sutton Coldfield, near Birmingham, and this entailed delivering an address at their annual meeting in January 1891. His subject, 'The programme of studies the students should pursue', allowed him to follow orthodox and politic lines in the main, but he also took the opportunity both to slate the unimaginative South Kensington design course he himself had taken and to advocate art as a means of enriching the lives of the poor. The latter, he suggested, would be through the media of art galleries, illustrated books — especially children's books — prints and posters. Poster-hoardings had a special place in his argument, being 'potential art galleries for the ordinary passer-by'.

Langley also advised the students to collect prints, as an inexpensive means of furthering their knowledge and appreciation of art. He often featured prints as wall decorations in his paintings, to fix the background perspective or point up a subject, and saw nothing incongruous in the notion that Newlyn fisherfolk might enjoy 'high' works of art.

Though his talk was well received, and reported at length in the local papers, Langley was never to repeat the experience. An aside, pencilled into the margin of his talk notes, may explain why: 'It is the duty of an artist to work first and talk afterwards, if he can and, whilst I should appreciate the gift of being able to talk well, I sometimes think it would lead me into talking too much and working too little.'

Langley returned to Penzance shortly before the worst winter on record reached its climax in the 'Great Blizzard', which cut Cornwall off from England and gave a local wag, 'Moonshine', an opportunity not to be missed:

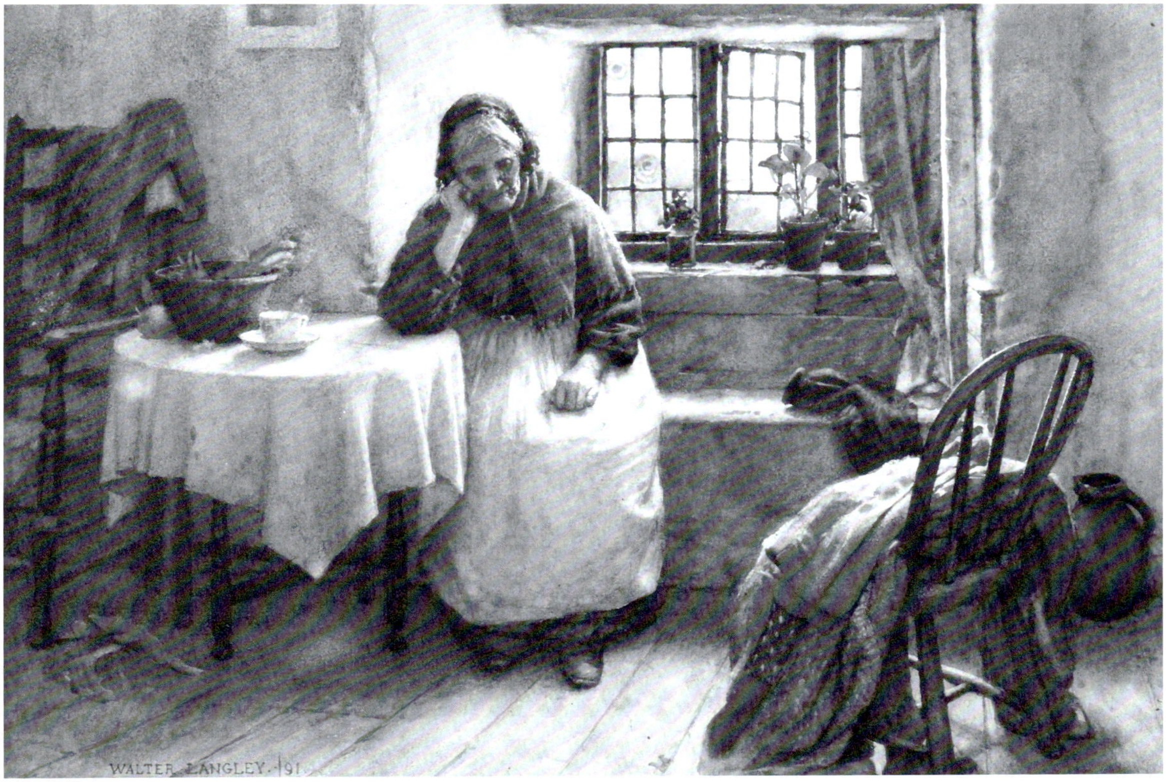

Old woman at a table 1891
watercolour, 32.4 x 47cm

Possibly *The Widow* 1891.

O painters of Newlyn how great your
Disgust at the storm. What a start
This latest subversion of nature
Must have given your version of art.

In the early spring of 1892, Langley's Academy painting was unveiled at the Newlyn preview. This was an annual event, when the artists threw open their studio doors to display the season's work before it went up to London. 'Open days' were great social occasions, the villagers seeing how well they and their friends looked on canvas, and the artists, after a hard painting season, assessing each other's work. Langley's Academy painting, *The Widow*, featured a countrywoman and her daughter against the background of a blossoming apple orchard. The painting was liked by the local reviewer but he took exception to its title, considering it inappropriate for such a sunny painting. Recognising the

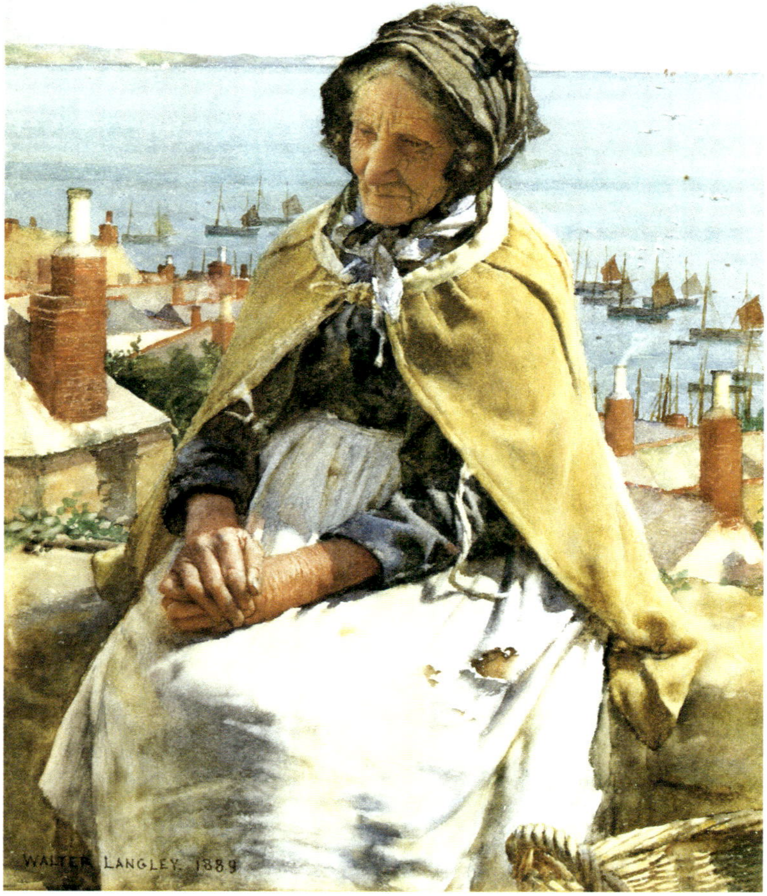

reviewer had a valid point, Langley changed the title and it was as *Sunshine and Shadow* that the painting was accepted by the Academy. He was doubtless relieved at its acceptance but it may be significant that the fate of the painting, when the Academy exhibition ended, is not known for certain.

The Academy behind him, Langley next concentrated on his one-man show, due to take place in February 1893, and all went well until July 1892, when the lease of Pembroke Lodge expired. The local newspaper advertising the auction of some of Langley's furniture exaggerated somewhat when it announced this was 'prior to the family's departure from the country' — they only moved as far as 43 Morrab Road, Penzance. Caught, once again, by a shortage of suitable property in the district they had to move to 40 Morrab Road in the autumn of 1892, then back to number 43 in the following spring and finally, in the autumn of 1893, to 6 St Mary's Terrace, Penzance, which was to be home for the next two years.

In the midst of that unsettled interlude Langley's exhibition, 'Water Colour Drawings Illustrating Fisher Life', opened in London. Notwithstanding the exhibition's title, the 69 paintings shown included a few oils, one of which drew a particularly appreciative comment from Alice Meynell, in her prefatory note to the exhibition catalogue:

> ... Mr Langley deals with no tragic stories; the most eloquent figure in his series expresses only the inevitable and inseparable potential grief of the title, *Maternity*, and no actual loss. This is, by the way, one of his few oil paintings, and its rich but cool tone, its full but simple execution, give you a taste for more in the same manner. It shows the infrequent pleasure that an out-of-door painter, who has exercised his eyes on opaque and diffused effects, takes in the transparent gloom and localized light of an interior ...

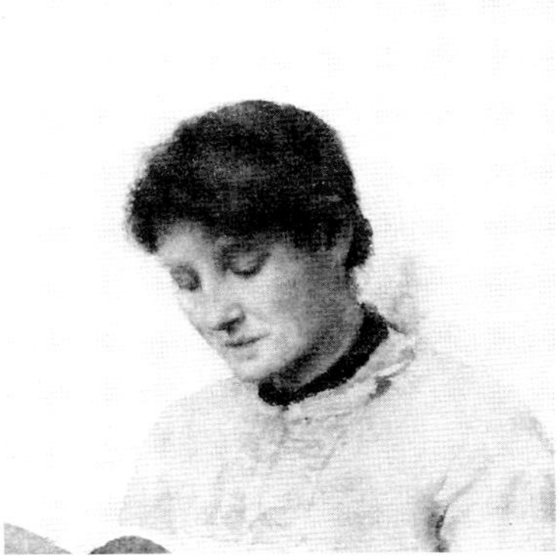

Head study early-1890s
watercolour, 14 x 15.3cm

PAGE 94
Sunshine and Shadow 1889
watercolour, 35.5 x 25.4cm

The title is taken from the RI catalogue though, confusingly, Langley refers to it as *Sunlight and Shadow* in his sales records, a title by which it has more recently been known.

BELOW
At Mousehole, Cornwall 1892
watercolour, 22.2 x 29.7cm

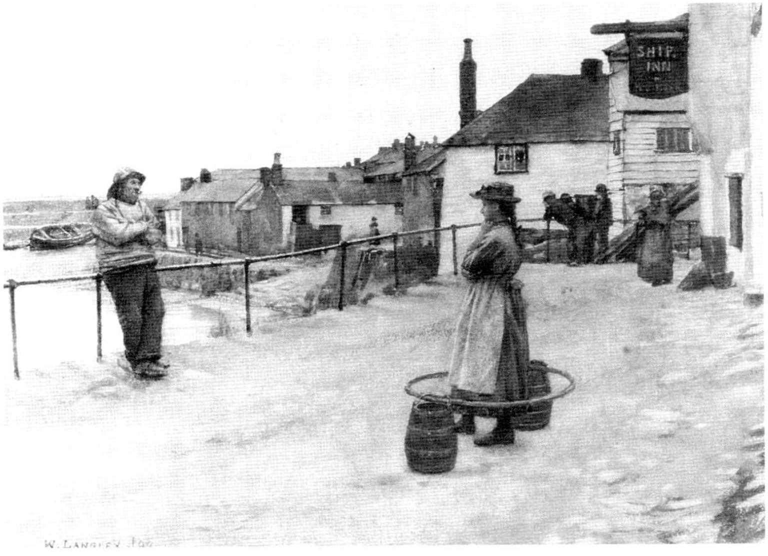

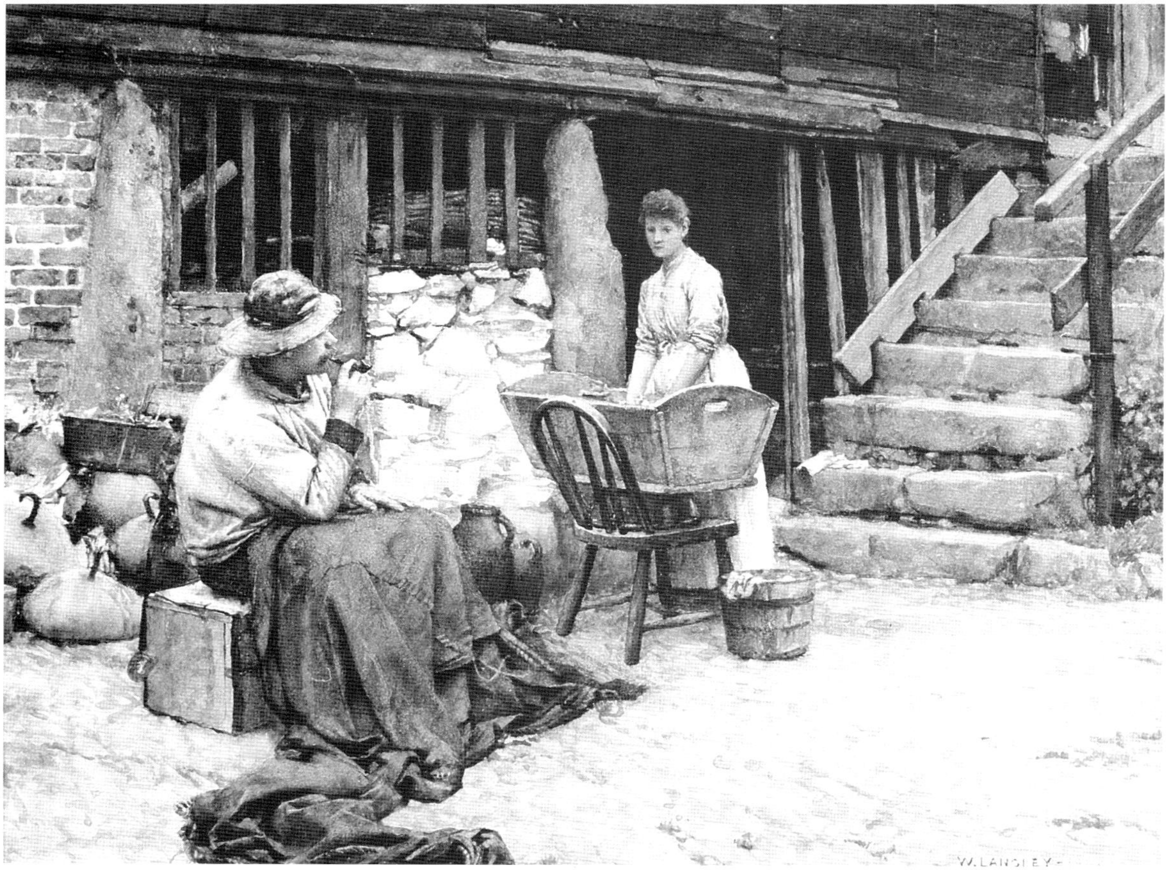

Washing Day 1893
watercolour, 29.7 x 38.5cm

There is a study for this subject, also 1893. The same courtyard with steps appears in a later watercolour of two women watching a man reading a newspaper, not positively identified but known as *Waiting for the News*.

The *Magazine of Art* included an appreciative review of his exhibition, at the same time highlighting the important difference in training between Langley and his contemporaries:

> Mr Walter Langley, RI ... differs from his fellows in his training. He never studied in a French atelier; and his art is purely English, and developed from within himself. He gives us the fisher-folk of the Lands End district with unidealised strength and fidelity. The comeliness of his buxom maidens and the patient dignity of his old men owe nothing to the imagination, everything to accurate observation ... His light is silvery grey, all pervading; and the moist sea air holds it in solution. As a master of the actual technique of water colours he has few living rivals. The quality of some of his work is matchless — so simple, direct and serene.

Holding the exhibition may have fulfilled an ambition of Langley's, but it did so at some cost. The catalogue value of the 69 paintings was £1,400, but only 21 sold at Bond Street and the final tally for the work shown was £850, spread over three years.

Perhaps Langley gained greater satisfaction in 1893 from the award of a gold medal for watercolours by the World's Colombian Exposition in Chicago, for *Disaster* and *Departure of the Fleet*. He never actually received the medal, his somewhat spirited reply to the United Kingdom excisemen's demand for duty on its supposed gold content ensured that it went instead to reduce the National Debt.

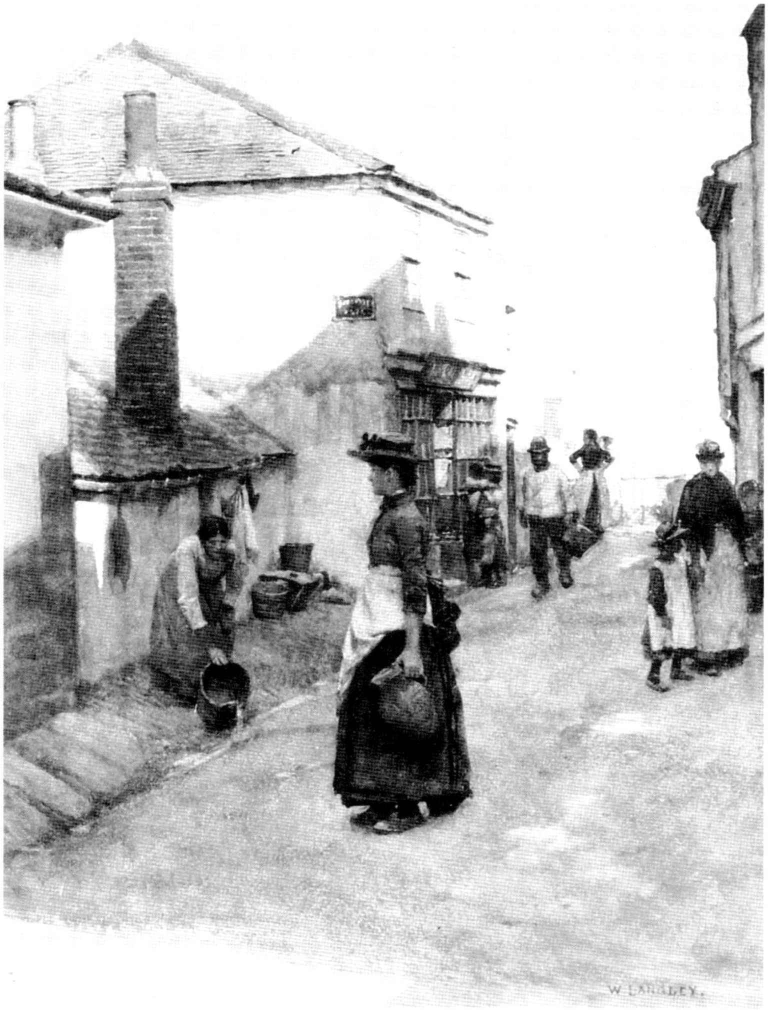

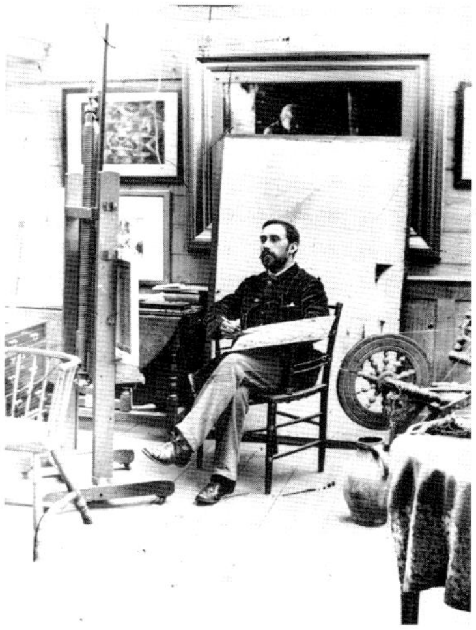

Walter Langley in his studio in Newlyn, c1890s
photographer unknown

LEFT
Street scene c1893
watercolour, 36.8 x 28.3cm

Possibly *A Street in Newlyn* 1893.

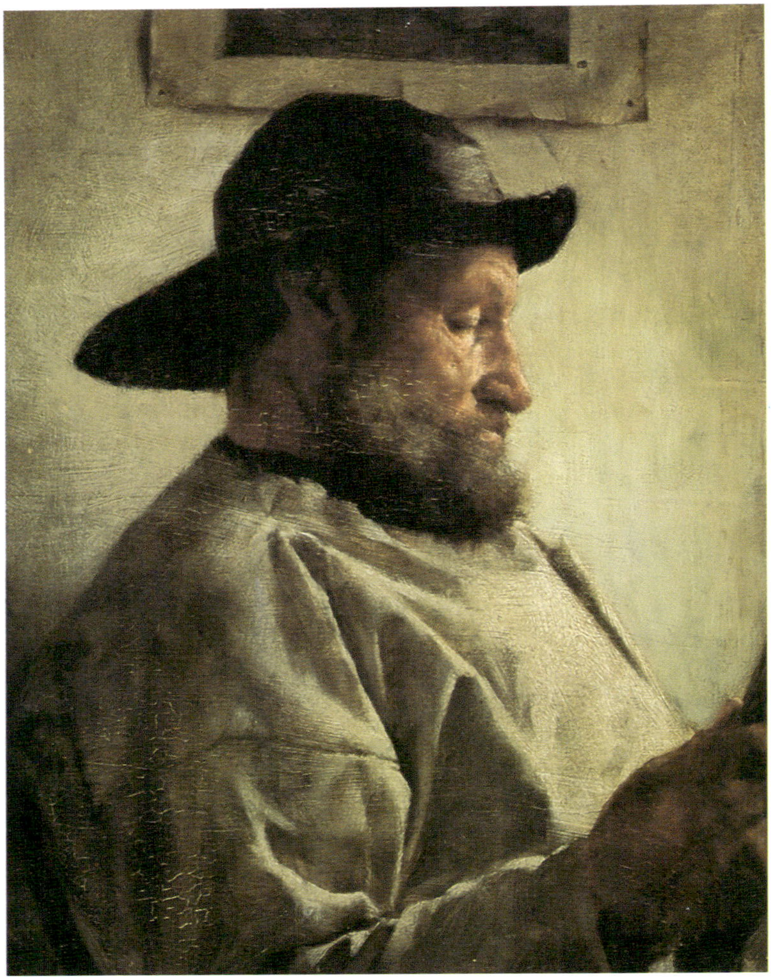

1894-1903 Newlyn

CHAPTER FIVE

The demands of his one-man show had allowed Langley no time in which to prepare for the Academy's 1893 exhibition but he returned there in 1894 with *Never morning wore to evening, but some heart did break*, a powerful work signalling his determination to spend more time painting in oils. *Never morning wore to evening* was sold direct from the easel, normally the occasion for much rejoicing, but then the Chantrey Bequest approached Langley with a view to purchasing it for the nation. Dismayed, he sought to repurchase it at a price half as much again as the owner had paid but the latter, pleased at this confirmation of his own good taste, responded with a further cheque. This, in turn, embarrassed Langley and he promptly reciprocated by sending the owner a study for the painting. At that point the exchanges ended and, as this book is published, there is still no painting by Langley in a national collection.

Never morning wore to evening was not the only major work Langley exhibited in 1894 for the year was marked by one of his last large watercolours for the Institute, *After the Storm*. This painting, set at Coverack on the Lizard peninsula rather than at Newlyn, was his only work to include in its composition the body, or rather legs — for only they can be seen — of a storm victim. *After the Storm* sold almost immediately, for £300, and was later presented to Birmingham Art Gallery. Regrettably, the painting's present whereabouts are not known. Lastly in 1894, Langley exhibited a three-quarter length portrait in oils of his 15 year-old daughter, Eleanore, at the West Cornwall Art Union biennial exhibition in Penzance. His execution of the portrait was much admired but this

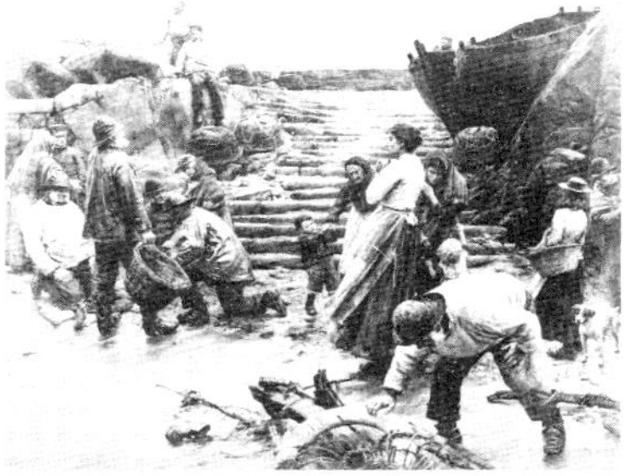

After the Storm 1894
watercolour, 113 x 134cm
(whereabouts unknown, reproduced from a photograph; presented to Birmingham Art Gallery by Richard Peyton, 1903).

PAGE 98
Reading the News c1900
oil, 33.5 x 25.5cm

was a labour of love and he still refused on principle to accept portrait commissions.

In 1894, for the first and so far as is known the only time, Langley took part in the colony's annual theatre show. This was not the usual serious production but two nights of 'Melancholy Minstrelsy by the Matabele Family' alias 'Lubly Lobengula's Impecunious Impi'. Lobengula, a Zulu chieftain, was very much a thorn in the side of British interests at the time. The concert was well publicised and questions were asked in the council chamber about the fly-posting of large posters 'gorgeous in hue and grotesque in design'. Perhaps it was wise of the artist responsible for the poster to remain anonymous; a copy preserved by Langley suggests a lithographic background was brought to bear in its production.

The artists went to great lengths to ensure their audiences enjoyed themselves and that they succeeded is apparent from the review in the *Cornishman*:

> The programme was unique and, where all did well, very well, it seems invidious to particularise; but candour claims extra praise for the corner men, Messrs Birch and Blackburne (bones) and for Mr Langley (tambourine). The latter gentleman's song and dance 'The little coon' brought down the house ... Mr Langley again delighted his audience with his clever dancing in his 'King of Carribee'.

Langley was clearly in his element, unlike Stanhope Forbes — at least initially — as he explained in a letter written in April 1944 to John Langley:

> How well I recollect the Concert. Your father came with another friend and took me to the Hall to take the part of Middle Man, for the chap who was to have done it got injured and, on the afternoon of the Concert, they found themselves with no-one to take this important part. I had sternly declined to take any part in such a low down affair, for I was keen on Classical music and highbrow stuff, but they forced me to go on and I quite enjoyed it in the end. Your father was splendid. I can recollect his jokes now quite clearly for I had to learn them up for the answers I had to make for them.

Henry Rheam was the injured actor for whom, according to the *Cornishman*, Forbes proved a more than adequate substitute.

For the artists of Cornwall as a whole, perhaps the most important event of 1894 was the Nottingham Castle Museum and Art Gallery exhibition 'Painters of the Cornish School', which was held in September of that year. Most of the 223 exhibits were oil paintings but Langley was represented by nine watercolours, the organisers having failed to secure *Never morning wore to evening*. Disappointingly for Langley, the newspaper coverage of the exhibition almost completely ignored the watercolour section. One ingenious reporter, having run out of space after devoting many column inches to the oils, concluded: 'Mr Langley's work is so well known that we shall not attempt to describe it here'. The *Studio* review was infinitely more pleasing, though hardly of greater length: 'In water colours Mr Walter Langley stands first, with a series of his well-known drawings, delightful in handling, and filled with truth.'

The sales of *Never morning wore to evening* and *Among the Missing* ensured that 1894 would be one of Langley's best years and it was only to be expected that in 1895 he would be represented at the Academy by another essay in social realism. The local reviewers, seeing *Motherless* at the Newlyn 'open day' were full of praise for Langley's faithful and unsentimental depiction of a situation all too familiar to the Newlyn folk but the *Times* reviewer of the Academy exhibition was not so impressed — 'It is as clever as might be expected, but infected with mannerisms which seem to grow upon this artist.'

As the spring of 1895 gave way to summer, there was nothing to suggest the year then unfolding would be much different from its predecessors. Then, late in June, Langley received a letter from the Uffizi Gallery, in Florence. No linguist, he had to curb his excitement until a translator could be found:

> The celebrated collection of portraits of the most eminent painters of every nation executed by themselves, which was founded by the Cardinal Leopoldo di Medici, and was continued by the Medici family and, thereafter, by the various Administrators of the Royal Gallery of the Uffizi, is still deficient

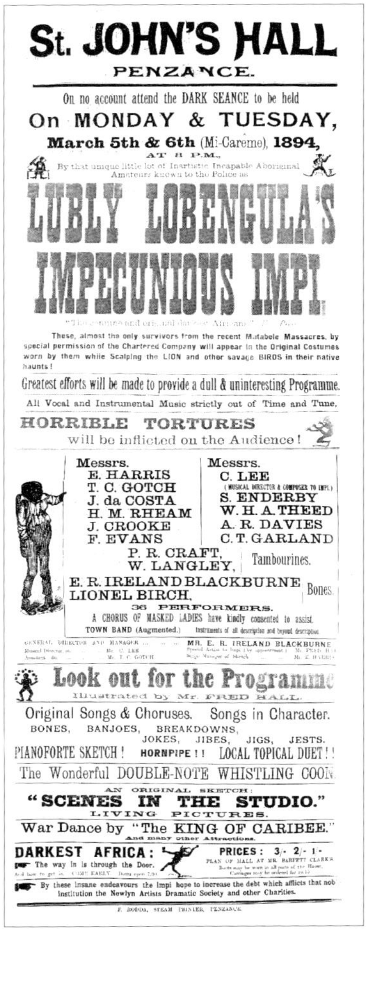

Poster for theatricals in Penzance, 1894

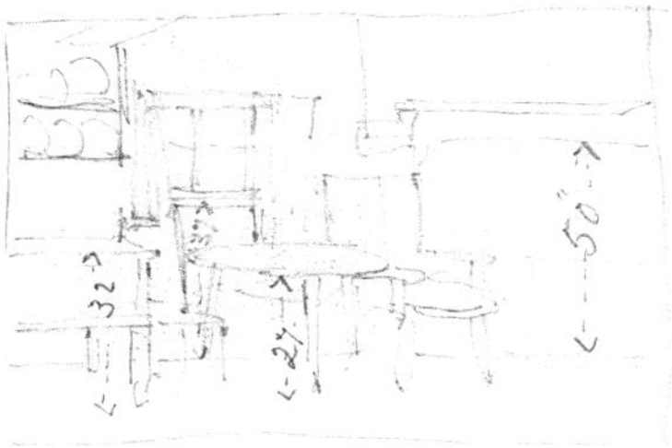

Interior study c1897
pencil, 8 x 13cm

From a pocketable sketchbook, this study with measurements shows the care with which Langley prepared the scenes for his paintings.

RIGHT
An old man with a pipe late-1890s
watercolour, 38.7 x 38cm

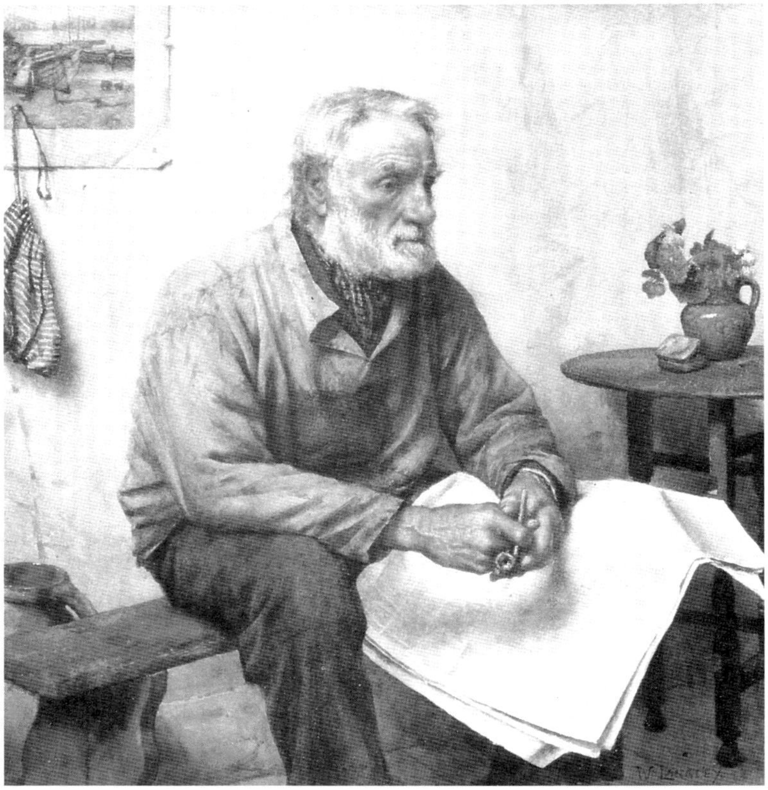

> in the portrait of yourself, whose name is so distinguished and whose notable works are the boast and honour of modern art; and I deem it a very great privilege to enlist your extreme courtesy, cordially requesting you to make a donation of your own portrait to the said Gallery, so that it may take the position of which it is so worthy in the celebrated collection.

One can only imagine Langley's feelings on finding himself thus honoured among a company that included Raphael, Rubens, Rembrandt and Velasquez and, nearer to his own time and country, Millais, Watts, Herkomer, Rossetti and Holman Hunt. It was an achievement to be savoured, the pinnacle of his career. There was, though, one question that Langley felt he needed to resolve, and when he wrote to the Uffizi early in July to accept the commission he asked whether he might paint his portrait in watercolours. They replied that he could use whatever medium he desired, but added that most portraits in their collection were in oils.

The Uffizi's reply left Langley in something of a quandary, but he had no time to decide what medium to use. Early on August 7 Clara, in her 44th year, suffered a stroke from which she died the same day. The household was plunged into gloom and all work ceased as Langley and the children sought to cope with their loss.

Clara's support and encouragement had been particularly important to Langley, especially in the early stages in his career when he first abandoned lithography. Then, as he became more established, she provided much-needed help in the management of his day-to-day business matters. The similarities in their backgrounds had been a unifying force, though there is a suggestion she may not have been entirely happy in Cornwall, giving rise to her wish, which Langley honoured, to be buried in Birmingham next to her mother and where, within a year, her father would also lie.

Clara's death did not precipitate any immediate changes in the Langley household. The two youngest children, Gabriel and Cecil, had still to complete their education. Eleanore had just finished her schooling and doubtless assumed some responsibilities in the house while, as in her mother's lifetime, a housekeeper and maid undertook most of the household chores. Lorraine, the eldest son, was still at home but being proficient on the 'cello was seeking a post in a London orchestra.

Family obligations dictated that work must carry on and Langley set to with a vengeance on his largest-ever work, *Breadwinners*, for the 1896 Academy exhibition. *Breadwinners* measured 117cm x 216cm and since it was no easy task for Langley to work on it in the cramped confines of his cottage studio he probably welcomed a brief interlude from work in January 1896, when he was empanelled into the Grand Jury at Penzance Quarter Sessions. The jury had quite an artistic flavour to it, also including Norman Garstin, J C Uren and H M Geffroi.

The difficulties Langley encountered when manoeuvring *Breadwinners* in his cottage-studio convinced him of the need for a purpose-built workplace. In June 1896 he engaged a local builder, Caldwell, to extend the cottage, at the same time gutting it to form one large studio room with a floor-to-rooftop north light. This work

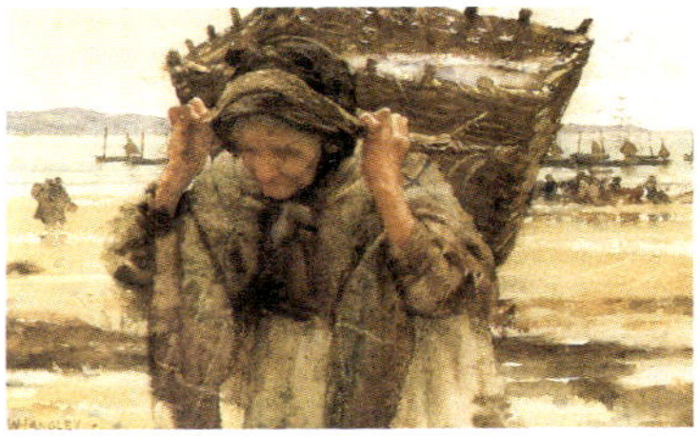

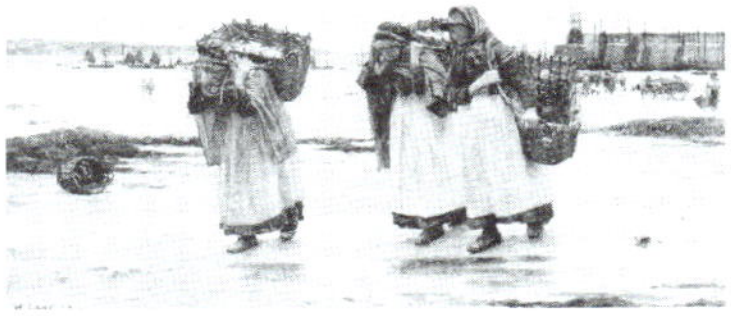

Breadwinners 1896
watercolour, 23 x 43cm
(Penlee House Gallery and Museum, Penzance)

See page 23 for the oil of this subject.

TOP
Study for *Breadwinners* c1896
watercolour, 12 x 19.7cm

This study has also been known as *Weary Toil*.

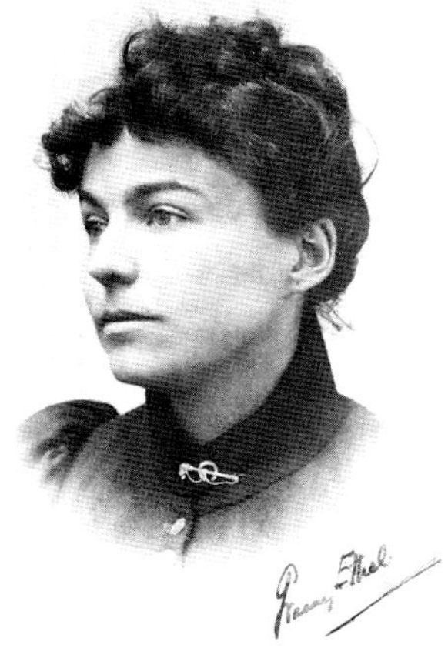

Ethel Langley c1896
photographer unknown

was completed in September, the sale of *Breadwinners* in the previous month paying for the conversion.

In October Langley attended the opening of the Passmore Edwards Art Gallery in Newlyn, which had been given for the artists by the well-known Cornish philanthropist, John Passmore Edwards. The gallery marked a new phase in the colony's existence and the end of the studio 'open days'. The air of formality was cemented by the time-honoured formula of placing the management of the gallery in the hands of a committee. Langley, who had been in the deputation of artists who first broached the question of an art gallery with the donor, served on the management committee from its inception.

At this point in his life, Langley faced an uncertain future. Widowed at 43, he was young enough to contemplate remarrying but even the most sanguine of his friends would have recognised that four teenage children represented a formidable challenge to any aspiring partner. Once again, however, a change was to come about in Langley's life through the intervention, albeit indirect this time, of his longtime friend Edwin Harris. Harris, who had been widowed in 1887, left Penzance for Plymouth in 1895 and there married a Penzance girl, Sally Cornwell. Sally and a close friend from her childhood days, Ethel Pengelly, were friends of the Langleys and when Sally left Penzance, Ethel and the recently widowed Langley were naturally drawn to each other.

Ethel had a very different background and upbringing to Langley's. Her father, John Russell Pengelly, had been one of a long line of farmers and market-gardeners in the village of Madron, near Penzance, where he was also churchwarden. On retirement, he moved to a smallholding in Penzance and a house there in Clarence Street. Her father's family, worthy though it was, could hardly compete with the Harveys, from whom her mother was descended. They boasted no fewer than fourteen doctors and surgeons, including three Fleet Surgeons, in a distinguished line stretching back over several hundred years. Through her mother, Ethel was also first cousin to Harold Harvey, probably the most gifted locally born artist.

An only child, and a local beauty in her younger days, Ethel had the usual accomplishments her upbringing would suggest: singing, playing the piano and painting competently in watercolours. She also enjoyed the undivided and spoiling attention of her parents and a host of unmarried uncles and aunts. Her sheltered, conventional life in Penzance was interrupted only once, when she briefly became governess in Chard, Somerset, to the children of a former Penzance vicar. Perhaps that experience was an added attraction to a widower beset by four teenagers. On her part, the opportunity at the comparatively late age of 34 to marry an artist of considerable renown may have seemed too good to miss. Matters progressed well

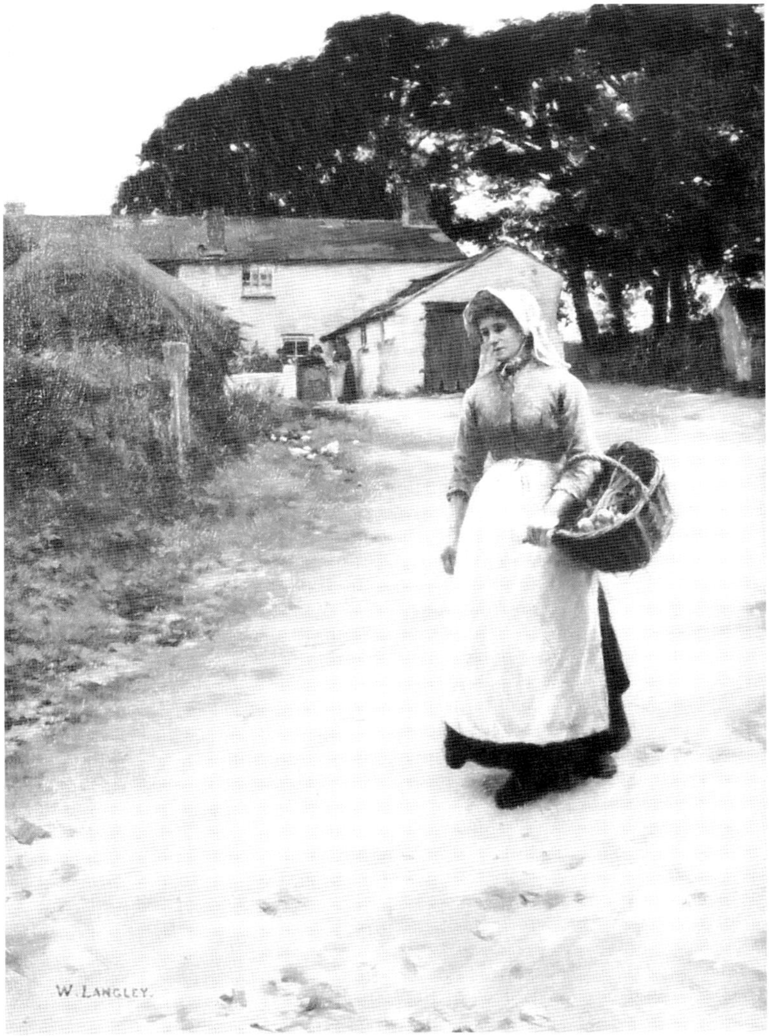

A Country Lass 1898
oil, 76 x 55.8cm

A scene at Chyvellan farm, just inland from Marazion.

The End of the Story 1898
oil, 74.2 x 62.2

Shown at the Royal Institute of Painters in Oil in 1898, this clearly shows the equivalence for his finest watercolours that Langley achieved in oil towards the end of the 1890s.

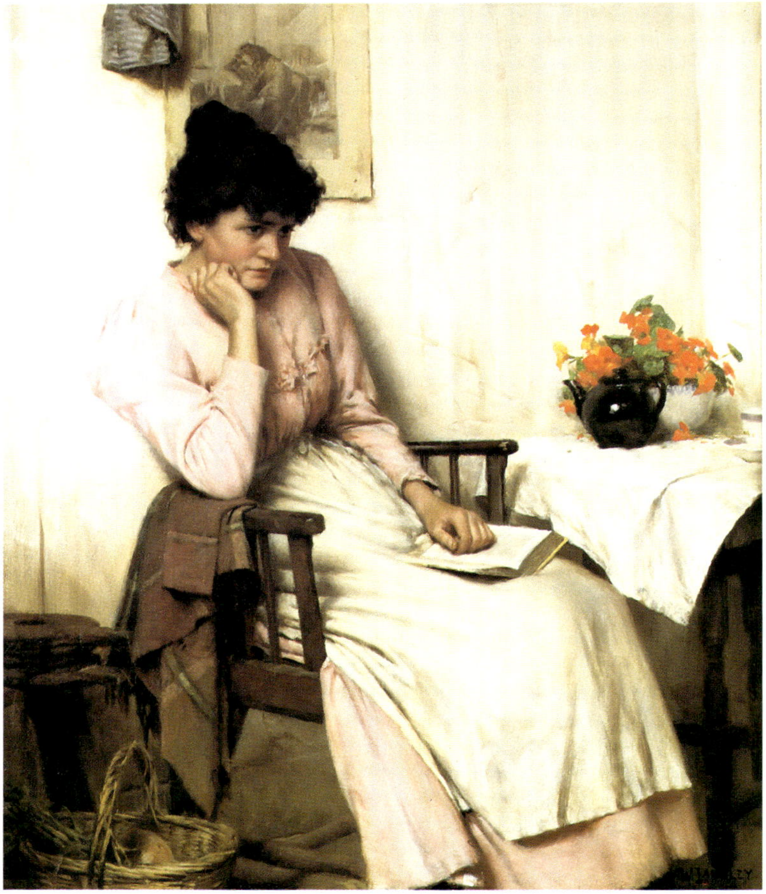

and a wedding date was fixed for the summer of 1897.

While plans were made for the wedding, work proceeded as usual. Langley had decided, somewhat regretfully one feels, that he had better follow the majority after all and paint his Uffizi commission in oils. This — a 'speaking likeness' according to one reviewer — was completed early in 1897 and occupied the place of honour at the spring exhibition of the Royal Birmingham Society of Artists, before being despatched to Florence.

At the Academy in 1897 Langley exhibited an interior scene, its title taken from Pope's 'An Essay on Man':

In faith and hope the world may disagree
But all mankind's concern is charity

Charity so moved Thomas Faed, the Scottish artist and poet, when he saw it at the Academy that he sent Langley a poem 'that might have been written expressly for the painting'. Such a generous tribute from a fellow artist was remarkable enough but the appeal of *Charity* went further, to Russia, where Tolstoy was composing his essay 'What is Art?':

> Next in the same book of Academy pictures comes a picture by Langley, showing a stray beggar boy, who has evidently been called in by a woman who has taken pity on him. The boy, pitifully drawing his bare feet under the bench, is eating; the woman is looking on, probably considering whether he will not want some more; and a girl of about seven, leaning on her arm, is carefully and seriously looking on, not taking her eyes from the hungry boy and evidently understanding for the first time what poverty is and what inequality among people is, and asking herself why she has everything provided for her while this boy

In faith and hope the world will disagree But all mankind's concern is charity 1897
oil, 125.7 x 165.7cm

This is the painting praised by Tolstoy. The text is from Pope's 'Essay on Man'; the same hearth with a wooden partition to one side appears in *His Only Pair* 1905 and *The New Arrival* 1910. There is also a study titled *An Old Cornish Kitchen* 1897 (watercolour 30 x 39)

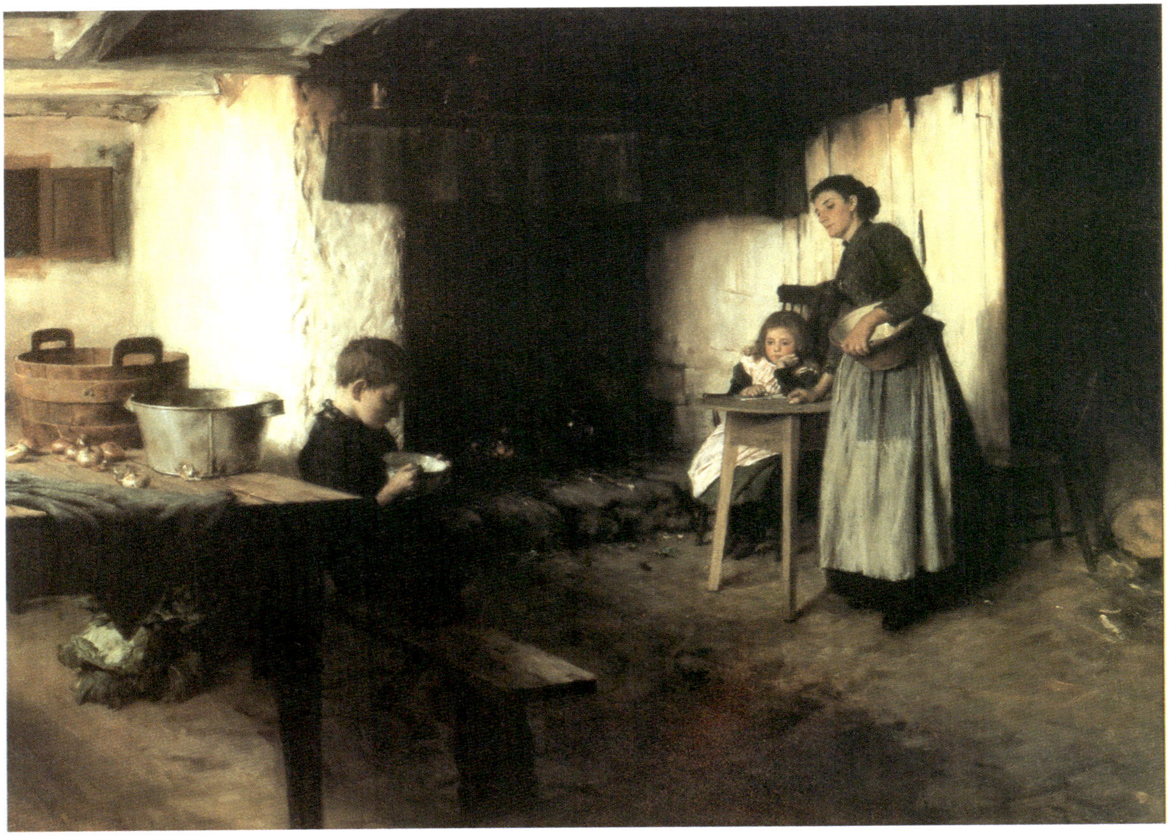

goes barefoot and hungry? She feels sorry and yet pleased, and she loves both the boy and goodness. And one feels that the artist loved this girl and that she too loves. And this picture, by an artist who, I think, is not very widely known, is an admirable and true work of art.

Charity was to be one of Langley's most successful paintings, yet he at first had no great expectations of it. At the Academy 'varnishing day' he realised all was not well with his work. 'My little boy,' he wrote to Ethel, 'I found looking rather muddled in the lower limbs. I tried to alter it but could not do much. Strange I did not notice it before, although I had a dim notion something was not quite right. It is not pleasant to find anything wrong in one's picture when it is too late to rectify it — but I don't think it will be noticed much.' He seems to have been justified in his last surmise, judging by the many requests he had to exhibit the picture.

Despite the change of emphasis towards oils in his larger works, watercolours were still Langley's main source of income, though he sent only one small work to the Institute in 1897, *At Porthgwarra,* and that was a donation to the Art Union charity draw. The need to complete his Uffizi portrait, combined with a desire to submit a major oil painting to the Academy, probably contributed to his comparative neglect of the Institute that year.

Langley also had important domestic matters on his mind. Ethel had no wish to live in a home that was formerly Clara's domain and, early in 1897, Langley left 6 St Mary's Terrace and moved a short distance to 'Westbourne', a newly-built house in Alexandra Road where there would be room for himself and Ethel, four children and two live-in domestics. Their new home as they wished it, Langley and Ethel married in St John's parish church, Penzance, on June 24. Langley did not record where the newly-weds spent their honeymoon, but it was unlikely to have been in the Midlands. His sister, Minnie, had visited Penzance in the past year and reported back unfavourably on Ethel.

Settling down to work once again, and possibly reflecting that he had neglected watercolours of late, Langley produced a major work for the Institute's 1898 spring exhibition. *In the Fishing Season* depicts a group of villagers sitting in the warmth of the afternoon sun at Porthgwarra, along the coast from Newlyn, awaiting the return of their hamlet's few fishing boats. The good humour of this painting also spilled over into Langley's Academy picture *A Cousin from Town*, in which a young lad endeavours to impress a group of Newlyners with his banjo playing. From the looks on their faces, it is clear his skills were of a modest order.

After despatching his work to the spring exhibitions, Langley

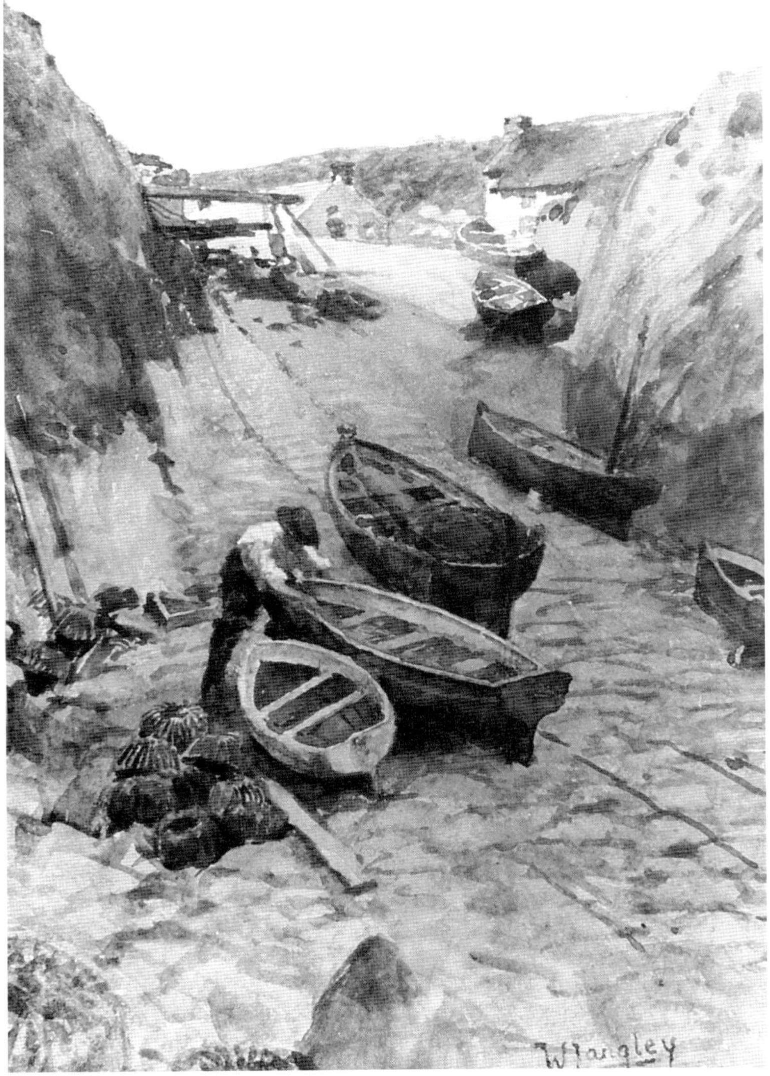

At Porthgwarra, Cornwall 1900
watercolour, 25.4 x 17.8cm

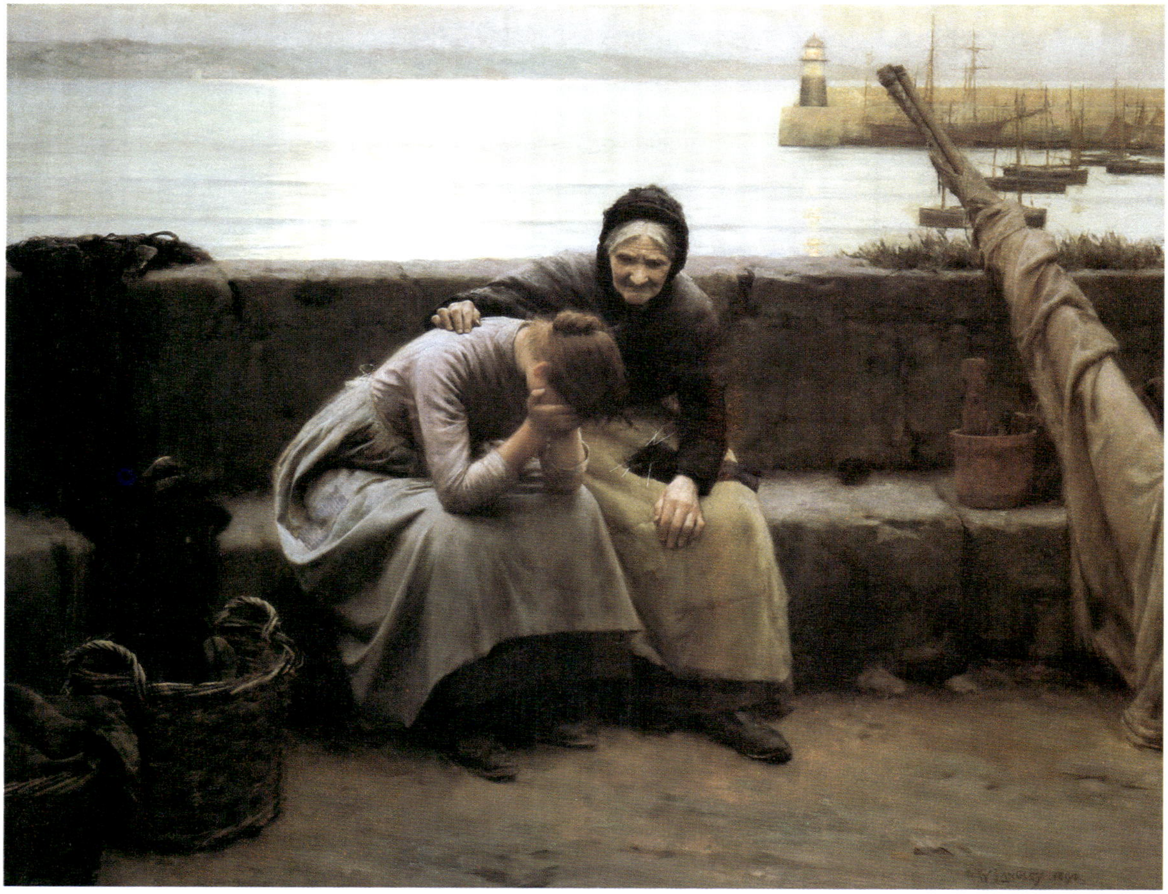

Never morning wore to evening, but some heart did break 1894
oil, 122 x 152.5cm
(Birmingham Museums and Art Gallery)

Shown at the RA in 1894 and engraved for the *Graphic*. The lines are from Tennyson's 'In Memoriam'. Though he had first shown an oil at the RA in 1892, it was between 1894 and 1897 that four of Langley's most important large oils appeared there. This painting was followed by *Motherless* in 1895, *Breadwinners* 1896 and ... *Charity* 1897.

would usually set off on his annual visits to London and Birmingham but in 1898 his routine was pre-empted by the news from Minnie that their mother had died, in her 79th year. It was her selfless action some 35 years earlier that set Langley off on a road that had but recently taken him to the Uffizi, and her death was a forceful reminder of the tremendous debt he owed her.

Perhaps it was nostalgia that prompted Langley to return to Worcestershire in the summer of 1898, to sketch at Elmley Castle, Eckington and Cropthorne. What was intended to be only a short break, since Ethel was expecting their first (and only) child in September, became even shorter with the news from Penzance that Batten, Carne and Carne's Bank had collapsed. It is not known to what extent Langley was affected by the collapse but he certainly attended the resulting depositors' meetings in Penzance. There he heard that Batten's was to be taken over by Barclays Bank, which had already established itself in the town via another old Penzance bank, Bolitho's. To a person of Langley's political leanings it was all doubtless an unpleasant reminder of the fickle nature of the capitalist system. There was little time for Langley to reflect on the Batten's debacle, however, for John (the writer's father), was born on September 19 1898, at 'Westbourne'.

Langley's response to the demands of a new baby, coupled to those of Eleanore, Gabriel and Cecil who were still at home and of Lorraine in London, was to bury himself in his work. For the Academy exhibition of 1899, he drew inspiration from his visit to Cropthorne in a painting entitled *The Wandering Musicians*, depicting a group of young itinerants by the village cross.

When Langley went to see how *The Wandering Musicians* fared at the Academy he also found there a bronze portrait medallion of himself in profile, submitted by a friend of his Birmingham Art School days, G W de Saulles, who had risen to be Head Designer at the Royal Mint. Langley later acquired the medallion though, as he revealed in a letter to Ethel, he was not too keen on the likeness.

The highlight of 1899 was in Birmingham, a retrospective of 39 paintings included within the Society's spring exhibition. That the honour was justly deserved was made clear by the *Birmingham Post*:

> ... Mr Langley unites that distinction in his profession, without which no one would be entitled to such an honour as this, with the fact, appealing to our local patriotism, that he is a Birmingham man — almost more a Birmingham man than he could be called from an accident of birth, and the fact of his boyhood, youth, and early manhood having been spent amongst us. He has the genuine Birmingham character, independence, strong individuality, and a sense of insistent force with great tenderness. In his art he has restricted himself to a limited range: he is the painter of the humble and hardworking folk, and those of restricted locality, and principally in their moments of sorrow, of emotion, of brooding care. In thus bounding himself he has done but as other painters have done who have made great and enduring reputations.

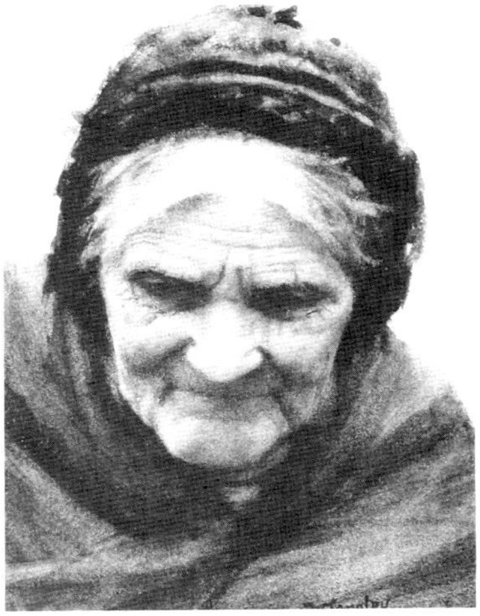

Old Grace 1894
watercolour, 34 x 25cm

A study for *Never morning ...*

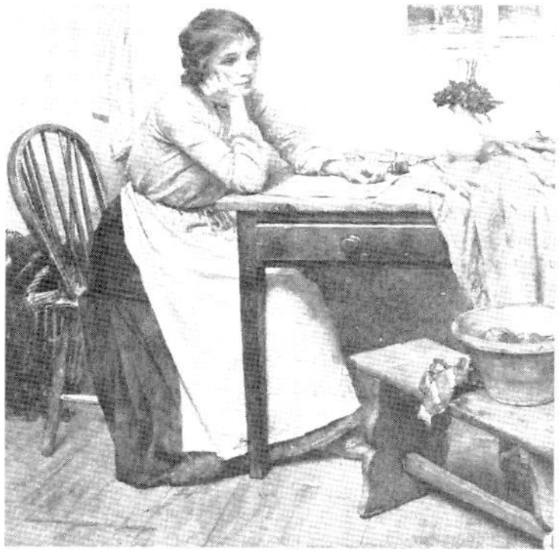

Woman at a table, early-1900s
watercolour, 43.1 x 40.6cm

This may be *A Letter from Home* 1903. There is a crayon drawing of the same subject.

> In Mr Langley's art there is never anything mean or base or ignoble; if he has portrayed mainly the remembered joys and present sorrows of Cornish fisher folk he has in doing so but taken a picturesque phase of what is co-extensive with human nature.
>
> In all we feel above all — technical accomplishment being assumed — the absolute sincerity of the artist; the aim not primarily to make a beautiful picture, but to present a bit of human life, with all its natural accessories, as it really is; and in working out the aim we are conscious that he has reached a very high level of poetic feeling, far beyond those who, making a poetic conception primary, have tried to tame facts to their will. Byron spoke of Crabbe as 'Nature's sternest painter, yet the best' and the phrase might be said of Mr Langley. He is uncompromising in his fidelity to fact, but his innate artistic sense has moulded every touch.

Though a 'limited range' served Langley well he sought to change artistic direction from time to time, but without success. His most recent attempt was with *The Wandering Musicians* but, as had happened with *Betrayed* some years earlier, while the painting was welcomed by the critics as a variation from his usual Newlyn scenes it was rejected by the market precisely because it was an unfamiliar subject. As before, Langley was unable to ignore the dictates of the market and reverted to Newlyn work for the while.

Other artists in Newlyn had also 'chafed at the bit', as witness the comments of the art correspondent of the *Cornish Telegraph*, in the spring of 1899:

> The Newlyn men, in their early days, were content with studies in wild nature and in Cornish cottage houses; they gave practical proof of their adhesion to the doctrine that in the eyes of the artist nothing is common and unclean, simply because Philistines pass it every day with blind eyes and tell you they see nothing in it. But the present day Cornish painters wander far afield; all the world is their parish; their canvasses glow with all the hues of the rainbow, and in place of Cornish fishermen and fisherwomen and Cornish village scenes we get glimpses of Parisian

> boulevards, caves of lapis lazuli tenanted by sea maidens illuminated by 'a light that never was on sea or land', angels, saints, heathen worshippers and goodness knows what besides. A great deal of it is very clever I dare say, but is there not something that smacks of decadence?

While the writer of that review might rail against the artists who deserted Newlyn, those who remained had to recognise and accommodate in their art the structural changes that had taken place in the village over the years — new quays, shops in place of cottages, and workshops where none had existed before.[13] Portraying the old harbour as if the new quays did not exist, or cottage interiors that were impossibly 'dated', could only postpone the facing of real problems of content and presentation. Another reason for Langley to change his approach and subject matter was the relatively improved economic situation of the Newlyn fisherfolk. It seems likely this point had not been lost on him, as witness the Institute and Academy paintings for 1898.

There were also changes at home. As the new century dawned, Lorraine moved to London to play the 'cello in the Queen's Hall orchestra, Eleanore left Penzance to work in the Post Office at Plymouth, Gabriel joined the commercial staff of the Great Western Railway at Newton Abbot and Cecil took an apprenticeship at Starley's engineering works in Coventry. Cecil owed his apprenticeship to a transaction that had taken place some years earlier when James Starley, wishing to purchase two Langley watercolours through a Birmingham dealer, agreed instead to barter a like number of his company's 'Rover' safety cycles for the paintings. Cecil may have thought his parents got the better bargain — his exchange was of home comforts for a 12-hour working day, a wage of 14 shillings a week and a shared room in a Coventry lodging house. No wonder his father wrote to Ethel from Birmingham that he thought the experience might come as a considerable shock to his seventeen year-old son and felt constrained to treat Cecil to his first theatre show by way of consolation.

The household reduced, Langley might have hoped for some assistance from Ethel with his administrative work, but this was not

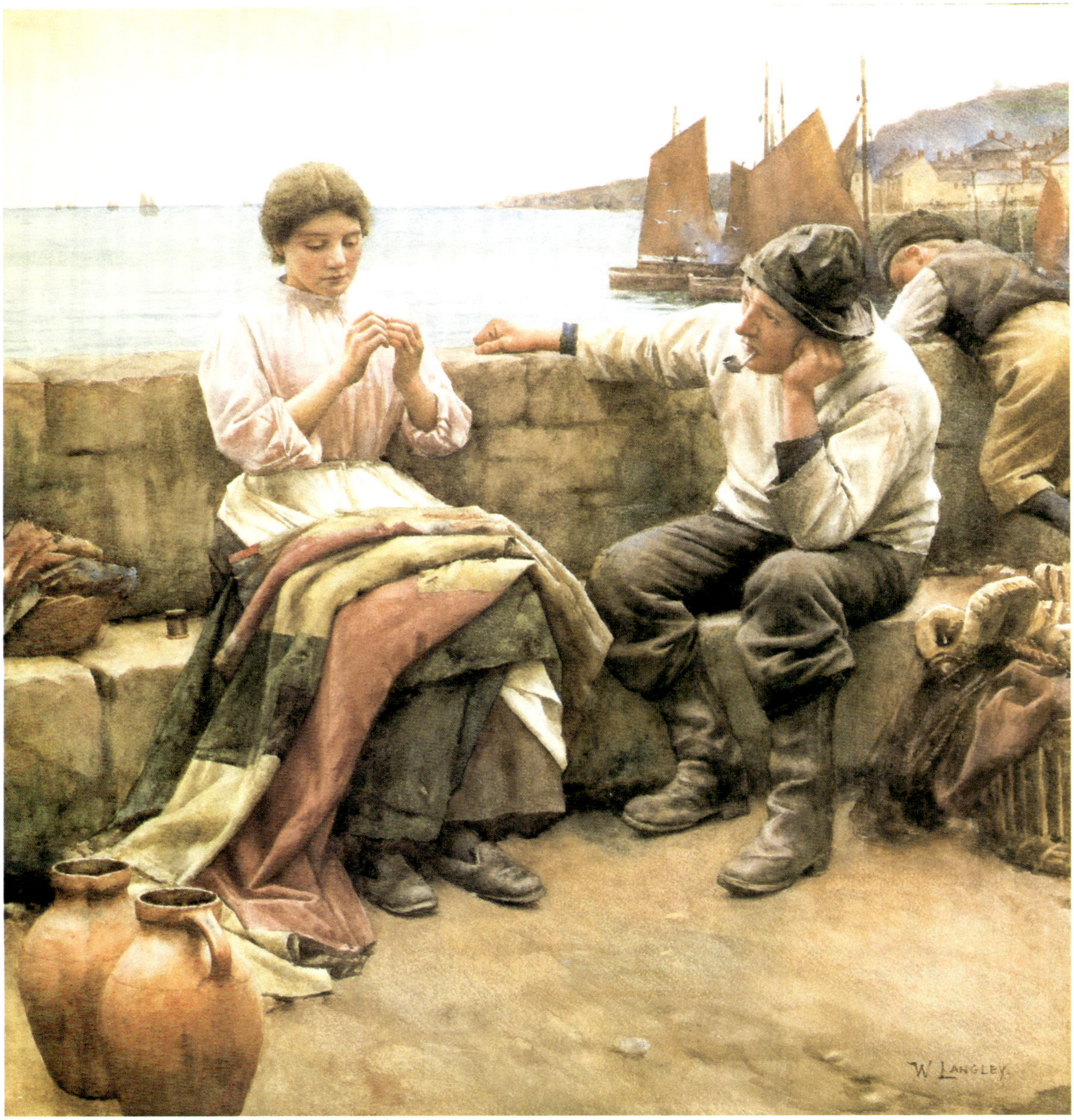
W. LANGLEY

forthcoming. This could possibly have contributed to his reduced output of paintings in later years. Two letters about one painting, in a year when over fifty were consigned to exhibitions or dealers, give some hint of the volume of administration he had to cope with. Both letters were to G H Wallis, of Nottingham Castle Museum:

> Your letter of 20 March to hand. My picture *Charity*, the last of the three works you mention, is at your disposal after the 7th of May, when the Glasgow Exhibition closes. Can you get the picture from Glasgow and keep it for your exhibition as I do not want to have it sent all the way down here and back to you. Kindly let me know and I will give you an order for removal. [April 25, 1900]

> I have directed the Glasgow people to send on my picture *Charity* to you. If you find the frame is in a very poor condition, will you kindly get an estimate from a local frame maker for re-gilding it and let me know, as I should not like it to look bad in your Exhibition. [May 10, 1900]

The re-gilding of a frame was a tedious but minor matter when compared to the risk that a painting might be damaged or lost in transit, but Langley's records disclose only two minor claims against his insurers, a remarkable tribute to those handling his paintings over the years.

Correspondence was the main means by which business was conducted throughout the year. Occasionally dealers and private purchasers would visit Newlyn but personal contacts were more usually made during Langley's visits each spring to London and Birmingham. Business was not, however, his only reason for travelling up country and days spent on business were more than compensated for by evening visits to the theatre, concerts, family and friends. There is some evidence, from his letters, that Ethel and John joined Langley on at least one excursion to London but they otherwise had to rely on his bulletins for news of the metropolis.

In May 1900 Langley wrote to Ethel from the Howard Hotel ('6s 6d for bed and breakfast and quite as much as I can afford'):

PAGE 114
A Cornish Idyll 1902
watercolour, 58.5 x 56cm

This is the larger of two watercolour versions of one of Langley's most popular subjects of the early 1900s. The oil version (in the Walker Art Gallery, Liverpool) was his Academy painting of 1902; it and *The Greeting* (see cover and page 30) each fetched £300, close to his best price for an oil.

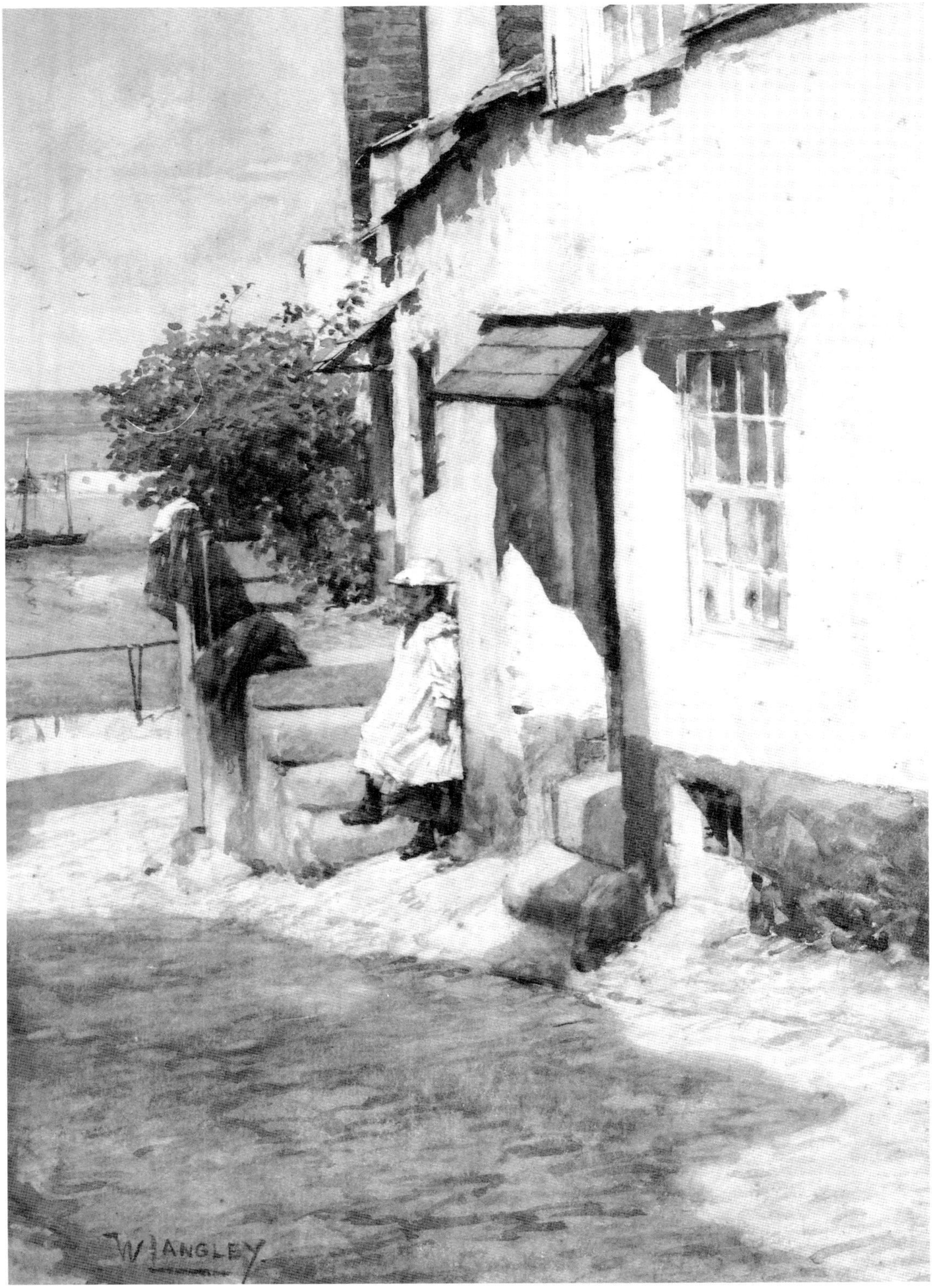
W LANGLEY

PAGE 116
A Sunny Afternoon, Newlyn 1902
watercolour, 43 x 30.5cm
(Cornwall County Museum, Truro)

BELOW
Study of a child in a pinafore c1904
crayon on tone paper, 25 x 9.6cm

Monday was rather a dark day for seeing one's pictures. Mine are in the large room [at the Academy]; one [*A Signal of Distress*] above the line and not far from Frank Dicksee's, which is a very fine work in the centre. It can be seen very well but of course it does not look so large and I cannot say I took much interest in it up there ... my other, smaller one [*Fading Light*] is also above the line, so that I am decidedly off this time ... Harris did not send, I believe. Sargent is wonderful, better than ever, the smaller one of his, a portrait group in a large room, is almost miraculous in the masterly way it is done. I saw Mr de Saulles there, he has some things well placed. I was at their house last night and found Mrs de Saulles very well. They may be coming down our way this year and I asked them to stay with us if they did.

I hope to hear a good concert on Friday night at the Queen's Hall. I tried to get in on Monday night but could not get a ticket so went to the Empire and got rather tired over it as it was not quite what I wanted.

I just missed Mrs Forbes' show ['Children and Child Lore', at the Fine Art Society], I did not know the last day was Monday. I did not see anything of Evans at the RA [Frederick McNamara Evans, briefly a member of the Newlyn colony]. Mrs Dicksee and her sister are still at Florence. Frank is going back for them in about a month's time ...

Both Academy paintings of 1900 fared badly and in the following year Langley sent in a single, large painting, *Between the Tides:*

I have seen my picture in the RA and it is placed very well indeed, on a low line which suits the perspective splendidly. I saw one of the RAs pointing out how well I had given the said perspective, which is something in its favour. Chevallier Tayler [who had left Newlyn some years earlier] has made a new departure and has a costume picture, something on the lines of Abbey, but I think he would be well advised to chuck it if he cannot do it better, for it is decidedly poor ... On Saturday I went to Joachim's quartette party at St James' Hall and as you

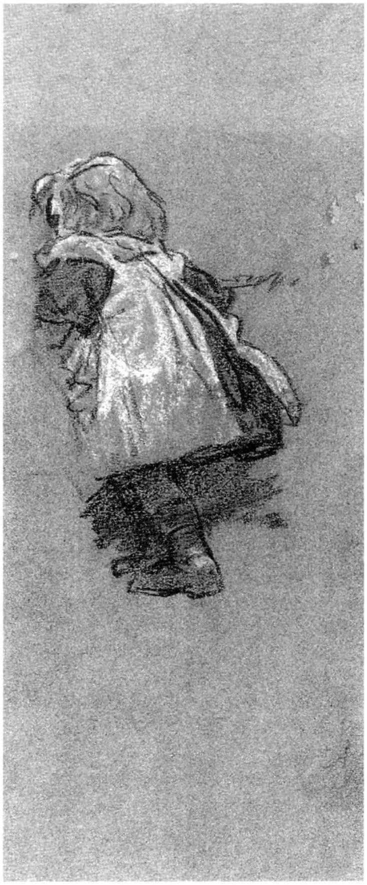

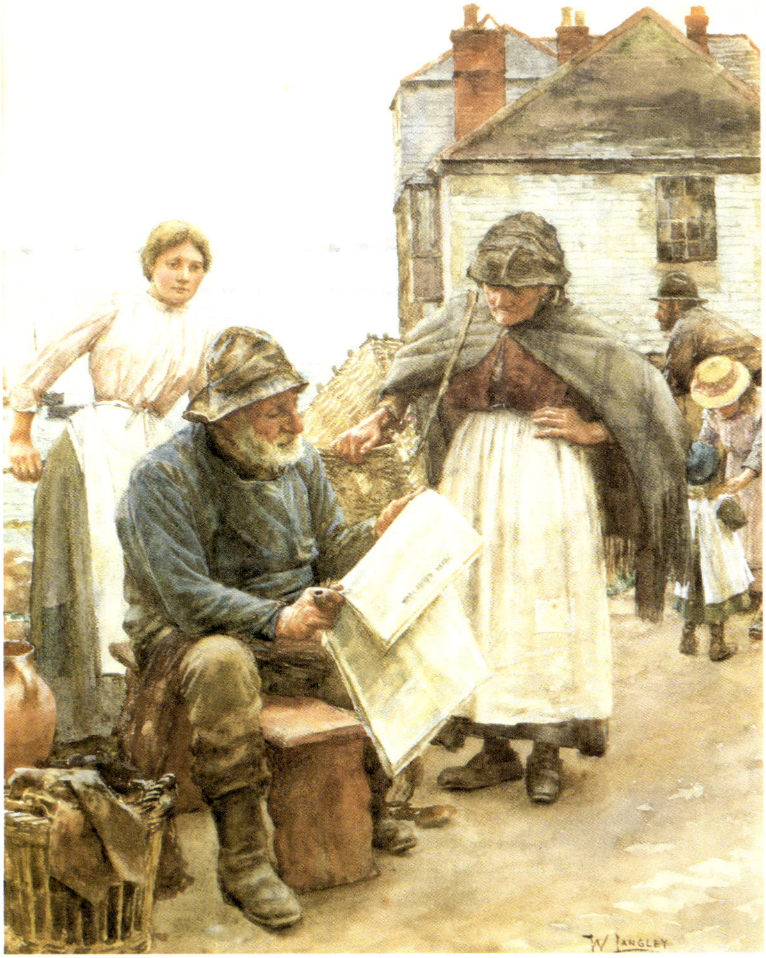

may expect enjoyed it immensely ... I had a pleasant evening at the Bonners', who asked after you ... I dined with the Dicksees last night [and] tonight with some friends of my first wife's family ... Mr de Saulles asked me to spend a few days of my stay with them ... I went with them yesterday to see a collection of pictures at the Guildhall, some Velasquez and some Fortunys, which are magnificent; the latter especially fairly took my breath away. I never saw anything like them in this particular line ... [To Ethel, May 1, 1901]

Frank Dicksee, the Academician, and his family are mentioned in several letters to Ethel and were clearly good friends, as were the Bonners — Hypatia Bonner being Charles Bradlaugh's daughter. Joachim's programme of chamber music by Brahms, Mozart and Beethoven reflected a love he in turn passed on to his children.

Birmingham provided more business opportunities for Langley but he had a social round there also. Edwin Harris had inherited a country cottage in the Midlands ('in the nick of time', according to Langley) and settled down there with Sally and their baby daughter, Queenie. There was talk that the Langleys might rent a cottage nearby for part of the summer, but Ethel would not travel

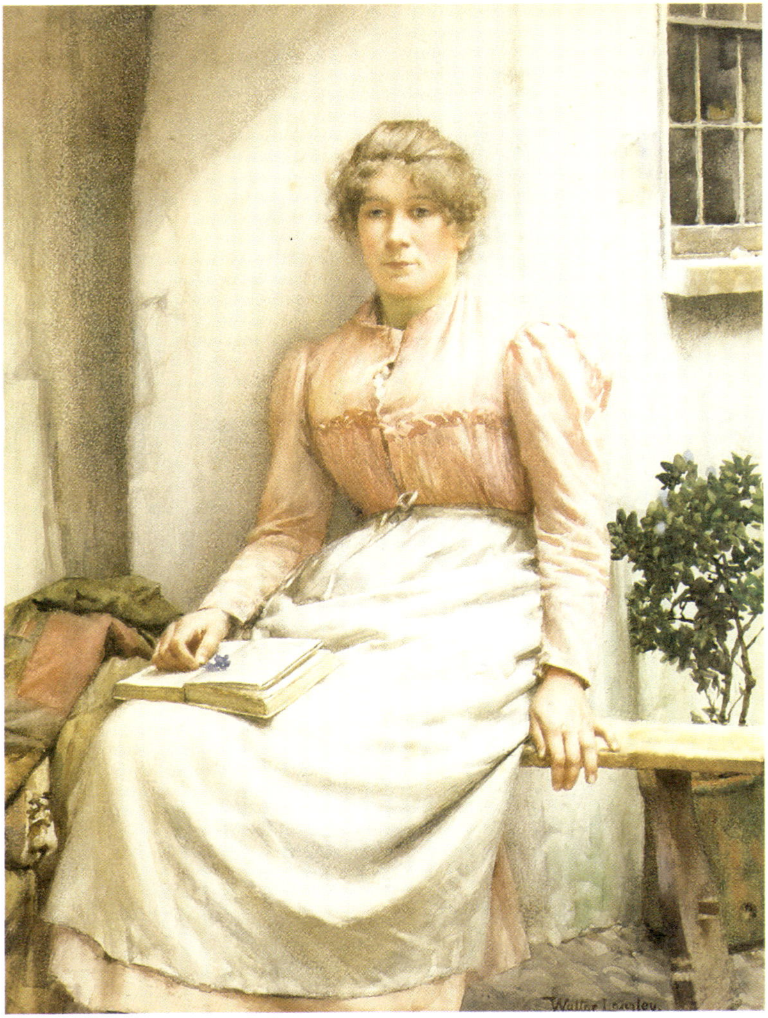

Woman in a pink blouse, early-1900s
watercolour, 52 x 47cm

Has been called *Daydreams*; the pink blouse appears on different models in many works from the 1890s onwards, one being *The End of the Story*, see page 106. Tessa Sidey reports that the blouse had belonged to a Mrs Tregurtha of Newlyn and was originally white, but was dyed pink. The colour didn't suit Mrs Tregurtha's complexion and she was going to discard the blouse but instead gave it to Langley for a model.

PAGE 118
Study for ***When the Boats are Away***
1903
watercolour, 40.6 x 31.7cm

Related to several paintings, watercolours and oils, in which a man reading a newspaper is watched by a woman. The newspaper is often identifiable as the *Cornishman* or the *Cornish Telegraph*. This is a smaller version of Langley's Royal Academy oil for 1903 (137 x 107cm).

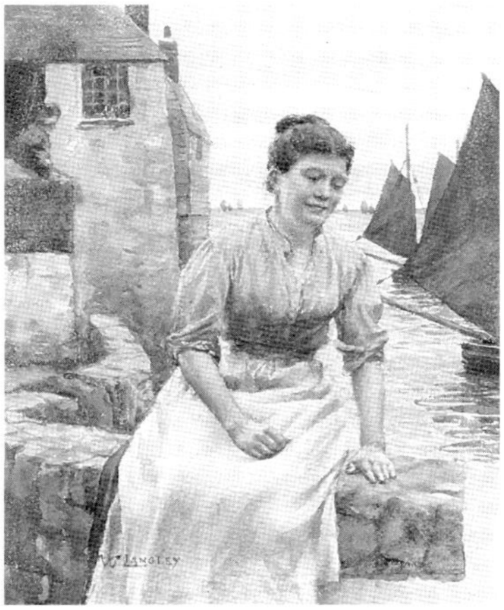

that far with John. Family visits, which had begun in London, continued in Birmingham, where Langley stayed with his sister Minnie, and even determined the progress of his homeward journey, with stopovers at Newton Abbot to see Gabriel and at Plymouth for Eleanore. John, in Penzance, was not forgotten and letters to Ethel might include messages for him and a drawing of 'the usual puffer', consolation until his father returned home and could once again recount bedtime stories about the traction engines of West Penwith.

Langley clearly enjoyed the visits up-country, though the business rewards were not always forthcoming. Since 1892 he had painted few large watercolours and real financial success could only be achieved through the sale of the year's Academy picture. In 1901, the sale of *Between the Tides* for its first asking price would have increased Langley's earnings from £532 (equal to £21,000 in 1997) to £850, whereas in fact the painting remained in his hands until 1904 when it netted only £150. In recent years *Between the Tides* has been reproduced in print, postcard and jigsaw puzzle form and it is unclear why a painting that is now so popular should have remained so long in Langley's hands. He had better fortune with his Academy painting of 1902, *A Cornish Idyll*, which was purchased privately for £300 and later presented to Liverpool's Walker Gallery. This was a highly gratifying outcome since, some years earlier, they had been frustrated in an attempt to purchase *But men must work*.

The 1903 Academy painting, *Local News*, depicted a fisherman studying the front page of the *Cornishman* newspaper. This was not the first of Langley's paintings to feature such a subject but he committed a rare solecism in his choice of title. The front page of that paper carried only advertisements, prompting a dig from the rival *Cornish Telegraph* that 'perhaps in this particular paper there was no local news inside'. Langley promptly changed the painting's title to the less contentious *When the Boats are Away* but, having got off to a bad start, it remained unsold for three years and then fetched only a third of its original asking price.

Langley exhibited at the Academy from 1892 to 1917 but

only in 1904 did he sell a painting there. The work which achieved that signal success was *The Greeting*, in which a returning fisherman is seen waving from his boat to his infant daughter, who waits on the quayside with her mother. *The Greeting* sold for £300 in a year when the highest price Langley obtained for a watercolour was £53, for *A Fisherman's Daughter*, further emphasising the point that oils were now, and would remain, Langley's principal source of income.

The proceeds from *The Greeting* paid a handsome dividend, enabling Langley to make his first working visit to the Continent since 1881. An early influence had been Jozef Israels, to whose work his own had once been likened, and it was towards Holland that Langley now turned.

Study for ***The Greeting,*** c1904
watercolour, 17.8 x 11.5cm

BELOW
Waiting the Return of the Fleet 1903
watercolour, 50 x 53cm

There is a study for the old woman, and a drawing for this composition showing that Langley changed the background for this watercolour. Whereas in the drawing the main figures are against houses, for the watercolour the viewpoint has swung round to show them against Mount's Bay.

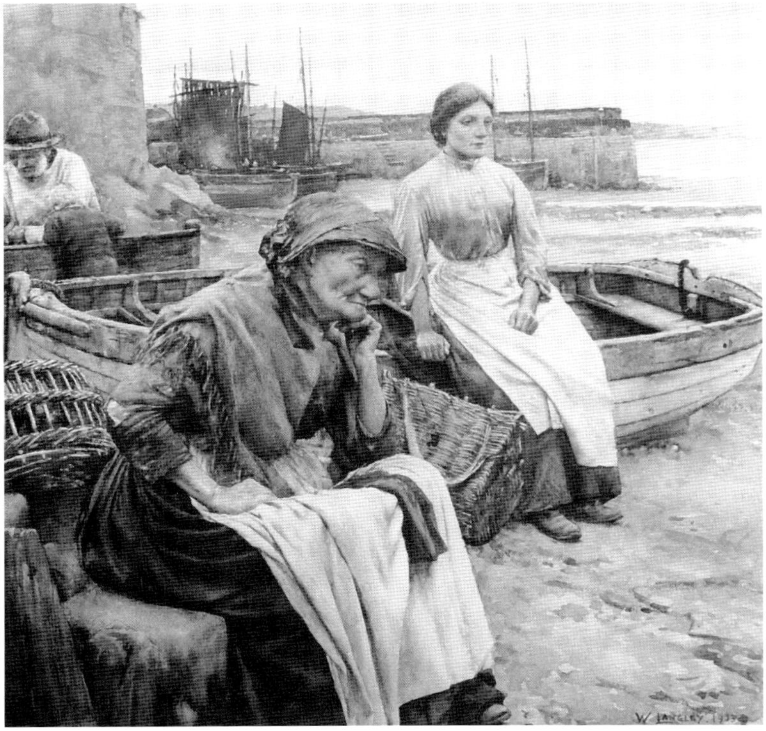

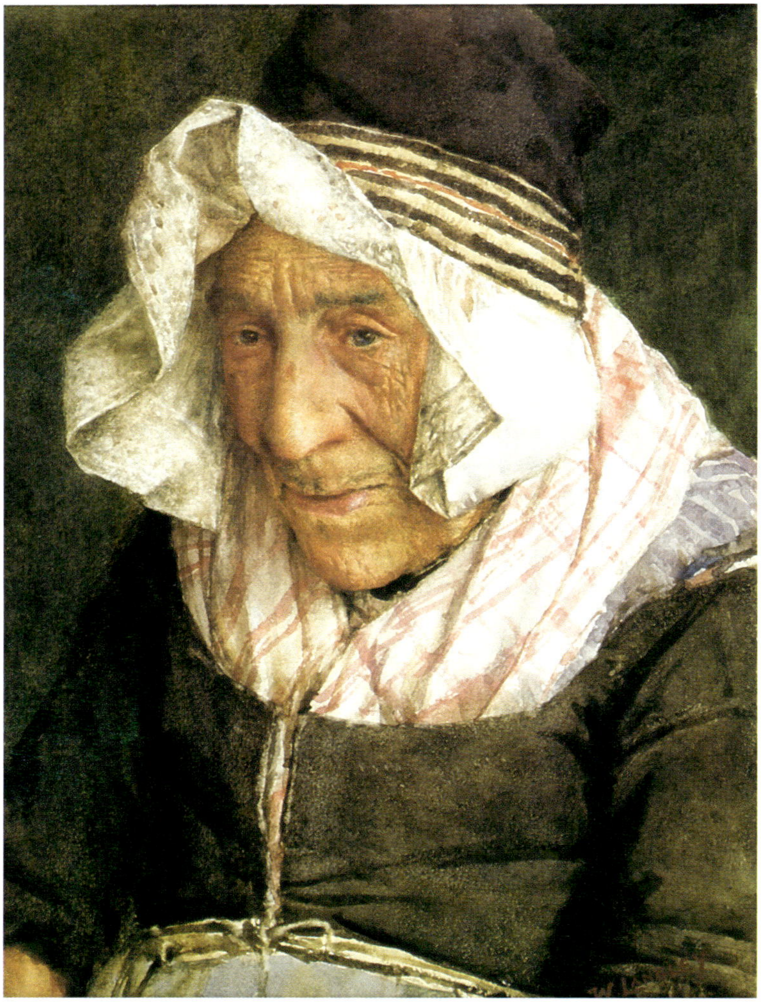

1904-1906 Newlyn, Holland & Belgium

CHAPTER SIX

Langley and a fellow artist from Newlyn, R Harry Carter, set off late in July, 1904 for Holland, making their headquarters at Volendam, a fishing village on the Zuider Zee. There they met up with a flourishing colony of artists, led by two younger members of the Hague School, Willy Sluiter and Albert Neuhuys. Convivial evenings were guaranteed at the local hotel, the Spaander, where Langley and Carter stayed.[14]

The Newlyners remained in Volendam for probably no more than three weeks and Langley's output of Dutch paintings in 1904 was consequently small. Captivated, however, by the Dutch scene, the colour and variety in the dress of the fisherfolk and the company of other artists at the Spaander, he resolved to return there in 1905.

The straitened circumstances of the Dutch fisherfolk, reminiscent of Newlyn in the 1880s, may have prompted a return by Langley to social commentary for his 1905 Academy painting. This proved to be a biting statement on the division of labour in the Newlyn fishing community. In *The Woman's Part* he depicted an old fisherwoman trudging along Newlyn's harbourside, carrying on her bent back a basket laden with fish to sell on the streets of Penzance while, nearby, a sturdy fisherman lights his pipe as he leans nonchalantly against the harbour-rail. Two young children play on the pathway and in the background a group of heavily laden old fisherwomen make their way to town. In the same year, Langley's Institute painting, *His Only Pair*, depicted an old Newlyn woman patching up her grandson's trousers, a more gentle allusion to the harshness of the times. Apart from the Academy and Institute paintings, and

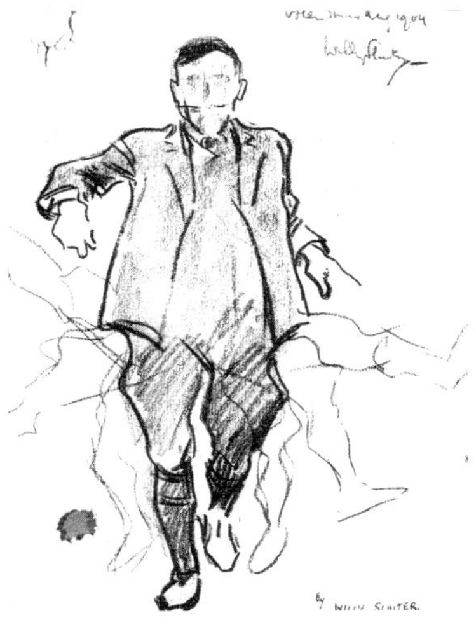

Willy Sluiter, drawing of Walter Langley tap-dancing, Volendam, August 1904.

PAGE 122
An Old Inhabitant 1905
watercolour, 34 x 25cm

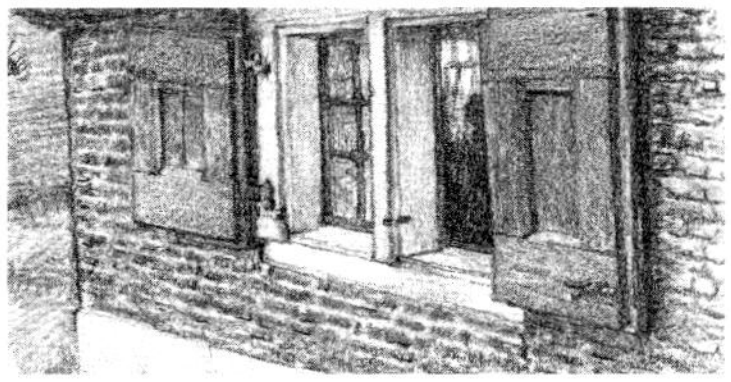

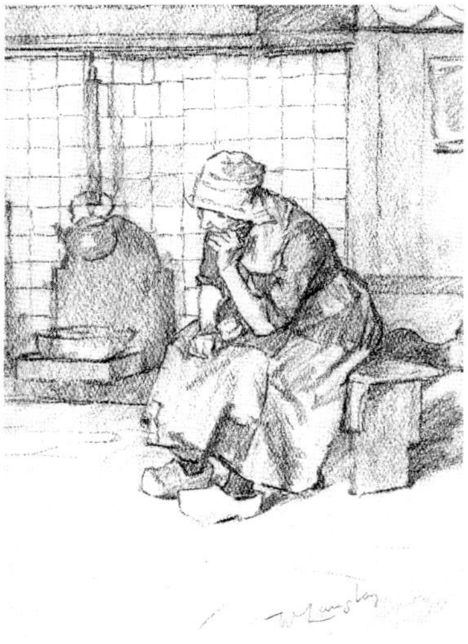

A Dutch Kitchen 1905
crayon, 34 x 24cm

TOP
Window study, Holland c1905
crayon, 12 x 21.6cm

a small number of Dutch works, Langley exhibited little in 1905, the main event of which was to be his second visit to Holland.

Perhaps buoyed by the prospect of a return to the camaraderie of the previous year, Langley planned to spend upwards of two months in Volendam staying, as before, at the Hotel Spaander. Ethel remained in Penzance and it is from his letters home to her that details of his stay in Holland are taken:

> I arrived here about midday, after a good crossing. It was somewhat rougher than when I came last time, but I felt no qualms; we got to the Hook of Holland about 5 o'clock and it was very cold indeed. I only had time to get a cup of coffee and a bite on board and perhaps that made me feel the cold more. I had a better meal when I got to Amsterdam and the weather also brightened up so, between the two, I felt more myself again. I found the Spaanders all well but there is no-one here and I had lunch all by myself and felt lonely. Also, they are Spring cleaning with the carpenters making alterations so that it is not so pleasant.
>
> You will gather from the foregoing that I am conscious of making a rather poor start. I'm afraid I have come a bit early but two old friends are coming, I understand this week, so that will make it more pleasant. I do not yet know if I have a studio. I hope there is one, as it is yet too cold to work out. Volendam itself seems much the same and when I can get onto some work I shall feel happier. I enclose some views of Amsterdam, which I got there this morning, and am sending one to the boy [John] ... The enclosures in your last letter re RI and Falmouth were the usual sort. I have accepted both providing they pay the commission. I do not know if they will come to anything ... [May 3, 1905]

Langley had little assistance from Ethel in the management of his business affairs while he was away. A few days later things were looking up, but there were still causes for dissatisfaction:

> .. I am feeling very well and gradually getting into work but it is certainly difficult among a people alien in language and almost impossible to do any serious subject work, it makes one regret

one's own people are not so picturesque. I think I shall have to do my most important work in my own country as I shall never pick up the language and am at a great disadvantage.

We have two Swedish girls here at present, which makes it somewhat better. One speaks French and the other English, very well, but the former has all the gift of the gab and is talking incessantly to a Frenchman, while the other seldom speaks at all, excepting I address some remark to her, so I do not get much out of it. I understand, however, that an American artist and his wife — whom I met here last year — are coming today and I need hardly say I shall be very glad to see them ... to hear a lot of talk going on in a foreign tongue I think emphasises the feeling of loneliness.

I have got an old Dutch room for a studio and I hope to make something out of it. We had a very fine day on Sunday here, but a cold wind. Yesterday it was dull and dreary and made me feel low spirited; today it has been sunny, but still cold in the wind ...

Am glad to know my picture came out well in Cassells. I hope it will find a purchaser. Am glad to know also my RI picture has sold. I agreed to take £60, free of commission, this is the price I shall get, the other £10 goes to the gallery. They will not send a cheque until the close of the Exhibition. Wish some of the others would sell. Have heard nothing from the B'ham Ex', things seem rather bad.

After I had written the above the two Americans arrived and it was very pleasant meeting [them] and has added to my sum of enjoyment for there is now someone I can talk to over meals, which makes them go better.

I have been painting this morning in a house, from an old man, but there is an overwhelming sense of wanting to hurry it up to get away which I do not seem to be able to get over, so different to working in one's own studio, but I hope to get more at home in the work. It will be better when the weather allows working out-of-doors. It is a beautiful day here today and looks like taking up ... I see on the notice from the Oldham Ex', which you sent, they draw my attention to the 'enclosed card', which you did not send. Is it anything in particular? [May 9, 1905]

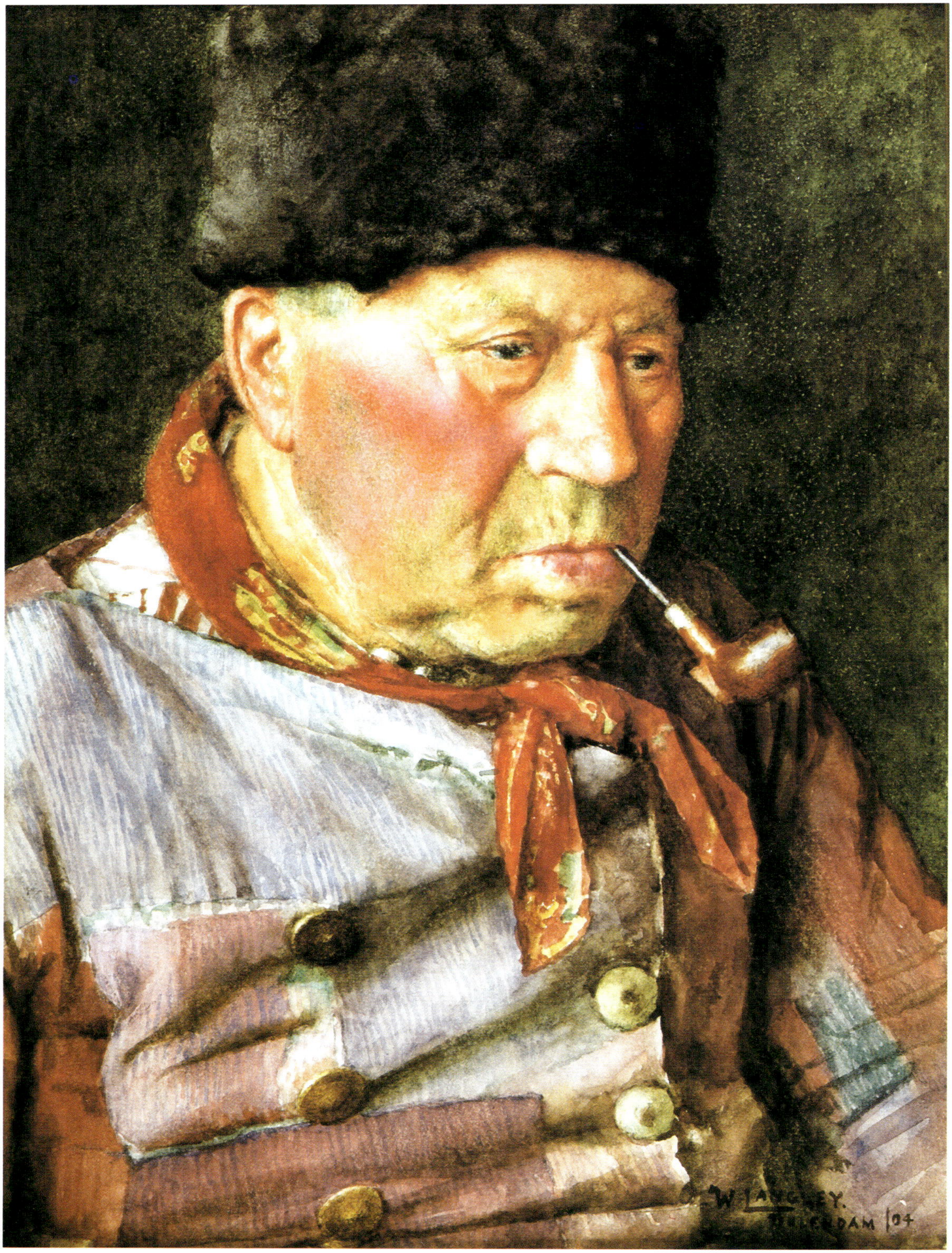
W. LANGLEY.

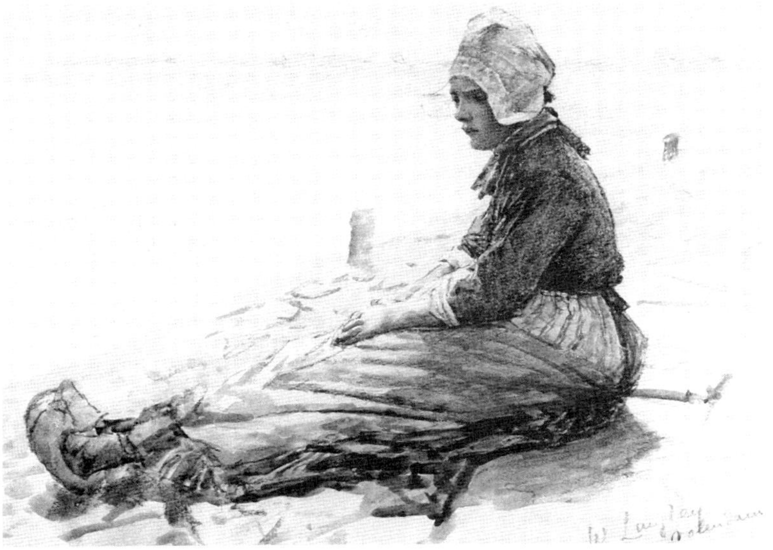

A Dutch Fishergirl, Volendam 1905
watercolour, 23 x 32cm

PAGE 126
A Dutch Fisherman 1904
watercolour, 32 x 23cm

In this and the portrait of an old woman, see page 122, the renewal by his visits to Holland in 1904 and 1905 of Langley's most intense vision and painterly ability with watercolour can best be appreciated.

It is clear from Langley's next letter that Ethel was not going to let him escape the minutiae of home life. She sought his opinions on the replacement of oil lamps and the inefficiency of the kitchen boiler and, as a consequence, he had little space in which to report on artistic matters:

> ... I am feeling rather tired today, having been working hard in my studio. These interiors are dreadful things to paint, so many things about and the colour in them so heavy it is difficult to do in watercolour.
>
> The lady whose letter you enclose must be Dutch. I have written her asking if she could postpone her article on my work as, being away from home, I could not supply her with the photographs she requires; I hope she can as I would like it to appear, it might do me some good. The other [letter], about Lords cricket ground is stupid for me and I do not think requires any answer as I am no cricketer, neither do I want to appear in the crowd. [May 18, 1905]

A week later, Langley was getting into his stride, and the band of artists in Volendam had swollen to fill the Spaander. There was also the prospect of a visit from Ethel, but this turned out to be a good-humoured leg-pull on her part. In early June, Langley took the opportunity to take a boat trip in search of local colour:

> ... the packet of letters etc came this afternoon. I am now trying to get on with the canvas I brought with me but after being used to working quietly in a glass house it is very difficult to paint carefully and well out of doors for, what with the wind and the uncertain weather, there are so many difficulties. I am not sure I shall be successful with it; the other day, for example, I went down to the edge of the sea at the back of the Hotel with my model and canvas and I had not been there long when it started to rain, so I had to go back to the Hotel and wait. I took it down again and the same thing happened, so I gave it up for the time ...
>
> Yesterday, being Ascension Day, was a Church festival here and like a Sunday so there were no models to be got and I worked on a background in my studio in the morning and made a trip out to Marken with three other painters, two Scotchmen and a Dutchman, in the afternoon. I had not been there before and enjoyed it very much. We went over from Volendam in a Marken fishing boat; a good breeze sprang up and the boat went along fine, heeling over to the side like a yacht. The island is very interesting and the costume of the women and girls grand for colour, quite barbaric in effect, it would make a fine costume for a fancy-dress ball. I hope to be able to get over for a day to make a sketch of one of the girls, just to show you what it is like. The little children are splendid and have flaxen hair and very ornamental caps. We returned by motor boat to Monnikendam, took the steam train back to Edam and then walked back to Volendam in time for dinner. Altogether very enjoyable. [June 2, 1905]

There is a gap of a fortnight in the news to Ethel, the missing bulletin being from the village of Laren, as the next extract suggests. In that fortnight the Imperial Russian Fleet was annihilated by the Japanese and John was given a dog. He received a letter from his father, congratulating him on his acquisition but also asking him to work harder at his lessons and music. The correspondence to Ethel continues:

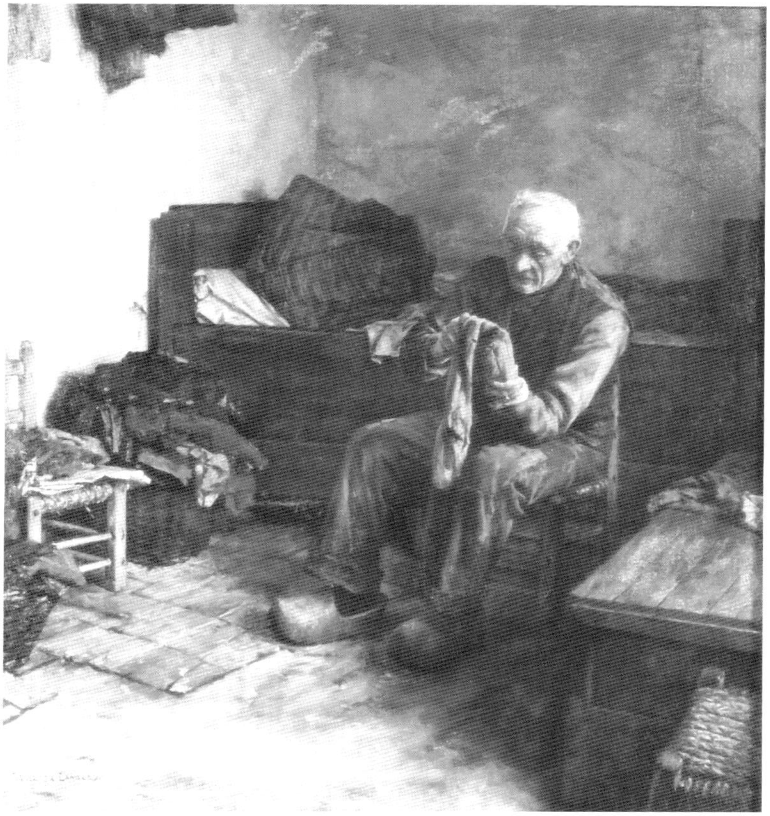

A Flemish Peasant 1907
oil, 102 x 92.7cm

When it was exhibited at the Academy in 1907 *A Flemish Peasant* measured 102 x 137cm, but having failed to sell it after five showings up to 1910, Langley cut it down. He removed about a third at the left-hand side, which had been occupied by a large rough-hewn pillar.

I got your letter dated 13th today, which seems quick delivery. You do not, however, enclose the acknowledgement from the RI as you state in it; from the amount you mention I suppose they have deducted my subscription to the RI, £5.5s, which would make it the £60 I agreed to accept. Do not forget to send it in your next ...

... you will have got my letter I wrote from Laren. We returned to Amsterdam by steam train and saw more of the country by doing so; it was very interesting. We have been having a lot of very sunny weather here which does not suit any of the painters, so we all complain — which is the only thing to do. I wish we could get a spell of grey, as I want to get on with one or two things and I do not care much for Holland in sunny weather.

Have you been receiving my *Clarion*? I asked them to send it on to me here. Also the *Literary Guide*. If you have this month's I wish you would send it on. You have never said how the case was

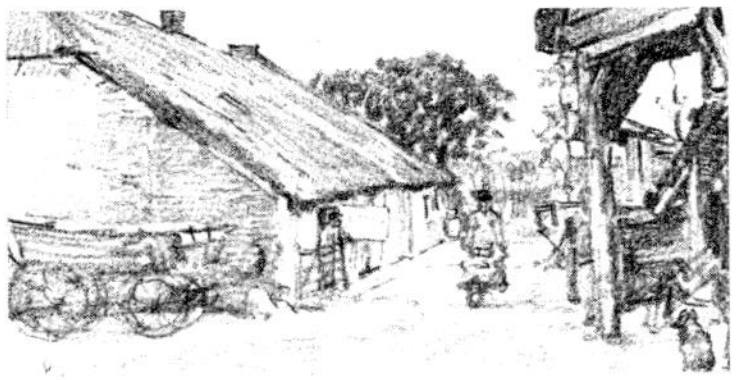

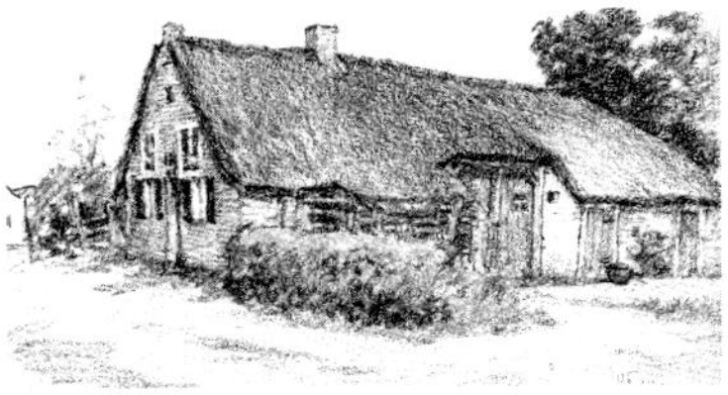

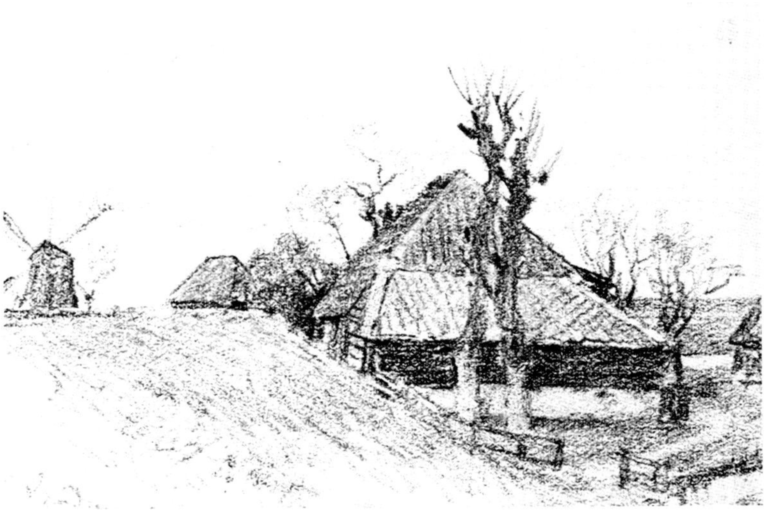

Study of a Dutch house c1905
crayon, 12 x 21.6cm

RIGHT
Study of a farm, Volendam 1905
crayon, 12.7 x 17.9cm

TOP
Study of a farmyard, Laren c1905
chalk, 11.9 x 21.6cm

decided regarding the fishermen of Prussia Cove and the despotic resident. I should like to know.

I got £2.2s the other day from a German firm of publishers for allowing them to reproduce in black and white my picture *The Greeting*, which will come in handy for paying models, and the firm has [written] about my copyright of the picture in [the] RA, but I do not think we shall come to terms. You did quite right in refusing the low offer for my picture in Newlyn Art Gallery, if it was the one you mention; it is astonishing what some people will do in the offer line. [June 14, 1905]

... myself and a Belgian painter are going tomorrow on a visit to Katwijk, a small fishing village on the north coast. I want to see the place as I hear it is very good. We go to the Hague first to see two good exhibitions of pictures. I return here on Monday evening.

I have been working hard, but have not touched the canvas I brought for some time. We have had so much sunny weather and when it is not sunny it is often windy so I am not getting on with it, but I am doing other things. I have made a purchase and spent some few pounds on a beautiful little picture by a Dutch artist ... as fine a bit of technique [as I] have ever seen ... The artist is very pleased to know I have bought it ...

You will have received notice of removal of picture from the RA, with a ticket for the Conversazione, will you send them on? Do not forget. I will conclude this letter now as I must go to work (the light in my studio is not good for long in the afternoon) ... [June 24, 1905]

The Belgian painter mentioned by Langley was Jakob Smits, an artist based near Mol, in Belgium.

... we had a dreadful storm the night before last, the worst I have seen here. The lightning was terrific and seemed to be all over the place, darting all about. I sat in my room watching it, not without a sense of awe ... two houses here were struck slightly and I expected every minute to see the hotel struck. Some of the flashes were composed of three and four streams of electric fluid, it was very grand but awful and I shall never forget it.

Last week I went to see Katwijk ... it is on the north coast, and is something like St Ives only finer, the boats are grand and the beach is very interesting ... Mr Willy Sluiter made my visit a very pleasant one. He has a delightful little house and studio. I secured a small picture from him, for which I am to send him one of mine.

I have now been away from home 10 weeks yesterday and am thinking of getting back as I cannot do my large picture, and I am beginning to feel I have had enough for the time, so I shall just finish up one or two things I have on hand and return in a week or so. I do not think I should do any important work here without better studio accommodation; also the few friends I got to know have gone, Mr and Mrs Burr and two Scottish artists ... Do not forget to send me the invitation to the RA Conversazione with the form for removal of picture.

... I have been over to Marken in a small fishing boat with three others. We were caught in a slight thunderstorm as we left Marken but it was soon over and I only got a wetting and enjoyed the trip.[15] [re the enclosed photograph] Mr Adams is a German American and a good painter. Mr Scharf is an Austrian, a painter too, Madam Scharf is French. Only Mr Adams speaks a little English so I could not talk much. [July 2, 1905]

There is a pencil note on the top of the first sheet of this letter: 'Labour is the source of all wealth'. That, combined with his concern to receive the *Clarion*, adds more weight to the argument that his sympathies lay with the political left.[16]

> The weather is still very sunny and hot here so that it is difficult to get on with anything. Yesterday was a delightful day, fine with a good breeze, and being invited to sail round Marken in the afternoon I went ... It was in one of the fishing boats — five or six Volendamers, young fellows, were with us for the outing and before we got back they had imbibed quite sufficient. The steersman was, however, a fine tall young chap and kept steady all through, which we were very glad of as the others were very rollicking, singing and rolling about, but they steadied up well when we reached the harbour again in the evening. We had rather a bad thunderstorm again but it does not seem to have made the weather cooler.
>
> I intend leaving here on Monday next and am returning by the Flushing route, as I want to visit Dordrecht and Middleburg, in South Holland, and Veere, which is close to Middleburg in the island of Walcheren, where Mr and Mrs Burr are staying. I might as well see these places whilst I am so near and at Dordrecht I want to get one of the brass milk cans, which are so picturesque. I hope to cross over on Thursday night next and get down to Penzance on the Saturday following ... I should have liked to have got away this week but I could not finish up. [July 14, 1905]

Despite the low-key note in Langley's letters concerning his work, the ten weeks in Holland were extremely productive, except that the 30 or so Dutch watercolours and three oil paintings included nothing for the 1906 Academy exhibition. Probably the oft-mentioned large canvas had been intended for that.

On his return to Penzance, Langley sent in three Volendam studies to an exhibition at Newlyn Art Gallery — *A Fisherman of the Zuider Zee*, *An Old Dutchman* and *An Old Inhabitant*. The *Cornish Telegraph* critic, commenting on these paintings, raised a chronic and notorious contention:

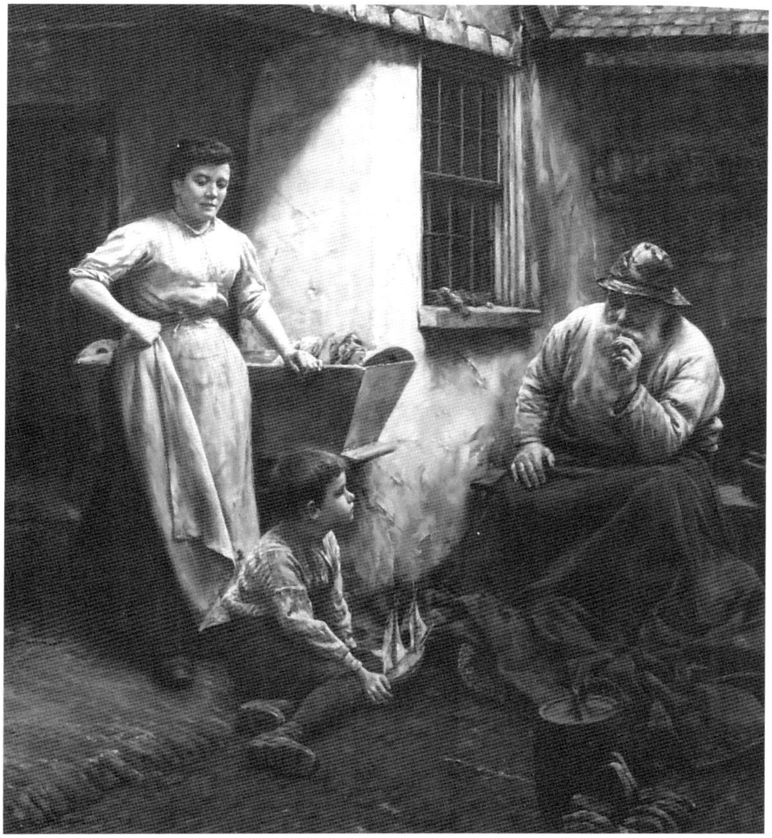

A Chip off the Old Block 1905
oil, 91.5 x 81cm
(Ferens Art Gallery, Kingston-upon-Hull)

> The works from the brush of Mr Walter Langley, RI, are in his very best style and are eloquent tributes to the power he holds in reproducing scenes from everyday life ... three small pictures of typical Dutch folk, which are very fine examples of this artist's ability and quite photographic in lifelike expression, to use a term which to painters may not be acceptable, though it is possible artists are at last beginning to appreciate the valuable assistance which may be gained from the practice of photography!

From the camera obscura on, artists had sought a means of 'fixing' the image they wished to paint but Langley's only use for photography, aside from family snapshots, was the engagement of professional photographers to make a record of his major finished works.

In February 1906, Langley gave a clue to his attitude towards art

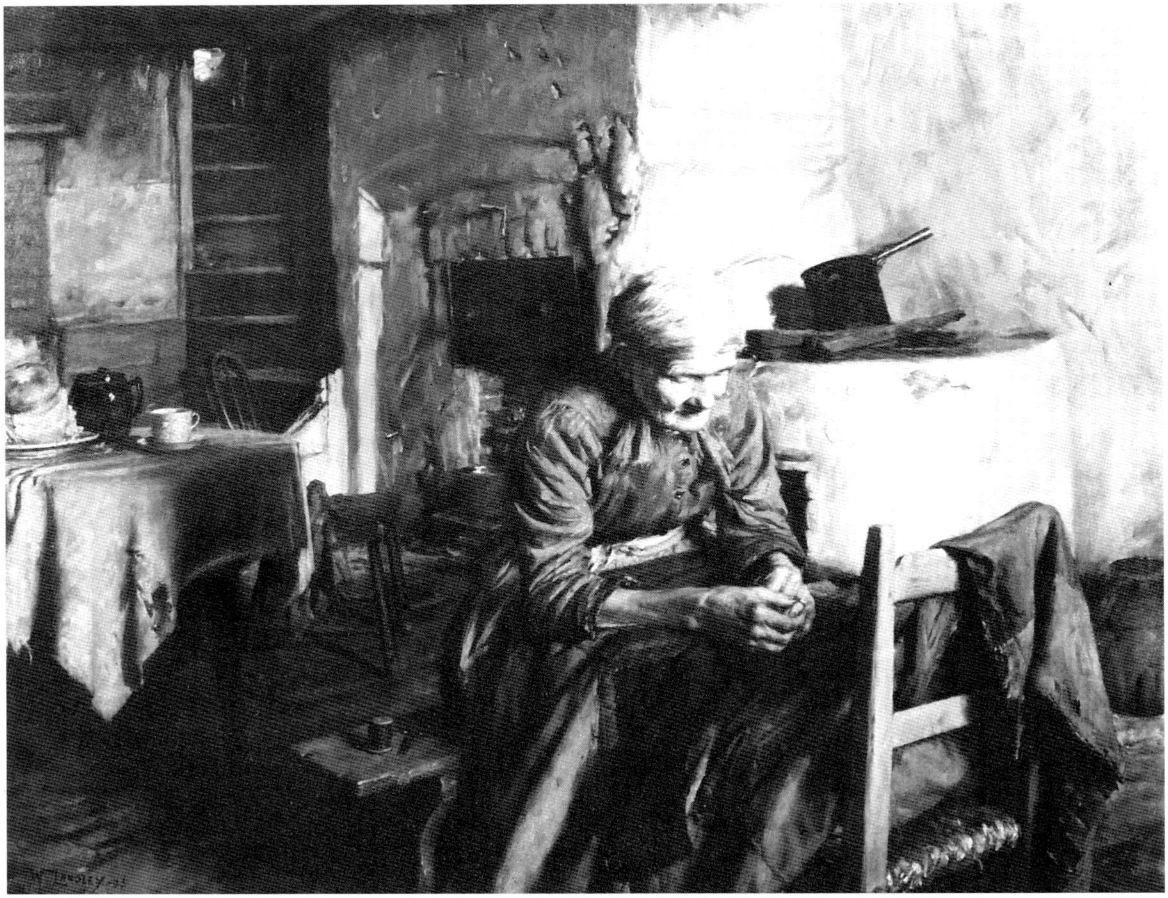

Memories 1906
oil, 109 x 133cm
(Ferens Art Gallery, Kingston-upon-Hull)

There is a smaller oil of this subject, looser in treatment and with sunnier colouring. Langley rarely made two oil versions in this way.

as a business, in his reply to the toast of 'The Visitors', at the annual dinner of the Penzance Chamber of Commerce. The painter, he said, was somewhat of a dreamer and could therefore say very little about commercial matters. Commerce had something to do with art and art therefore got some good from it but if there was too much commerce mixed up with art 'the result would not be altogether satisfactory' to the latter.

What reads as a mild complaint was more than somewhat heartfelt. While he considered his Dutch work to be among his very best, yet again the dealers desired traditional subjects and he returned to Newlyn for the 1906 Academy exhibition. *The Fisherman's Widow* was priced at £250 and sold only after being much exhibited over the following years. He had better luck with a painting at the Oil Institute, *Thinking it Out* — a Newlyn fisherman reflecting on the contents of his local newspaper — which sold immediately for £74.

In response to invitations from Mr and Mrs Burr to join them in Paris and Jakob Smits to visit him at Mol, Langley set off again for the Continent in the spring of 1906. His letters tell of an enjoyable two weeks' sightseeing in Paris before moving on to Mol, where he planned to do some serious work. Mol lies just within Belgium in the Flemish-speaking region of Kempen, a desolate and sparsely populated country where the poor soil provided only a subsistence-level economy. It was hardly picturesque in a conventional way; few paintings resulted from the visit to Belgium, and all were interiors. Mol succeeded, however, where Volendam had failed by providing Langley with material for an Academy painting, *A Flemish Peasant*, which he submitted in 1907. This work conveyed a somewhat mixed message to the *Cornish Telegraph* critic:

> Poverty in actual life has little to recommend it, but under the magic of Mr Langley's hand it evidently has its compensations. The surroundings are poor but not squalid; the old man's countenance, on which the artist has bestowed infinite care, expresses contentment with his lot, and the bits of varied coloured clothing about the room and its general unstudied state, lend to the scene a charm which would be absent from the more precise arrangement of a room of the better class. We hear much nowadays of the 'simple life'. Mr Langley has here produced the simple life in its reality. The picture appeals to one, however, by its harmonious treatment; everything seems so natural and the colours blend with such a charming effect that one loses sight of the actual poverty of the scene and sees only the beauty which has entrapped the artist's inmost soul and which he has so successfully transferred to canvas.

A Flemish Peasant failed to sell and, at 55, Langley turned once more to subjects nearer to home.

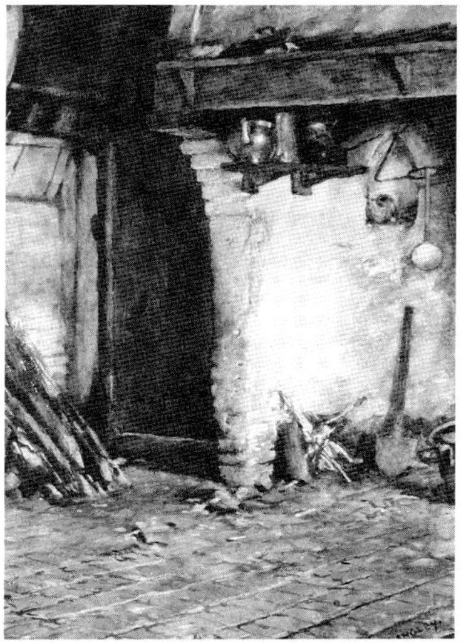

A Belgian Interior 1907
watercolour, 35 x 24.5cm

Later used for the oil of this title shown at the Academy in 1916.

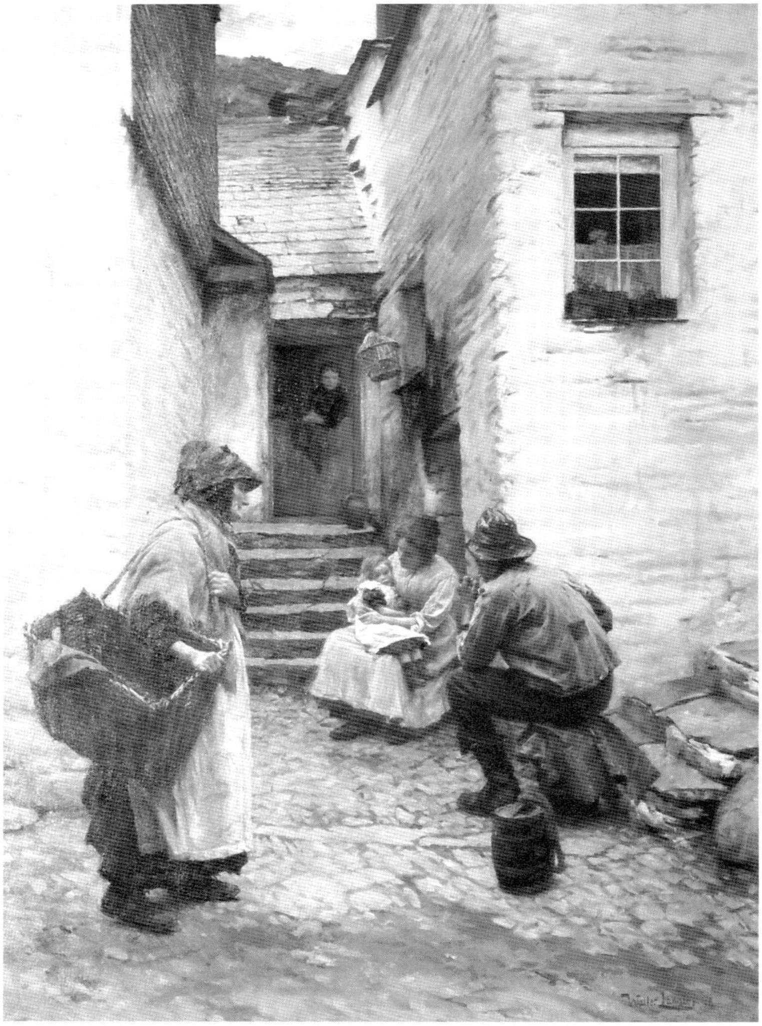

1907-1922 Newlyn

CHAPTER SEVEN

In this final period a sharp reduction in Langley's output was accompanied, with few exceptions, by a change of subject matter to domestic scenes. The peak of his career had passed, the financial demands on him had eased and he might reasonably have felt the time had come to take life more easily. The Newlyn colony of artists had also seen its best days and only four of the early stalwarts — Langley, Forbes, Garstin and Gotch — were still exhibiting Newlyn scenes. A telling indication of the diminished standing of the Newlyn artists was that the local papers now gave precedence to St Ives in their coverage of Academy shows.

Langley's Academy painting of 1908, *Cornish Fisher Folk*, proved over-priced at £250. In that year his total sales fell to an all-time low of £120, and when in the following year, he placed more paintings at exhibitions the financial result was little better. His Academy painting was, however, more acceptable and marked a brief return to typical themes:

The tender grace of a day that is dead
Will ne'er come back to me.

The lines, from Tennyson's 'Break, Break, Break', presaged a tragedy in Langley's own life. Cecil, his and Clara's youngest son, had become a skilled wood sculptor but his active preoccupation with working-class causes frequently prejudiced his keeping a job. After working on the new Chapel at Cheltenham Men's College he decided to emigrate to Canada, to take up farming under the Canadian Government's 'Homesteader' scheme to develop the

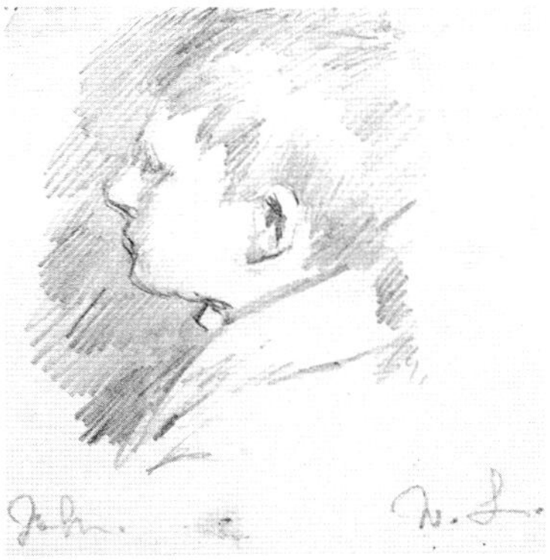

Study of John, Walter and Ethel's son, c1907
Pencil, 8.5 x 10cm

PAGE 136
Cornish Fisher Folk 1908
oil, 137 x 99cm
(Waverley Borough Council, Godalming)

Set in the same alleyway as *At Polperro* 1909, see page 140.

PAGE 139
Study of a girl, late-1880s
chalk, 25.5 x 17.5cm

outback. This venture ended with his death in his first Canadian winter, at Prince Albert, Saskatchewan, on February 25,1909, eight days after his 26th birthday.

Perhaps it was Langley's recollection of Cecil in happier days that prompted his change in 1910 to a hitherto neglected theme, epitomised by the title of his Academy painting for that year, *The New Arrival*. This was a successful move and was followed in 1911 by *Maternity*. These two paintings were well received by the *Cornishman's* reviewer, who also echoed an often expressed view of Langley's outlook on life:

> ... a homely story and a story full of interest, but a story ever new and from which is absent that note of sadness which sometimes overshadows Mr Langley's works. It is a beautiful picture and quite the best Mr Langley has done in this direction.

In 1890 an interviewer for *Edgbastonia* asked Langley why he generally chose subjects of a 'touching' nature. Langley responded that he had 'always been drawn insensibly to such subjects', though he was 'by no means of a sad turn of mind'. That the latter is true is borne out by the recollections of his family and doubtless would have struck those who witnessed his performance in 'Lubly Lobengula'.

The New Arrival sold well in 1910, contributing £210 to a financial result that must have seemed like a return to the good old days. It was not to be. The failure of *Maternity* to sell in 1911 prompted the temporary abandonment of what had seemed to be a promising line in subject matter. Compensation came, however, from an unexpected source. From time to time, paintings by Langley had been among those representing British art overseas and in 1911 he was similarly honoured when *The Fisherman's Widow*, his Academy painting of 1906, and two earlier watercolours, *Disaster* and *Among the Missing*, were included in the British Section of the International Fine Arts Exhibition, in Rome. This was the only such exhibition to include one of Langley's oil paintings.

The indications are that Langley was in poor health in the 1910/1911 painting season since *Maternity* and a small watercolour were the only new paintings he exhibited in 1911. In the following year, however, he sent three paintings to the Academy, *Preparing Dinner*, *A*

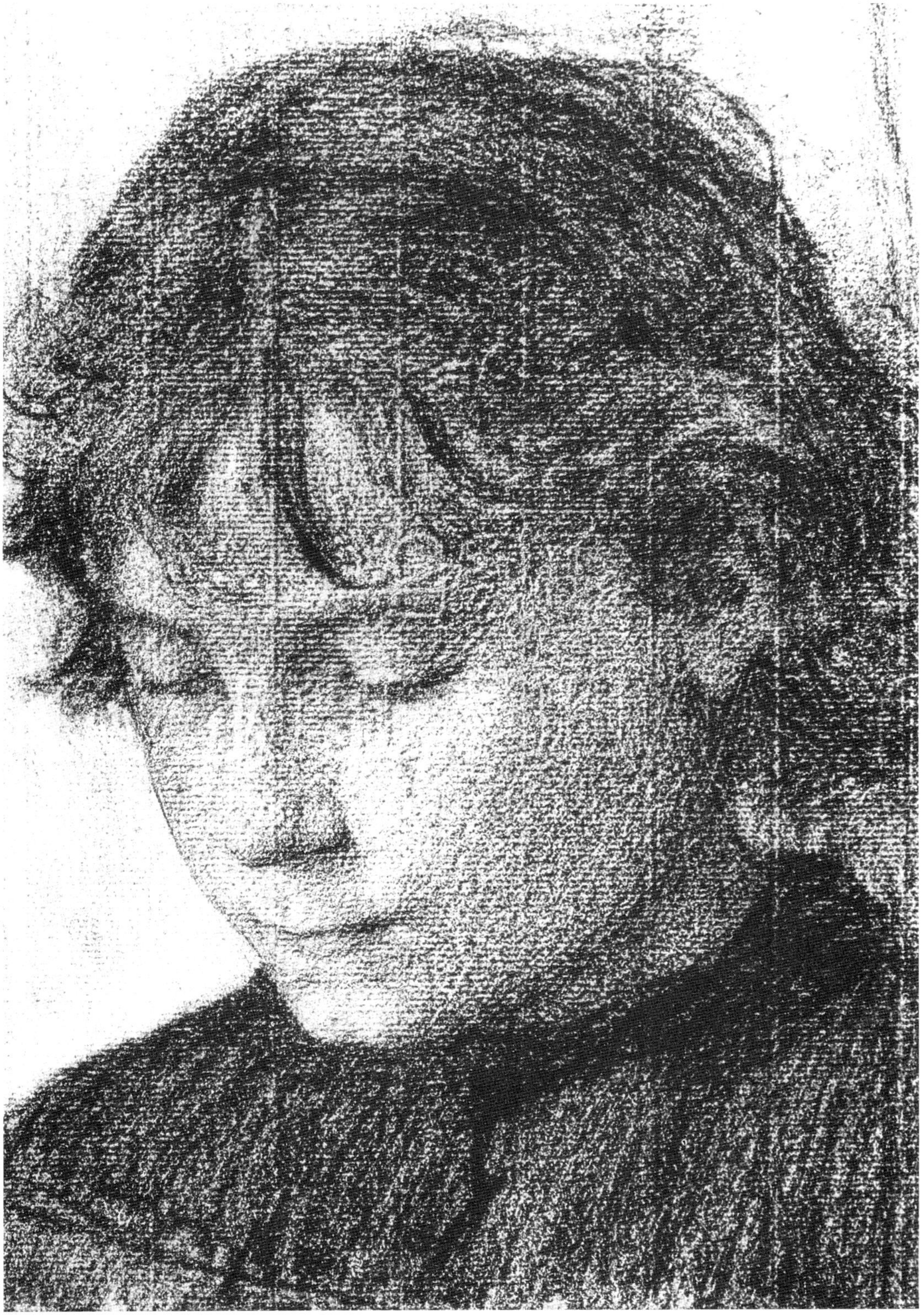

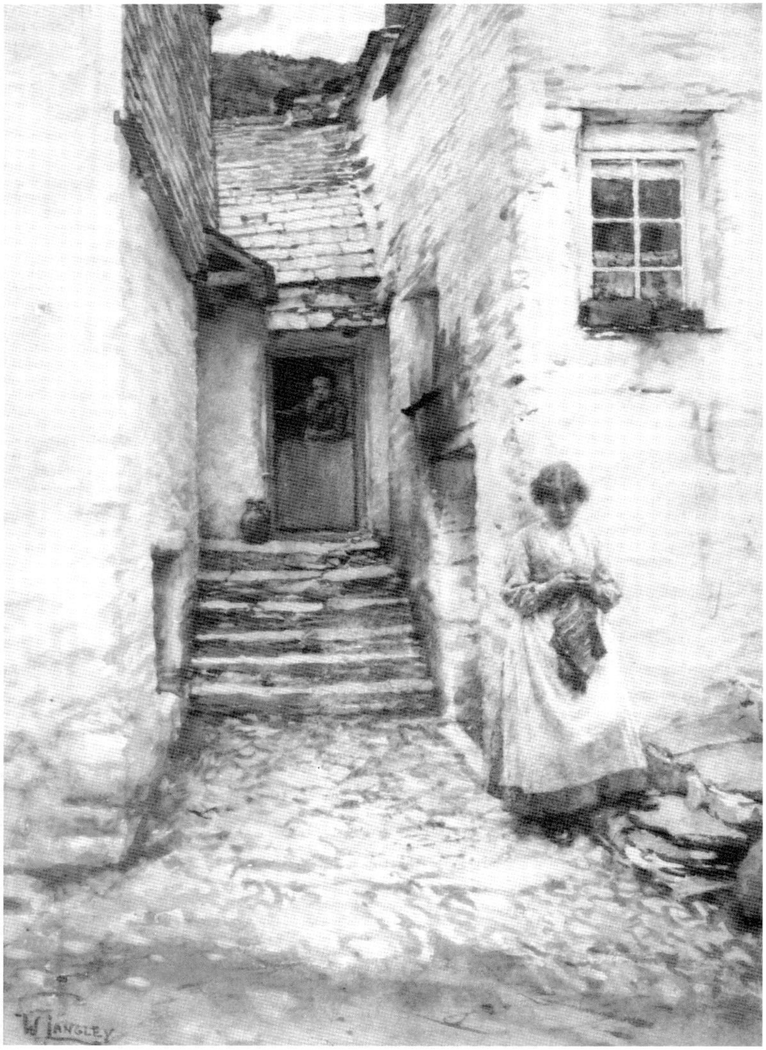

Crown of Years and *Mending the Quilt*. The first two were sombre studies and were not well received in the market; Langley then returned to the type of subject that had done so well in 1910.

Langley's work was now undertaken entirely in his studio in Newlyn, with the models and material to hand, which in some cases was used with considerable freedom. His outdated interior for the 1911 Academy painting, *Maternity*, had been more typical of Newlyn some thirty years earlier and in 1913 he took invention a stage further. When *Motherlove* and *An Old Inhabitant*[17] were exhibited in Newlyn the local reviewer commented that 'only Mr

Walter Langley, RI, could possibly have given us the two cottage interiors which awaited his coming before they revealed their possibilities to the Newlyn Colony. [They are] typical Langley pictures and in their way inimitable.'

Indeed, only Langley could have given the 'Cornish' interior for *Motherlove*, the original study for which has survived and is clearly inscribed 'Brittany' in the artist's own brushwork. Unless he made an unrecorded return visit to Brittany, after his first holiday in Paris, or following his painting trip to Belgium, the interior had not only been transposed by Langley in place but also in time, from 1881.

In the early years of the Newlyn colony Langley, with Clara and the children, had enjoyed a social life that was almost fully bound up with that of the other artists. As time went on, however, and particularly after he married Ethel Pengelly, Langley gained pleasure from activities in the town at large. His haven from work and family was The Penzance Club, where many an hour was whiled away at billiards, but Langley was also a keen chess and bowls player, and was Penzance singles bowls champion in 1912.

Early in 1913, another of Langley's interests surfaced when he presided at a public meeting in the Alverne Hall, Penzance, at which his old friend Mrs Hypatia Bradlaugh Bonner spoke on 'The Influence of Religious Belief on Morals'. The talk was sponsored by The Penzance Rationalist Society, of which Langley was a prominent member. In introducing the speaker, Langley gave a succinct account of his beliefs, which perhaps marks the final resting point on his journey from Unitarianism: 'I know of no higher tribunal than that of Reason for the guidance of human beings'.

As the war clouds gathered and 'Reason' was ignored, Langley returned to the theme of motherhood in his Academy paintings of 1913 and 1914, *Motherlove* and *Daydreams*. Writing of the latter, the local reviewer was as enthusiastic as ever, at the same time hinting at inside information:

> ... his latest work is one that will appeal to the thousands who will have the opportunity of seeing it. Nothing could exceed the simplicity of Mr Langley's method ... The lighting is done with rare cunning and later on the three colour process will reproduce this

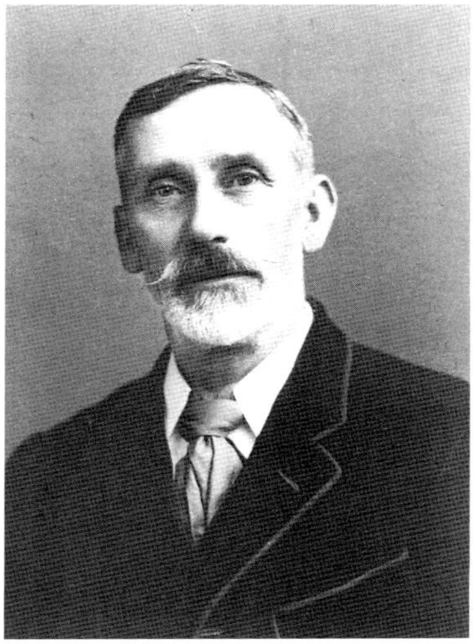

Walter Langley, about 1910-12, photograph by Russell of London

PAGE 140
At Polperro 1908
watercolour, 36 x 26cm

There is also an oil of this title of 1908.

picture so that thousands of mothering women will be able to look at it and be glad.

The painting was purchased in 1916 by Bristol Art Gallery but Langley had sold the copyright in it two years earlier to Forman, a Nottingham publisher who had seen in it a potential vehicle for a patriotic message.

To all intents and purposes, Langley had ceased painting when the war started and sales thereafter came largely from the clearance of old stocks. The war not only affected the art market but also made painting en plein air difficult, with prohibitions on sketching in sensitive areas. The artists complained about some of the more petty restrictions, especially when they were prevented from sketching around the St Ives coastline, earning them a reproof from Francis Meynell, who 'could see no reason why artists should be exempt from the law'. [18]

In the depths of the war, Langley's 1916 Academy painting *A Belgian Interior*, which was clearly derived from his Kempen sketchbook, echoed the prevailing admiration for Belgium's heroic stand against tyranny but nevertheless failed to sell. His output for the remaining years was minimal as he suffered increasingly from poor health. His last exhibits at the Academy and Institute were in 1917 and 1918 respectively. In 1920 he resigned from the management committee of the Newlyn Art Gallery and he exhibited that year for the last time at a Birmingham Society spring exhibition. Two sketches shown at the Newlyn Art Gallery in 1921 were his last recorded works.

Walter Langley died in Penzance on March 22, 1922, after a long period of failing health. The inscription on his tombstone in Penzance cemetery reads quite simply 'Walter Langley, R.I. Pioneer of the Newlyn Art Colony'. He was survived by Ethel and their son John, and by the three eldest children from his first marriage: Lorraine, Eleanore and Gabriel.

1 Among an undistinguished company of ancestors only William Langley, a late-seventeenth and early-eighteenth century sculptor, stands out. Rupert Gunnis, in his *Dictionary of British Sculptors 1660-1851* records that in 1724 William Langley '...was paid £12.8s for the two large stone figures of a boy and girl on the front of the Charity School at Frome, Somerset'. It is pleasing to report that the statues, known as 'Nancy Guy' and 'Billy Ball', are still in place and, having recently been cleaned, are in excellent condition. The female figure is not, however, of a girl but of an elderly dame.

2 Unitarianism rejects the doctrine of the Holy Trinity and the position of Jesus Christ as God. It emphasises the human condition and scientific progress, making its adherents especially responsive to the spirit of their own age. Unitarians are often leaders and translators of current thought. In Birmingham they were particularly prominent in the movement to improve conditions for the poorer classes, through education and the provision of amenities by the civic authorities. In this crusade Joseph Chamberlain became perhaps the most prominent lay Unitarian of the day.

3 The exhibition aimed to demonstrate the skills of the working people and to some extent it succeeded. There were, though, criticisms of the poor quality of the exhibits and a review of the catalogue suggests a hotchpot of good, bad and indifferent work. A financial success was somewhat marred by the inability of the organisers to determine how to deal with the surplus. The outcome was a wholesale distribution of medals, including bronze medals to people who, like Langley, may only have played a small part in providing an exhibit. It is recorded that the bronze medals cost tuppence each.

4 Sale prices were usually in guineas and half guineas of 21 and 10.5 shillings respectively. In the text, prices have generally been rounded to the nearest pound.

5 The Holyoake concerned is believed to have been Rowland Holyoake (active 1880-1907), the son of William Holyoake, also an artist. William was the brother of George Jacob Holyoake, after Charles Bradlaugh the most active free thinker of the day. It seems likely, but unproven, that Langley's introduction to Bradlaugh came about through his friendship with the Holyoakes.

6 Letter to his mother.

7 William Wainwright went on to describe Langley's watercolour technique: 'Langley in his handling was very practical. He looked upon handling as a means and not an end, yet by the nature of his training and his gifts he attached extreme importance to it ... He always preceded his painting by a black and white drawing, rubbed down or traced according to circumstances, to ensure good drawing and good handling ... In the application of his colour he was obsessed by no particular fad; he understood and appreciated the beauty of a wash of pure colour as well as anyone, but if a wash would not suit his purpose or would not realise it, he would resort to hatching, stippling, scrubbing etc, until he had effected his object. He appreciated a bit of good hatching or other manipulation, but if he could do without it he did not think it obligatory to introduce it because it was considered by some to be good practice, and the same with other resources of the art ... He was very particular as to his paper, and one sees very little variation in its texture, whatever the scale of work, and he was

very particular as to it being well and carefully strained ... So direct was his workmanship that he seldom had recourse to the sponge, but considered it necessary to be able to mend faulty places in a wash by skilful hatching or stippling as required, but as to be as unobtrusive as possible.'

8 The first members of the Birmingham Art Circle were Oliver Baker, William Breakspeare, S Currie, W B Fortescue, J Fulwood, E S Harper, Edwin Harris, John Keeley, Walter Langley, W S Lloyd, F Mercer, C Morgan, W J Morgan, Henry Pope, W F Roden, Harry S Thompson, W J Wainwright and Charles H Whitworth. Of the eighteen original members at least five — William Fortescue, Edwin Harris, Walter Langley, Henry Pope and William Wainwright — visited Newlyn or lived there.

9 The Royal Society of Painters in Water Colours, founded in 1804 and, by dint of seniority, known as the 'Old' Society was seen by some artists to be pursuing a policy of exclusiveness that hindered the development of watercolour painting and militated against those who were not members. In 1831, therefore, a new body was established, the Institute of Painters in Water Colours, with powers to recruit 100 members. Associates were elected between 1840 and 1878. The Institute took steps to increase its membership to 89 in 1882, which was still 11 short of the number permitted. Langley was admitted in 1883, filling one of the remaining vacancies.

10 Langley was an avid reader of poetry and on several occasions used lines and phrases from favourite poems as the titles or, as with *Alone*, sub-titles of his paintings. His taste in poetry ran to much which is now obscure but 'The Three Fishers', the tale of disaster at sea by Charles Kingsley which provided the title for *But men must work*, is a poem of lasting appeal.

11 Langley recorded every modelling session in his diary for 1883, the only diary that has survived. He named the models and itemised the fees paid — 6d per session to a man or woman, half that to a child. The models used in 1883 (allowing for mis-spellings through Langley being unfamiliar with Cornish pronunciation) were: Catherine Roseveare, Charles Jenkin, Jack Cotton, Annie Ellis, Mrs Lanyon, Sarah Madden, Annie Warren, Grace Kelynack, Lilly Rowe, Caroline Rowe, John Jenkin, Mary James (a 'little girl'), Sarah Stevenson, Mr Sampson, Mrs Marks, Ethel Runnals, Charles Strick, Mr Pender, Blanche Courtenay and Mr Beckerleg. To put the session fees into perspective, at that time a fisherman's family could earn about £1 in a good week.

12 Each member of the Easel Club was required to submit five sketches annually on given subjects, usually lines of poetry and lofty sentiments, and take part in debates.

13 Until 1885 Newlyn harbour comprised one tiny pier and in stormy weather the considerable fishing fleet of some 400 boats had to seek shelter in Penzance harbour. In 1885, however, the new 700ft South pier was completed and alleviated the inconvenience somewhat. The 1,760ft North pier was added in 1888 to bring the total enclosed area to 40 acres. By these measures, and the construction of a harbour road, Langley's studio, which once fronted the sea, became almost landlocked before the nineteenth century was out. The most recent developments in the harbour area place the studio behind a grassed space where boats formerly moored, with a road, a lorry park and the harbour piers further separating it from the sea.

14 The Hotel Spaander still stands at Volendam and contains on its walls a register in pictures of the artists who enjoyed the hospitality of the Spaander family. Langley's own contribution to the register is a watercolour study of a Dutch girl standing on the nearby dyke.

15 Despite Langley's obvious enjoyment of his sailing experiences in Holland, he did not once visit the Isles of Scilly, virtually on his doorstep. It must be said that the crossing to the islands had a fearsome reputation, epitomised by the thoughts attributed to the Bishop of Truro who said that before he started his first voyage over he feared he might be drowned and when he got half way across he prayed that he might be (J G Uren, *Scilly and the Scillonians*).

16 The editor of the *Clarion* was Robert Blatchford, author of *Merrie England*, a best-selling examination of the prevailing political and economic systems. He made clear the *Clarion's* political outlook in 'An Address To New Readers', on January 6, 1905: 'We suggest that the Nation shall own *all* the ships, *all* the railways, *all* the factories, *all* the buildings, *all* the land and *all* the requisites of national life and defence ... The nation directs the people's minds through a State Church which once a week teaches the wickedness of grinding the faces of widows and orphans. We claim that the nation should establish social conditions which will make oppression and injustice impossible all the year round.' The *Literary Guide*, which Langley was also keen to receive, was published by the Rationalist Press Association.

17 The cottage interior, *An Old Inhabitant*, has not been identified positively and is not included under that name in the catalogue.

18 Official sensitivity over security reached its peak when a Newlyn artist, Rolf Johnsson, was accused of signalling to enemy ships in Mount's Bay from his home in Rope Walk Studio, near Pembroke Lodge. The prosecution went to great lengths to prove their case — they had been out in boats and seen the signals — but Johnsson went one better, engaging the great advocate Marshall Hall to demolish their absurd case.

BELOW
Hand painted greeting card 1882
watercolour, 17.5 x 25cm

The central panel is a watercolour version of the Brittany painting *At the Well* 1882.

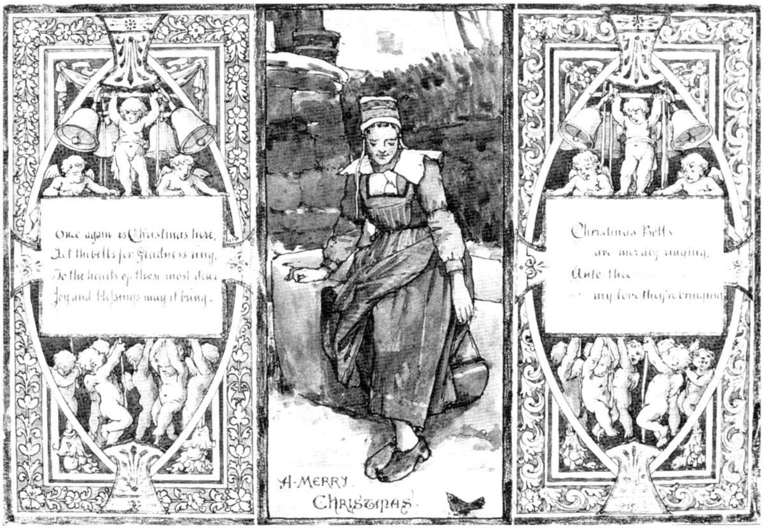

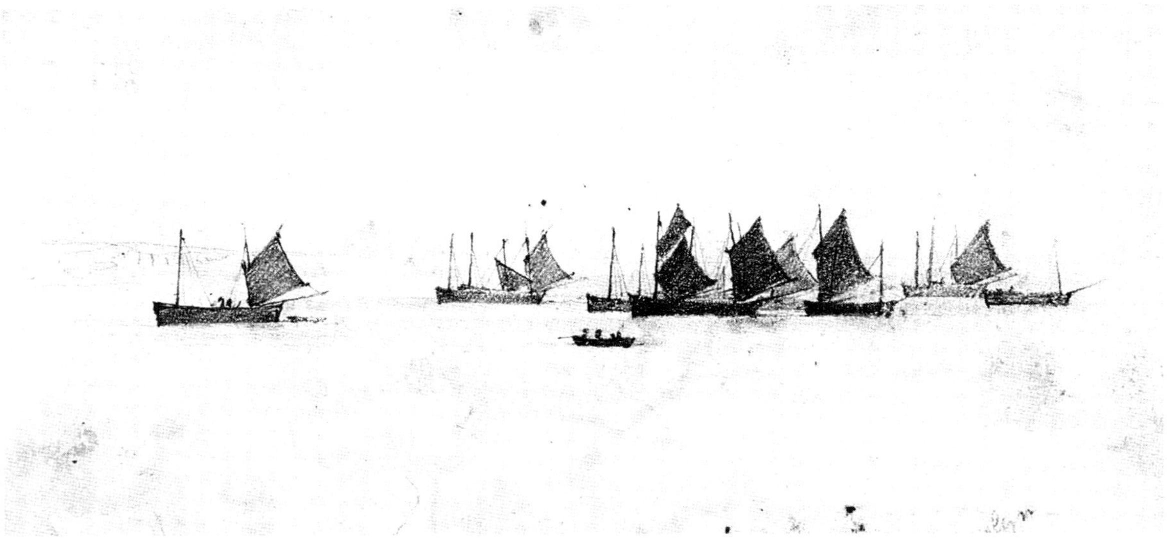

Postscript

When Walter Langley set out on his artistic career he could hardly have expected the success that followed. Hard work might always have ensured a reasonable living from painting but it was the inspiration he drew from the fisherfolk of Newlyn that brought the ultimate reward of an invitation to paint his self-portrait for the Uffizi.

He was primarily a watercolourist, and Langley's membership of the Royal Institute represented another major recognition of his standing as an artist and one of which he was most proud. Indeed it is worth remembering that his first inclination was to execute the Uffizi portrait in watercolours and that, despite exhibiting 29 paintings there, he never allowed his name to be put forward for election to membership of the Royal Academy.

As a contemporary commentator remarked, Langley was first and foremost a Birmingham man and his contribution to the reputation of that city's art was recognised in the year following his death by a memorial exhibition of 103 paintings and drawings, covering the whole range of his work, at the galleries of the Royal Birmingham Society of Artists. A further tribute to his memory was paid that year by his old friend and sometime studio colleague, William Wainwright, who made Langley the subject of his Clarendon Lecture to Birmingham students.

Sketchbook study of boats, Newlyn, early-1880s
pencil, 8.2 x 17cm

From a pocket sketchbook from Langley's earliest days in Newlyn, this shows the fishing boats out in Mount's Bay. Their red-brown sails make a frieze in the distance in many artists' paintings as well as in works like *Breadwinners* on page 23.

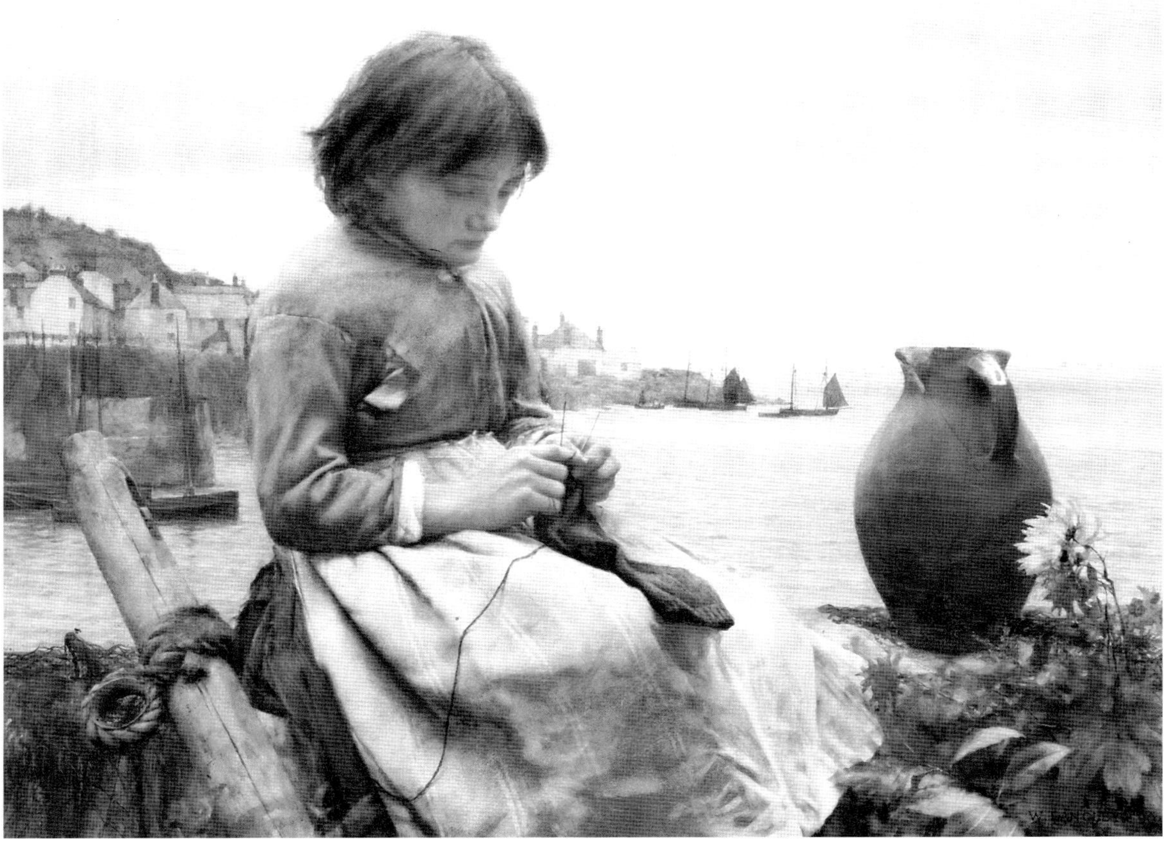

Catalogue raisonné

The catalogue is ordered both chronologically and alphabetically. Most of the works listed were exhibited by Langley and/or were named in his records of picture sales but the catalogue also includes works known to have been gifts from him. It does not include minor unsigned working drawings, studies or sketches, or works that cannot be identified to a name bestowed by the artist himself.

Some works are now known by other names and this is indicated in the alphabetical index by a note of the new name (prefixed aka - also known as). Longer titles, which may include lines of poetry, are given in full though they are now commonly abbreviated.

The date under which most works are listed is the earliest, of the year known at the time of writing to be inscribed on the work, the year in which the work was first exhibited, or the year in which it was sold. A few works are dated approximately and prefixed c (circa).

The medium in which the work was executed is indicated, where known, by an abbreviation:
bw = black and white [where known, specified as cr (crayon), ch (charcoal), pe (pencil), pi (pen and ink); c = coloured crayon; o = oil; pa = pastel; se = sepia; wc = watercolour.

Dimensions, where known, are given in centimetres, height x width. Where the Imperial paper size of a work is known but not its format (landscape or portrait) that paper size is named. The most frequently encountered Imperial sizes are given below, with their metric dimensions:
Octavo = 12.7cm x 20.3cm
Quarto = 20.3cm x 25.4cm
Demi = 25.4cm x 40.6cm

Knitting 1890
watercolour, 66 x 88cm

Where a work was exhibited during Langley's lifetime the venue and date are denoted in alpha-numeric code, for example RB79. The alpha segment is explained on page 151. The numeric segment runs from 73 (1873) through 00 (1900) to 20 (1920). Most exhibitions were regular events where works were offered for sale, for example the annual exhibitions of the Royal Academy and the spring and autumn exhibitions of the Royal Birmingham Society of Artists. Special and invitation exhibitions are indicated under the appropriate gallery heading. Exhibitions after Langley's death in 1922 are named in full.

The name of the buyer, or the dealer who took or commissioned the work (indicated by a D), is given where known. Langley did not distinguish between dealers and others in his sales records. Some indication is given of the relative importance to Langley of each type of sale in the Appendix 'Works Exhibited and Sold'.

Langley made gifts of paintings, sometimes omitted to record sales and did not always name the works for which sums of money were noted as received. Where the sales proceeds of individual works are shown, they are gross, in the case of commissioned works and private sales, or otherwise net of charges ranging from 5 per cent to 40 per cent or more for sales at galleries or to dealers.

Where the asking price for a work is known, but not the eventual proceeds, the asking price will be given, prefixed AP. Where Langley's first asking price for a work exceeded its eventual sales proceeds by a considerable margin, e.g. following its exposure at several exhibitions, the asking price is given in brackets, prefixed AP, as well as the sales proceeds.

All prices have been rounded to the nearest £. No account has been taken of the impact of inflation over the years but, as a rough guide, 1884 prices would need to be multiplied by over 40 times, to give an equivalent number of £s in 1997.

Public collections are given, where known.

Selected published statements about particular paintings (especially where they include a description of the work in question) are referred to in the chronological listing.

EXHIBITION VENUES DURING LANGLEY'S LIFETIME

AC
Birmingham Art Circle

BA
Birmingham Museum and Art Gallery - 1886 — 'Paintings by Walter Langley'

BL
Bristol City Art Gallery

BR
Bradford City Art Gallery

BU
Townley Hall Art Gallery, Burnley

CH
World's Colombian Exposition, Chicago 1892

DD
Messrs Dowderswell and Dowderswell

DG
The Dudley Galleries, London

DU
Dundee City Art Gallery

EX
Royal Albert Memorial Art Gallery, Exeter

FA
The Fine Art Society -1893 — 'Water-Colour Drawings Illustrating Fisher-Life'

GL
Glasgow Art Gallery and Museum (Kelvingrove, from 1901)

HU
Kingston-upon-Hull Art Gallery

LE
Leeds City Art Gallery

MA
Royal Manchester Institution, Manchester Art Gallery

ML
Moll (Belgium) - Kunsktenjoonstrung van schiderisjen der kunstenaats die te moll en omstreken hebben grubekt 1907.

NC
Nottingham Castle Museum and Art Gallery - 1894 — 'Special Exhibition of Pictures by Cornish Painters'

NE
Newcastle Art Gallery (Laing Art Gallery, from 1904)

OL
Oldham Art Gallery

PA
Paris — Exposition Universelle, 1889 and 1901

PL
Plymouth City Museum and Art Gallery

PM
Portsmouth City Museum and Art Gallery

PN
Newlyn, Passmore Edwards Gallery (RA previews are not listed)

PO
Institute of Painters in Oils (Royal Institute from 1886)

PZ
Penzance Art Gallery (now Penlee House Gallery and Museum)

RA
Royal Academy

RB
Royal Birmingham Society of Artists - 1899 — Retrospective

RI
Royal Institute of Painters in Water Colours

RO
Rome — International Fine Arts Exhibition, 1911

RS
Royal Society of British Artists

SA
'South African Exhibition', 1899 (venue not known)

SO
Southport Art Gallery

TR
Royal Institution of Cornwall, Truro - 1893 — Cornwall Fisheries Exhibition

WG
Walker Art Gallery, Liverpool (Liverpool Water Colour Society)

WH
Whitechapel Art Gallery

WO
Wolverhampton Art Gallery

WR
Worcester City Museum and Art Gallery

YO
York City Art Gallery

A Newlyn Byway c1883
crayon, 30 x 19.5cm

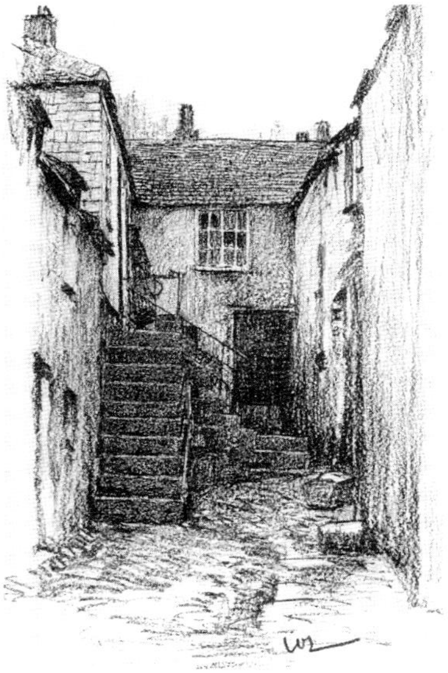

1923
Royal Birmingham Society of Artists: 'Walter Langley — Memorial Exhibition'

1927
Royal Birmingham Society of Artists: Centenary Exhibition

1929
Leamington Spa Art Gallery: Inaugural Exhibition

1955
Kidderminster: Arts Council Exhibition

1958
Newlyn, Bristol: 'Paintings by the Newlyn School, 1880-1900'

1968
Royal Birmingham Society of Artists: Royal Centenary Retrospective Exhibition

1975
Bradford: 'Edwardian Reflections'

1978
Truro: 'Painting in Cornwall, 1880-1930'

1979
Newlyn, Plymouth, Bristol: 'Artists of the Newlyn School (1880-1900)'

1983
Bucharest, Athens, Budapest: British Council — 'British Watercolours, 1760-1930'

1984
Hull: 'Trial & Innocence — Victorian Works from the Ferens'

1984
Exeter, Birmingham: 'Walter Langley 1852-1922'

1985
London (Barbican), Birmingham: 'Painting in Newlyn 1880-1930'

1987
Manchester, Amsterdam, Yale: 'Hard Times — Social Realism in Victorian Art'

1989
Truro County Hall: 'A Century of Art in Cornwall, 1889-1989'

1991
Tokyo, Gifu, Osaka, Kofu: 'British Watercolours from Birmingham, 1750-1900'

1992
London (Bankside), Birmingham: 'British Watercolours from Birmingham'

1993
Penzance: 'An Artistic Tradition (Two centuries of painting and craft in West Cornwall — 1750-1950)'

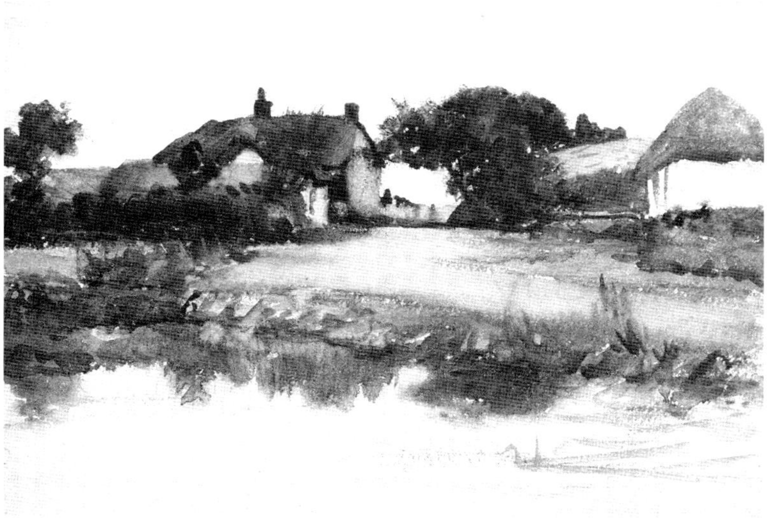

Study of Worcestershire cottages c1886
watercolour, 17.8 x 25.2cm

CATALOGUE LISTING

1871

The Dog and Duck Inn, Birmingham
bw,-
published in a Birmingham newspaper, 1938
see: illustration p20

William Langley
wc, 15.5 x 11.3
see: illustration p33

1873

Composure
-,-
exh: RB73
AP £5

La Pensiera
-,-
exh: RB73
AP £7

The Tired Gleaner
-,-
AP £3

1874

A Fisherman
-,-
exh: RB74
AP £2

On the Lyn, Devon
-,-
exh: RB74, RB97
Donated to New General Hospital, Birmingham

1875

Cottages at Fillongley, Warwickshire
wc, 25 x 36
exh: RB75, Exeter 1984

Evening, North Devon
-,-
exh: RB75
AP £5

Idle Moments
-,-
exh: RB75,WG75
AP £5

1876

At Marston Green
-,-
exh: RB76, Birmingham 1923
Dingley (D) 1880, £4

At the Well
-,-
exh: RB76
Remnant 1879, £2

Contemplation
wc, 28 x 23.5

A Country Lass
-,-
exh: RB76
AP £5

High Tor, Matlock
-,-
exh: RB76
AP £4

The Picture Book
wc, 31.8 x 22.2
exh: RB77, Birmingham 1923
Brooks (D) 1879, £3
see: illustration p21

1877

Dionysus, a Study from Life
wc, 29 x 21
exh: RB77
AP £5

A fisher-girl
(c.1877)
wc, 64.1 x 44.2
see: illustration p21

In the Hayfield
-,-
exh: RB77, Birmingham 1923
AP £13

Mary Ann Langley
(c 1877)
pe, 15 x 11.5
see: illustration p33

On the Alert
-,-
exh: RB77
AP £16

1878

The Bell Tower, Evesham
-,-
exh: Birmingham 1923
Cadbury

A Corner of the Studio
(c.1878)
wc, 37 x 28

A Cottage Home
-,-
exh: RB78
AP £21

I do remember an apothecary
wc,-
exh: RB78
Walford 1879, £7
see: *Birmingham Daily Post*, Aug 30, 1878

The Kitten
-,-
exh: Birmingham 1923
Cadbury

News from Abroad
-,-
exh: RB78, Birmingham 1923
Cadbury 1879, £8

A Tired Bacchanalian
-,-
exh: RB78
AP £5

The World Forgetting
-,-
exh: RB78
AP £13

1879

Rosa Adams
-,-
Adams (D) 1879, £5

Blossom and Decay
-,-
exh: RB79
AP £8

Daydreams
-,-
Langford 1879, £12

Fisherman's Pride
-,-
Adams (D) 1879, £15

The Gamekeeper
-,-
Remnant 1879, £3

In the Woods
-,-
Cohen (D) 1879, £4

Joanna
-,-
Harrison 1879, £8

The Letter
-,-
Brooks (D) 1879, £15

Musing on the roaring ocean,
Which divides my love and me
wc,-
exh: RB79
sold RB Exh, £16

News from an Absent One
-,-
Barford 1879, £12

An Old Resort for Young Gossips
-,-
exh: RB79, WG79
sold WG Exh, £13

A Pleasant Reverie
wc,-
exh: WG79
sold WG Exh, £9

A Quiet Afternoon
-,-
Jones 1879, £4

She gazed upon the golden gift,
Absorbed in pleasant reveries
wc, 71 x 46
exh: RB79
sold RB Exh, £19

Simple in structure but in
bounty great
wc, 38.7 x 48.2
exh: RB79
sold RB Exh, £25
see: illustration p50

1880

At Sutton Coldfield
-,-
exh: Birmingham 1923
Dingley (D) 1880, £2

Bedtime
-,-
Harrison 1880, £10

The Best in the Market
-,-
exh: RB80
sold RB Exh £28
see: *Birmingham Daily Post*,
March 30, 1880

Cottages at Marston Green
-,-
exh: Birmingham 1923
Dingley (D) 1880, £5

Miss Dingley
-,-
exh: Birmingham 1923
Dingley (D) 1880, £8

Dreams by night and thoughts by day,
Are with him that's far away
-,-
exh: WG80
AP £21

Fiction
wc,-
exh: RB80
AP £16

Home from Market
-,-
exh: WG80
sold WG Exh, £14

Lamorna Cove, Cornwall
-,-
exh: Birmingham 1923
Dingley (D) 1880, £2

Near Newlyn, Cornwall
-,-
exh: Birmingham 1923
Dingley (D) 1880, £2

Newlyn
-,-
exh: Birmingham 1923
Dingley (D) 1880, £2

The Old Well
-,-
exh: YO80
Franks (D) 1880, £8

Silent Sorrow
wc,-
exh: RB80
AP £32

A Street in Newlyn
-,-
exh: Birmingham 1923
Dingley (D) 1880, £6
and
-,-
exh: Birmingham 1923
Dingley (D) 1880, £2

Their task being ended with
declining day, Homeward the weary
peasants wend their way
-,-
exh: RB80
sold RB Exh, £28

A View of Eckington
-,-
Adams 1880, £3

Waiting for the Carrier
-,-
Cohen (D) 1880, £3

Weston-on-Avon Church
-,-
exh: Birmingham 1923
Dingley (D) 1880, £4

1881

Breadwinners
wc,-
exh: RB81
Clarke (D) 1881, £30

A Breton Mendicant
wc,-
exh: RB81, WG81, AC82
AP £15

A Breton Peasant Girl
wc, 40.6 x 28
exh: RB81
AP £15
see: illustration p46
and
wc, 38 x 22

A Brittany Interior
wc, 22.5 x 31
exh: Exeter 1984
see: illustration p57

A Cavalier
-,-
exh: Birmingham 1923
Dingley (D) 1881, £5

Convalescent
wc,-
exh: AC81
Clarke (D) 1881, £20

A Corner of the Kitchen, Brittany
wc, 30.5 x 22
see: illustration p56

A Cornish Kitchen
c1881
wc, 38 x 25

A Cottage at St Paul
wc,-
exh: Birmingham 1923
Dingley (D) 1881, £3

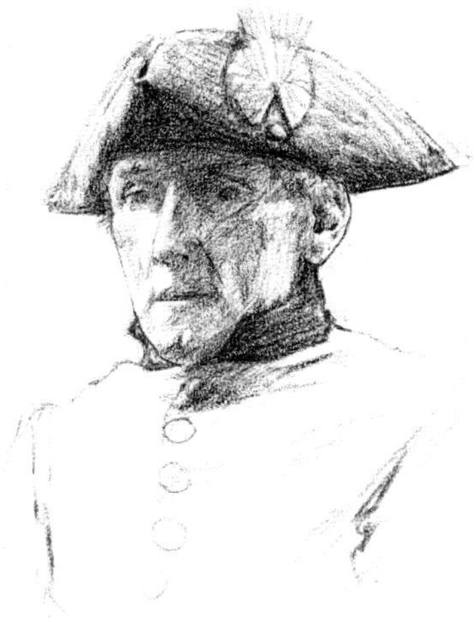

Study of a pensioner early-1890s
crayon, 25.4 x 17.6cm

Daydreams
wc,-
exh: AC82
Clarke (D) 1881, £15

Entrez
wc,-
exh: AC81
Clarke (D) 1881, £15

A Fisherman's Home
-,-
Clarke (D) 1881

Mr Franks
-,-
Franks (D) 1881, £5

Gossip
wc, 41 x 25
exh: RS81, NO94, RB99
AP £30
and
wc, 23 x 29
exh: BL81
sold BL Exh, £10

Harborne Church
-,-
Hewitt 1881, £3

In a Brittany Apple Orchard
wc, 74 x 41
ex: RB82, DD83, RB18, Birmingham 1923, 1927
Alldays 1881, £35

In a Cornish Fishing Village
wc,-
Clarke (D) 1881, £31

In a Cornish Village
-,-
exh: DG81
Sold DG Exh, £18

Left in Charge
-,-
Keeley (D) 1881, £7

Light in the Cottage
-,-
Hewett 1881, £8

The Midday Meal
-,-
Dingley (D) 1881, £1:

The Milkman
wc,-
Clarke (D) 1881, £6

A Mousehole Court
-,-
Alldays 1881, £16

My heart is light and gay
wc,-
exh: RB81
AP £16

The New Arrival
wc,-
exh: Birmingham 1923
Dingley (D) 1881, £10

Obstruction
-,-
exh: SO81
sold SO Exh, £8

An Old Breton Woman
-,-
Keeley (D) 1881, £8

The Picture Book
-,-
exh: Birmingham 1923
Dingley (D) 1881, £13

The Prayer
wc,-
Lloyd 1881, £15

A Shady Corner
-,-
Keeley (D) 1881, £4

A Street in Quimperlé
-,-
Clarke (D) 1881, £3

Sunshine, Brittany
wc,-
exh: AC81
Clarke (D) 1881, £20

A Telegram
wc,-
Clarke (D) 1881, £5
and
wc,-
exh: RB81
Clarke (D) 1881, £41
and
-,-
exh: WG81
AP £25

Washing Day
-,-
Hewett 1881, £6

The Wayfarer
-,-
Clarke (D), 1881

The Young Musician
wc, 33 x 24

1882

At the Well, Brittany
wc, ½imp
comm Alldays 1882, £20

An Authority
-, 64 x 48
comm Alldays 1882, £40

An Authority on Fish
-, 25 x 20
comm Alldays 1882, £8

Barking Nets
-,-
comm Alldays 1882, £20

The Beach, Newlyn
(c 1882)
wc, 11 x 14

But men must work and women must weep, Though storms be sudden and waters deep, And the harbour bar be moaning
wc, 90.5 x 53
exh: RI83, WG83, WH85, BA86, PZ87, RB08, Birmingham 1923, Leamington 1929, Newlyn 1958, 1979, Exeter 1984, London 1985, Tokyo 1991, London 1992
Ingram (D) 1883, £105 coll: Birmingham Museums and Art Gallery; see *Graphic*, Jan 3, 1884
see: illustration p.10
and
bw,-
exh: RB83
sold RB Exh, £40
and
wc, 33 x 20.3
Ingram (D) 1883, £10
coll: Leicester City Museums and Art Gallery
and
se, 90.5 x 53
exh: Newlyn 1958,
coll: Birmingham Museums and Art Gallery

A Corner of the Studio
-,-
comm Alldays 1882, £10

A Cornish Fishwife
-,-
comm Alldays 1882, £10
and
wc,-
exh: RB82, AC83, DD83
Chamberlain (D) 1883, £15

Daydreams
-,-
comm Alldays 1882, £20

The Evening of Life
-, 25 x 20
comm Alldays 1882, £15

The Fishing Fleet
(c 1882)
wc, 9 x 13

Gathering Seaweed
(c 1882)
wc, 11 x 17

His Opinion
-, quarto
comm Alldays 1882, £10

In a Cornish Village
wc,-
exh: RS82
comm Alldays 1882, £20

The Jackdaw of Rheims
wc,-
exh: AC82
Keeley (D) 1882, £14

La Blanchisseuse
bw, ½imp
exh: RB82
AP £20

A Lass that Loves a Sailor
-,-
comm Alldays 1882, £15

Left in Charge
-, quarto
comm Alldays 1882, £10

Lingering Hope
-, 51 x 71
comm Alldays 1882, £40

Mending the Sails
-,-
comm Alldays 1882, £50
and
bw,-
comm Alldays 1882, £8

A Moment's Rest
(c 1882)
wc, 16 x 11

Mounts Bay
(c 1882)
wc, 12 x 17

Newlyn
(c 1882)
wc, 11 x 17
and
(c 1882)
wc, 8 x 18

A Newlyn Woman
(c 1882)
wc, 20 x 12

Obstruction
bw,-
exh: RB82
AP £8

On the Beach
(c 1882)
wc, 7 x 12

On the Moors
(c 1882)
wc, 19 x 12.3
see: illustration p65

On the Rocks
(c 1882)
wc, 17 x 12

A Pensive Maiden
wc,-
exh: RB82, DD83
Ingram (D) 1883, £10
see: *Birmingham Daily Post,*
April l, 1882

Penzance, from Newlyn
(c 1882)
wc, 7 x 18

A Question of Quality
-,-
comm Alldays 1882, £10

A Quiet Afternoon
wc, 28 x 32
exh: Birmingham 1968, Newlyn
1979, Exeter 1984
comm Alldays 1882, £25
see: illustration p58

Rest and Rust
-, quarto
comm Alldays 1882, £10

Shipping Intelligence
-, 91 x 56
comm Alldays 1882, £60

Summer Morning on the Beach
-, quarto
comm Alldays 1882, £10

Time moveth not, our being
'tis that moves
bw, 26 x 16
exh: Exeter 1984
Ingram (D) 1883, £10
and
wc, 15 x 10
and
wc, 19.7 x 11.5
see: illustration p.15
and
wc, 55 x 21
exh: DG83, BA86, Birmingham 1927
Ingram (D) 1883, £60
see: illustration p60

A View of Newlyn
wc, 24 x 34
exh: Newlyn 1979

Wandering Thoughts
wc, 104 x 56
exh: AC82, RI83, MA83
comm Alldays 1882, £60
see: illustration p54

Weary Waiting
-, imp
comm Alldays 1882, £50

1883

A Child of the Village
-,-
exh: DD83
comm Chamberlain (D)
1883, £15

Consolation
wc, 18 x 25
exh: AC83, DD83
comm Ingram (D) 1883, £10

Contentment
-,-
Ingram (D) 1883, £16

A Cornish Fisherman
(c 1883)
wc, 20 x 13

A Cornish Village Maiden
-,-
Dearle 1883, £63

A Crown of Years
wc,-
exh: RI83, DD83

Early Reveries
wc,-
exh: AC83, DD83
comm Ingram (D) 1883, £10

The Evening of Life
wc,-
exh: DD83
comm Chamberlain (D)
1883, £15

The Gathering Storm
cr, 38 x 21
see: illustration p73
and
wc, 76 x 44
exh: DD83
comm Brunning 1883, £105
and
wc,-
exh: DD83
Brunning 1883, £11

In Memoriam
wc,-
exh: DD83
comm Chamberlain (D)1883, £15
and
o, 85 x 65
exh: PO83, RB84, Kidderminster
1955, Exeter 1984
Radcliffe 1883, £63
(AP £170)
coll: Birmingham Museums
and Art Gallery

Mrs Kathleen Lynam
(c 1883)
wc, 28 x 24

A Newlyn Byway
(c 1883)
cr, 30 x 19.5
see: illustration p151

Newlyn Harbour - Low Tide
(c 1883)
wc, 17 x 14

News of the Sea
wc,-
exh: PN84, RI84
comm Brunning 1883, £105

The Old Sailmaker
wc,-
exh: DD83
Ingram (D) 1883, £10

The Old Story
wc,-
exh: RB83, WG83, DG84
Starkey (D) 1890, £65
(AP £210)

Returning from Market
-,-
exh: AC83
AP £10

A Reverie
wc, 17 x 12.5
Ingram (D) 1883, £20
see: illustration p66

A Son of Toil
wc,-
exh: DD83
AP £10

A Stitch in Time
-,-
Ingram (D) 1883, £10

The Sunset of Life
-, octavo
Smith 1883, £21

A Toiler of the Sea
-, octavo
Ingram (D) 1883, £10

A View of Newlyn
(c 1883)
wc, 25 x 30

1884

Above Newlyn
(c 1884)
wc, 11 x 20

Among the Missing — Scene in a Cornish Fishing Village
wc,-
exh: RI84, RB84, BA86, PA89, RB99, BU03, RB08, RO11
Bolton 1884, £420
see: *Illustrated London News* May 3, 1884
see: illustration p16

The Apprentice
(c 1884)
wc, 19 x 12

The Beached Boat
(c 1884)
wc, 11 x 22

Constancy
wc, 54 x 32
exh: RS84
Brunning 1884, £52

Cork Cutting
o,-
exh: PO84, RB85
AP £105

The Country Walk
(c 1884)
wc, 12 x 18

A Daydream
wc, 34.3 x 24.1
exh: RB85
Franks (D) 1884, £32
see: illustration p69

Father's Boat
wc, 23 x 33
Chamberlain (D) 1884, £10

A Fisherman's Son
wc, 34.3 x 24.1
Franks (D) 1885, £32
see: illustration p68

The Fisherman's Son
(c 1884)
wc, 25.3 x 13.2
see: illustration p70

Fishing Boats, St Mawes
(c 1884)
wc, 8 x 12

A Garden by the Sea
wc, quarto
exh: AC84, DU85, FA93, AC93, LW94, PL94
Botteley 1895, £15

Idle Moments
wc,-
exh: RB84, WG85
AP £52

In the Cornfield
(c 1884)
wc, 11 x 16

Knitting
bw, 20 x 28
exh: AC84

Landing Fish, Newlyn
-,-
exh: AC84
Chamberlain (D) 1884, £10

The Last Chapter
-,-
exh: DD84
comm Ingram (D) 1884, £30

A Lover and his Lass
wc,-
exh: RI84, WG84, Birmingham 1923
Brunning 1884, £105

Near St Mawes
(c 1884)
wc, 6 x 15

A Newlyn Fisherlad
wc, 23 x 11

The Old Market Hall and Fountain, Birmingham
wc, 26 x 15
exh: Bucharest 1983, Exeter 1984
Keeley (D) 1884, £8
coll: Birmingham Museums and Art Gallery

On the Rocks
(c 1884)
wc, 19 x 11

A Quiet Pipe
-,-
exh: DG84
comm Ingram (D) 1884, £30

The Old Gardener
wc, 32 x 24

The seas are quiet when the winds give o'er, So calm are we when passions are no more
wc, 37 x 27
exh: RI84, AC84, RB99
see: illustration p42
and
ch, 35 x 25
see illustration p165

Wonderland
wc, 25.4 x 35.6
exh: AC84, Newlyn 1979, London 1985
Hewson 1884, £30
see: illustration p70
and
cr, 27.4 x 35.4
exh: Bucharest 1983, Exeter 1984
Chamberlain (D) 1884
coll: Birmingham Museums and Art Gallery

1885

Becalmed
wc, -
exh: RI85, MA85
sold MA Exh, £30

Going to Market
wc, 90 x 46
exh: RI86, Birmingham 1923
comm Dearle 1885, £105

In the Net Loft
-,-
exh: AC85
Chamberlain (D) 1885, £24

Memories
wc, 45.8 x 79
exh: AC85, NC92, NC96, RB07, RB09, Birmingham 1923, 1968, Newlyn 1979
Chamberlain (D) 1885, £100
coll: Birmingham Museums and Art Gallery
see: illustration p71

News from the North
-,-
Dale 1885, £31

A Reverie
wc, -
exh: RI85, BA86
White 1885, £40

Sad News
wc, 32 x 17
Chamberlain (D) 1885, £16
see: illustration p73

Spring
wc, -
exh: RB85, RB99
Holder 1886, £70

A Sunny Day, Cornwall
-,-
exh: AC85
AP £25

The Sunny South
o, 122 x 61
exh: PO85, RB86, WG86
Rigg 1886, £75
(AP £150)
see: *Birmingham Daily Post*, March 29, 1886
see: illustration p62

The Sunny South, a Study
wc, 22.6 x 11.1
see: illustration p63

The tender grace of a day that is dead, Will ne'er come back to me
wc, -
exh: RB85, BA86, RB99, NE04, WH08
Bunce 1885, £48

The Village Postman
wc, 14 x 8

Waiting for the Boats
wc, -
exh: RI85, RB85
Michael 1885, £315
and
wc, approx 16.5 x 48
see: illustration p59

1886

The Answer
wc, 43 x 37
exh: BA86
Franks (D) 1886, £45

By the Church, Welford-on-Avon
wc, 12 x 20

A Corner of the Village
(c1886)
wc, 13 x 18

A Country Inn
(c 1886)
wc, 14 x 22.9
see: illustration p76

Daydreams
-,-
exh: MA86
sold 1886, £32

The Fisher's Daughter
wc, 55 x 33
exh: RB86, BA86
Franks (D) 1886, £51
see: *Birmingham Daily Post*, April 19, 1886

In a Cornish Fishing Village — Departure of the Fleet for the North
wc, 61 x 122
exh: RI86, RB87, WC93, RB99, Penzance 1993
Franks (D) 1886, £420
coll: Penlee Art Gallery and Museum, Penzance
see: *Birmingham Daily Post* 'Birmingham Artist - Walter Langley', 1886
see: illustration p6

An Interesting Story
wc, 76 x 46
exh: AC86, RI87, WG87, OL88, PL88, NC88, PA89, LE90, RB99
AP £160

The Lych Gate, Welford-on-Avon
wc, 12.9 x 19.9
see: illustration p75

My Youngest Son, Cecil
wc, 25 x 38
exh: RB86, NC87, Newlyn 1979
see: illustration p77

Newly Enfranchised
wc, 36 x 25
exh: AC86, BA86, Exeter 1984
Chamberlain (D) 1886, £45

The New Novel
-, 48 x 34
Chamberlain (D) 1886, £21

An Old Servant
wc,-
exh: RI86
Evans 1886, £35

One of the Crew
bw,-
exh: AC86
Chamberlain (D) 1886, £8

A Story of the Sea
bw,-
Franks (D) 1886, £30

The Thatched Cottage
(c 1886)
wc, 19.3 x 26
see: illustration p76

A View of Newlyn
(c 1886)
wc, 71 x 43
exh: Exeter 1984

A Worcestershire Village
(c 1886)
wc, 11 x 23.2
see: illustration p75

1887

The Answer
wc, 46.4 x 60.3
exh: RI87
Franks (D) 1887, £80

Betrayed
wc, 75 x 120
exh: RI87, WG87, RB88, MA88
Craven 1889, £158
(AP £450)
see: *Magazine of Art* (annual), 1888
see: illustration p79

A Calm Day, Newlyn
(c 1887)
wc, 7 x 20

The Evening Hour
bw,-
Franks (D) 1887, £39
and
wc,-
exh: RI87, MA87, NC88, DG88, NE89, PL89
Starkey (D) 1890, £50
(AP £200)

The Evening of Life
wc,-
exh: NC87
AP £42

Eventide, Newlyn
(c 1887)
wc, 10 x 18

In Memoriam
wc,-
exh: AC88, MA88, NE99, SO90, GL90, PL90
AP £40

The New Novel
-,-
Starkey (D) 1887, £16

An Old Campaigner
wc,-
exh: RI87, RB99
Franks (D) 1887, £35

The Truant
wc, 52 x 25
exh: AC87
Chamberlain (D) 1887, £31
see: illustration p80

Waiting
-,-
Starkey (D) 1887, £16

Widowed
wc,-
exh: RB88, RB99
Wallis 1887, £200

1888

Convalescent
-,-
exh: AC88
Sold 1888, £34

Disaster! Scene in a Cornish Fishing Village
ch, 122 x 76
exh: Exeter 1984

Early Cares
wc, 63.5 x 40.5
exh: AC88, OL89
sold OL Exh, £20
see: illustration p86

Fishing Nets — Out to Dry
(c 1888)
wc, 15 x 25

An Interesting Letter
bw,-
exh: RB88
AP £30

In the Harbour, Newlyn
(c 1888)
wc, 13 x 18

The Last Gleam
wc, 31 x 22.5

The Last Gleaning
-,-
Starkey (D) 1889, £13

O! For the touch of a vanish'd hand,
And the sound of a voice that is still
wc, 67.3 x 95.5
exh: RI89, WG89, AC90, NC90, NC96, Leamington 1929, Exeter 1984
Starkey (D) 1890, £150
coll: Birmingham Museums and Art Gallery
see: illustration p28

The Orphan
wc,-
exh: WG88, LE89, PZ89, AC89
sold AC Exh, £30
and
ch, 67 x 87

The Steam Trawler
wc, 11 x 21

The Sunset of Life
wc,-
exh: RI88, NC94
Michael 1888, £45

Village Idyll — After the buoyant happy days of youth, Comes the calm eventide of age
wc, 75 x 121
exh: RI88, Birmingham 1923, Exeter 1984
sold RI Exh, £250
(AP £400)

Whisperings of the Past
wc, 48.2 x 66
exh: WO88
sold WO Exh, £42
see: illustration p78

1889

Absent Thoughts
wc,-
exh: MA89, PN89
sold PN Exh, £35
and
-,-
exh: RB90
Hill 1889, £105

A Cornish Fishwife
pa,-
exh: MA89, RB89
sold RB Exh, £50
(AP £100)
and
wc, 25 x 20
exh: SO89
sold SO Exh, £23

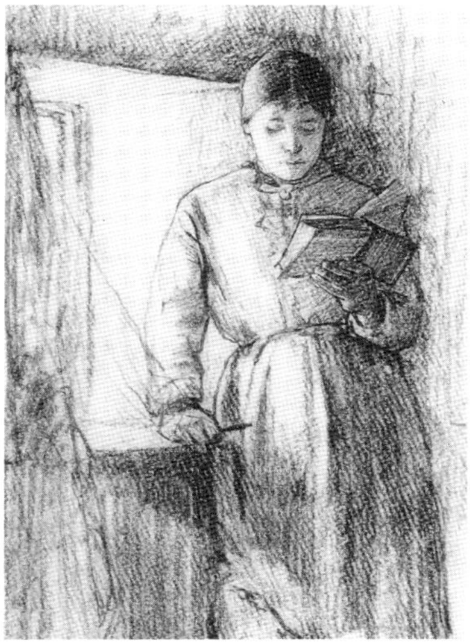

Study of a girl mending a net and reading, mid-1880s
chalk, 24.8 x 17cm

Disaster! Scene in a Cornish Fishing Village
wc, 122 x 76.5
exh: RI89, MA89, PA89, RB90, WC93, NC94, RB99, WH02, RO11, Birmingham 1923, Newlyn 1958, 1979, Exeter 1984
sold RB 90 Exh, £250
(AP £350)
coll: Birmingham Museums and Art Gallery
see: illustration p74

The Evening of Life
o,-
exh: PZ89
sold PZ Exh, £50

In St Ives Harbour
wc, -
exh: RB89
Starkey (D) 1889, £15

In Times of Trouble
bw, -
exh: LE90
sold LE Exh, £8

Jilted — The fraud of man was ever so, Since summer first was leafy
wc, 90 x 67
exh: AC89, RB90, NC94, RB99
Starkey (D) 1889, £55
see: illustration p85

Knitting
wc, -
exh: RB89
Starkey (D) 1889, £8

Leisure Moments
-, quarto
Starkey (D) 1889, £21

An Old Fisherman
wc, 37 x 22
exh: Exeter 1984
Starkey (D) 1889, £25

The Orphan
wc, 66 x 87.5
exh: NE89, Truro 1989
Starkey (D) 1889, £120
(AP £200)
see: illustration p38

A Reverie
-,-
exh: AC89, NE90, OL91
Blackhurst 1891, £16

A Street in Clovelly
-,-
exh: AC89
Chamberlain (D) 1890, £10

Sunshine and Shadow
wc, 35.5 x 25.4
exh: RI89, Birmingham 1923
Sully 1889, £32
see: illustration p94

Tired Out
wc, 56 x 34
exh: SO89, Exeter 1984
Keeley (D) 1889, £35

1890

Alone - Borne on the swift though silent wings of time, Old age comes on apace
wc,-
exh: RI90, RB99
Walton 1890, £150

By the Sea
wc,-
exh: DD90
sold DD Exh, £113

Cottage Steps, Newlyn
(c 1890)
wc, 36 x 25
see: illustration p85

The Fish Cellar
(c 1890)
wc, 28 x 23
exh: Newlyn 1979
see: illustration p83

Knitting
wc, 66 x 88
exh: RI90, WG90, NE91, RB91, PN91, SO92, MA92, Exeter 1984
AP £210
see: illustration p148

A Newlyn Fisherman
(c 1890)
wc, 22 x 14

Sunshine and Shadow
(c 1890)
wc, 36 x 25
see: illustration p12

Sympathy
wc,-
exh: AC90, PN91, FA93
AP £26

A Toiler of the Sea
-,-
exh: AC90
AP £17

Waiting for the Crew
-, octavo
Starkey (D) 1890, £16

When the Boats are Away
wc, 25 x 17
Starkey (D) 1890, £16

1891

At Coverack, Cornwall
wc, 30 x 21.6
exh: FA93, NO93, RB94, PN95
AP £20
and
wc, 30 x 21.6
exh: FA93
AP £21
see: illustration p87

Convalescent
wc,-
Starkey (D) 1891, £32
and
o,-
Halder 1891, £25

In a Cornish Fishing Village — Naval Manoeuvres
wc, 58.4 x 120
exh: FA93
Starkey (D) 1893, £84
(AP £157)
see: illustration p90

In a Cornish Village
-,-
exh: OL91, FA93, NO93
Luton (D) 1894, £17

Local News
-,-
Starkey (D) 1891, £21
and
wc,-
exh: FA93
sold FA Exh, £20
and
wc,-
exh: FA93
Harris 1894, £11

Maternity
o,-
exh: AC91, PN91, FA93, PN99

An Old Pilot
wc, 56 x 39
exh: RI91, RE91, LE92, NE92, CF93, NC94, SO95, YO95
Starkey (D) 1896, £45
(AP £315)

Watching for the Fleet, Cadgwith
wc, 44.5 x 63
exh: FA93
AP £37
see: illustration p90

When the Boats are Away
wc, 76 x 86
exh: RI91, AC91, NE92, LW92, BL93, PN94
Starkey (D) 1895, £53

The Widow
-,-
Starkey (D) 1891, £74

1892

At Mousehole, Cornwall
wc, 22.2 x 29.7
exh: FA93
sold FA Exh, £16
see: illustration p95

Critics of the Newlyn School
wc,-
exh: FA93
sold FA Exh, £35

One Man, One Vote
wc,-
exh: FA93
sold FA Exh, £23

One of the Crew
wc,-
exh: FA93, CF93, RB93, LE94, RB99, Birmingham 1923
sold RB93 Exh, £100
(AP £157)
see: *Cornishman*, July 27, 1893

Orchard Scene
(c 1892)
pa, 56 x 81
exh: PN21

A Quiet Time
wc, 25 x 36
exh: FA93
AP £23

Sunlight and Shadow
o, 107 x 152
exh: RA92, RB92, LE93, MA93
AP £400

Trereife Avenue, Penzance
(c 1892)
o, 37 x 25

Trouble
o,-
exh: RB92
sold RB Exh, £25

Waiting for the Crew
wc,-
exh: RI92
Cooper 1892, £34

The Way to School
wc, 38 x 26.7
exh: FA93, BL93
Waite 1894, £20
see: illustration p67

1893

Alone
wc,-
exh: FA93
sold FA Exh, £4

At Blakeney, Norfolk
wc,-
exh: FA93, NO93
AP £25
and
wc,-
exh: FA93
AP £16

At Cadgwith, Cornwall
wc,-
exh: FA93
Lanham 1895, £5

At Low Tide
(c 1893)
wc, 8 x 13

At Paul, near Newlyn, Cornwall
wc,-
exh: FA93
AP £8

At St Ives, Cornwall
wc,-
exh: FA93
AP £37

At the Capstan, Southwold
wc,-
exh: FA93, AC93, CF93
sold FA Exh, £28

At Walberswick
wc,-
exh: FA93
sold FA Exh, £10
and
wc,-
exh: FA93
AP £8

At Walberswick, Suffolk
wc,-
exh: FA93
AP £5

Barking Nets
wc,-
exh: FA93
AP £21

The Cliff Road, Newlyn
wc,-
exh: FA93
AP £37

Coming from the Shoot
wc,-
exh: FA93
AP £8

A Cottage by the Sea
wc, 37 x 23
exh: FA93
sold FA Exh, £35

A Cottage Home, Cropthorne, Worcestershire
wc,-
exh: RB93, Birmingham 1923
sold RB Exh, £10

A Daydream
wc,-
exh: FA93
sold FA Exh, £28

Deferred Hopes
wc,-
exh: FA93
sold FA Exh, £20

The Evening of Life
wc,-
exh: FA93
AP £21

The Fisherman's Courtship
wc,-
exh: FA93, LW93, RB93, LE94
Hawker 1894, £35

The Gentle Craft
wc,-
exh: FA93, NE93, BR94
AP £31

A Good Catch
wc,-
exh: FA93
Waite 1894, £8

An Interesting Chapter
wc,-
exh: RI93
Oliver 1893, £35

In the Harbour, Coverack
wc,-
exh: FA93
sold FA Exh, £8

In the Pilchard Season
wc,-
exh: FA93
sold FA Exh, £28

Kynance, Cornwall
wc, -
exh: FA93
AP £10

A Lass that Loves a Sailor
wc, -
exh: FA93
Jacob 1893, £10

The Last Gleam
wc, 25 x 36
exh: FA93
Hiddersley 1898, £12

The Limpet Gatherer
-,-
Starkey (D) 1893, £20
and
-,-
Starkey (D) 1893, £15

Mending the Net
wc, 27 x 24
exh: FA93
sold FA Exh, £14

My Neighbour
wc, 32 x 22
exh: FA93, Newlyn 1979,
Exeter 1984

Near Coverack, Cornwall
wc,-
exh: FA93
AP £8

A Newlyn Character
wc,-
exh: FA93
AP £16

Newlyn, Evening
wc,-
exh: FA93
AP £21

A Newlyn Fisherman
wc,-
exh: FA93
sold FA Exh, £8

A Newlyn Fishwife
wc,-
exh: FA93
Aste 1893, £8

News of the Fleet
wc,-
exh: FA93
sold FA Exh, £39

An Old Fishwife
wc,-
exh: FA93
sold FA Exh, £6

The Old Story
wc,-
exh: FA93, MA93, NC94,
LE94, PN95, SO95,
Starkey (D) 1896, £42
(AP £84)

The Old Windmill
(c 1893)
wc, 11 x 26

On the Beach, Southwold
wc,-
exh: FA93
AP £8

On the Cliff, Southwold, Suffolk
wc,-
exh: FA93
Jacob 1893, £26

Poor Weather
wc,-
exh: FA93
AP £8

A Quiet Chat
wc,-
exh; FA93
AP £8

Resting
wc,-
exh: FA93
AP £50

A Reverie
wc,-
exh: FA93
sold FA Exh, £23

The Road to the Village
wc,-
exh: FA93
AP £19

St Ives, Cornwall
wc,-
exh: FA93
sold FA Exh, £4

A Street in Newlyn
wc,-
exh: FA93, AC93, BR94, PN94
Starkey (D) 1895, £12
(AP £35)
and
wc,-
exh: FA93
AP £10

Sunlight and Shadow
wc,-
exh: FA93
AP £26

A Sunny Afternoon, Cornwall
wc,-
exh: FA93, Birmingham 1923
sold FA Exh, £20

Technical Instruction
wc,-
exh: FA93, LW93, RB94, Birmingham
1923
sold RB Exh, £70

Waiting for the Boats
wc,-
exh: FA93, NE93, AC93,
CF93, NC94
Starkey (D) 1894, £40
see: *Cornishman* July 27, 1893

Walberswick
wc,-
exh: FA93
AP £8

Washing Day
wc, 29.7 x 38.5
exh: FA93, Newlyn 1979,
Exeter 1984
see: illustration p96
and
ch, 26 x 38

Watching Father's Boat
wc,-
exh: FA93
AP £21
and
wc, 16 x 10

The Yarn
wc,-
exh: FA93
sold FA Exh, £28

1894

After the Storm
wc, 113 x 134
exh: RI94, RB99, RB03,
Birmingham 1923
Lethbridge 1894, £300
(AP £450)
Presented to Birmingham Museums
and Art Gallery
see: illustration p99

Convalescent
wc, 50 x 67
exh: RI94, RB95, RB99,
Exeter 1984
Jacob 1894, £50

A Cornish Cottage
-,-
exh: RB94
AP £3

The Epps Door
(c 1894)
o, 41 x 51

Idle Moments
wc, quarto
exh: PL94, LW94
Waite 1895, £25

An Interesting Story
o,-
exh: PO94
sold PO Exh, £42

Eleanore Langley
o, 102 x 64
exh: PN94

A Lass that Loves a Sailor
wc,-
exh: PN94, NC94, RB96
Starkey (D) 1896, £31

Never morning wore to evening,
But some heart did break
o, 122 x 152.5
exh: RA94, RB94, RB99, WH02,
Newlyn 1979, Exeter 1984
Jewell 1894, £328
coll: Birmingham Museums
and Art Gallery
see: illustration p110

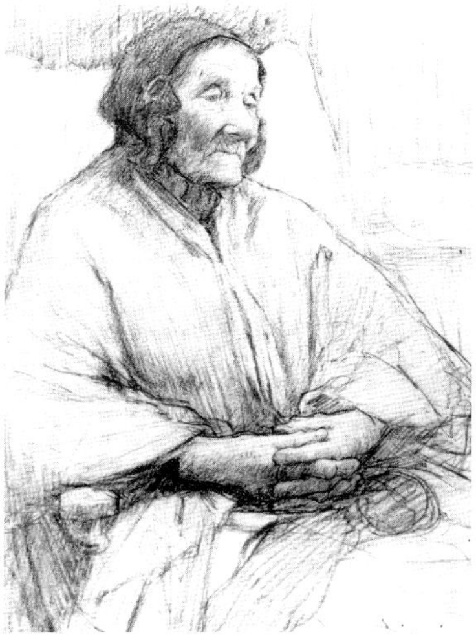

The seas are quiet 1884
chalk, 35 x 25.2

Old Grace
wc, 34 x 25
exh: PN22, Birmingham 1968,
Exeter 1984
see: illustration p111

1895

A Country Lass
o,-
exh: PN95
Read 1896, £15

Evening at Coverack, Cornwall
o, 48 x 60
exh: PN95, RB97
sold 1898, £25
(AP £60)
coll: Walsall Art Gallery

The Hand-bell
(c 1895)
wc, 20.4 x 12.7
see: illustration p191

Her Only Care
-,-
exh: RB95, Birmingham 1923
sold RB Exh, £20

Idle Moments
wc,-
exh: RI95, RB95, RB99
Hedges 1895, £150

Motherless
o, 122 x 152
exh: RA95, WG95, RB99
Davis 1896, £260
(AP £350)
see: *Cornish Telegraph*,
April 4, 1895
and
wc, 24 x 32
exh: Exeter 1984

A Newlyn Fisherman
wc,-
exh: RI95
sold RI Exh, £21

A Newlyn Fishwife
wc,-
exh: RI95
sold RI Exh, £10

An Old Campaigner
wc,-
exh: PN95
sold PN Ex, £30
See: *The Yellow Book*,
October 1895

Once upon a Time
wc, 53 x 75
exh: RI96, WG96
Starkey (D) 1897, £53
(AP £105)

On the Dart
-,-
Luton (D) 1895, £15

On the Lookout
bw,-
exh: RI95
sold RI Exh, £21

A Sentinel of the Sea
wc, 34 x 20
exh: RB95, PN95, LE96, YO96

A Stitch in Time
-,-
Cheadle 1895, £25

When One is Old
wc,-
exh: RI95
sold RI Exh, £13
and
o, 78 x 45
exh: RB95
Davis 1895, £25
and
-,-
Cheadle 1897, £32

1896

At Porthgwarra
wc,-
exh: RI96
Donated for prize draw, Art Union 1897

Breadwinners
o, 117 x 216
exh: RA96
Booth 1896, £315
see: illustration p23
and
wc, 23 x 43
exh: Truro 1978, Penzance 1993
coll: Penlee House Gallery and Museum, Penzance
see: illustration p103

Indecision
wc,-
exh: RB96
AP £31

Old Age is Lonely
-,-
exh: AC96
AP £40

An Old Soldier
wc,-
exh: RI96
sold RI Exh, £10

On Guard
-,-
Starkey (D) 1896, £40

Pensive Thoughts
wc,-
exh: RI96, RB96
Starkey (D) 1896, £35

A Reverie
o,-
exh: PO96, LE97
Cohen (D) 1898, £20
(AP £42)

Waiting for the Boats
o,-
Starkey (D) 1896, £53
and
wc,-
exh: SO95, YO95, PN95
Cheadle 1896, £30

Waiting the Return of the Boats
o,-
exh: PN95, RB96, RB19
Bellingham 1896, £65

1897

A Council of Three
-,-
Starkey (D) 1897, £60

In faith and hope the world will disagree, But all mankind's concern is charity
o, 125.7 x 165.7
exh: RA97, RB97, SO99, YO99, GL00, NC00, NE00, Birmingham 1923, Exeter 1984, Manchester 1987
AP £300
see: Tolstoy 'What Is Art?'
see: illustration p107
and
-,-
exh: PN98
Wightman 1898, £30

An Interesting Book
-,-
Starkey (D) 1897, £23

Walter Langley — Self Portrait
o, 77 x 64
exh: RB97
coll: Uffizi Gallery, Florence
see: frontispiece

Local News
-,-
exh: RB97
Starkey (D) 1897, £40

Nothing Doing
-,-
Williams 1897, £9

Old Billy
o, 64 x 43
Saloman 1897, £42

An Old Cornish Kitchen
wc, 30 x 39
exh: RB99, Exeter 1984

An Old Fisherman
-,-
exh: AC97
AP £8
and
-,-
exh: AC97
AP £8
and
o,-
exh: PO97, RB98, RB99
AP £65

A Reverie
-,-
exh: AC97, PN98
Luton (D) 1900, £32

The Widower
-,-
Starkey (D) 1897, £30

1898

Companions
wc,-
exh: BL98
sold BL Exh, £22

Confidences
-,-
Harris 1898, £15

A Country Lass
o, 76 x 55.8
exh: RB98
sold RB Exh, £30
see: illustration p105

A Cousin from Town
o, 152 x 109
exh: RA98, WG98
Tooth (D) 1899, £200
see: *Cornish Telegraph*,
March 24, 1898
and
o, 41 x 30
exh: Newlyn 1979
Wightman 1898, £30
coll: Victoria Art Gallery, Bath

A Crown of Years
wc, 36 x 25
exh: RB98, SO99

Daydreams
wc,-
exh: RI98
Ward 1898, £30

The End of the Story
o, 74.2 x 62.2
exh: PO98
Stannage 1899, £45
(AP £75)
see: illustration p106

An Impromptu Exhibition
-,-
Starkey (D) 1898, £52

In the Fishing Season
wc, 105 x 71
exh: RI98, RB99
Fieldhouse (D) 1900, £65
(AP £210)

The Letter
-,-
Starkey (D) 1898, £23

A Quiet Corner
wc, 65 x 33
exh: RB98, OL99
sold 1900, £32
coll: Huddersfield Art Gallery

A Quiet Pipe
wc,-
exh: RB98, SO99, YO99
sold YO Exh, £23

Stories of the Battlefield
o, 32 x 42
Starkey (D) 1898, £30

Trouble
-,-
Starkey (D) 1898, £35

1899

Absent Thoughts
wc, 41 x 38
Fieldhouse (D) 1899, £25

An Anxious Moment
wc, 71 x 54
Fieldhouse (D) 1899, £55

Between the Tides
-,-
exh: RB99
sold RB Exh, £38

A Cornish Fisherman
-,-
exh: SA99
sold: SA Exh, £35

The Evening of Life
-,-
exh: RB99
AP £30

The Grandfather
-,-
Cohen (D) 1899, £40

An Interesting Chapter
o,-
exh: OL99
sold 1901, £20

Maternity
wc,-
exh: WG99, EX00, RI02
sold 1902, £22

News of the Fleet
wc, 69 x 53
Fieldhouse (D) 1899, £55

A Quiet Time
-,-
exh: RB99, OL00
AP £42

The Waif
o,-
Cohen (D) 1899, £25

Waiting for the Tide
wc,-
exh: RI99
sold RI Exh, £71

A Wanderer
-,-
Fieldhouse (D) 1899, £25

Wandering Musicians
o,-
exh: RA99, YO00, RB01, BR01
AP £250
see: *Cornish Telegraph*,
March 23, 1899

The Widower
o,-
exh: RB99, BR00, EX00, PN02
sold PN Exh, £42

1900

At Porthgwarra, Cornwall
wc, 25.4 x 17.8
exh: RI00
sold RI Exh, £4
see: illustration p109

A Cornish Fisherman
wc,-
exh: RI00, RB01
AP £30

Fading Light
o, 109 x 122
exh: RA00, RB00, LE01
sold 1901, £105
coll: Leeds City Art Gallery
and
o,-
exh: RB00, WR00, YO01, PN01
sold PN Exh, £30
(Ap £52)
and
wc,-
Gibbons 1918, £10

An Interesting Paragraph
-,-
Luton (D) 1900, £65

In the Mackerel Season
-,-
Fieldhouse (D) 1900, £24

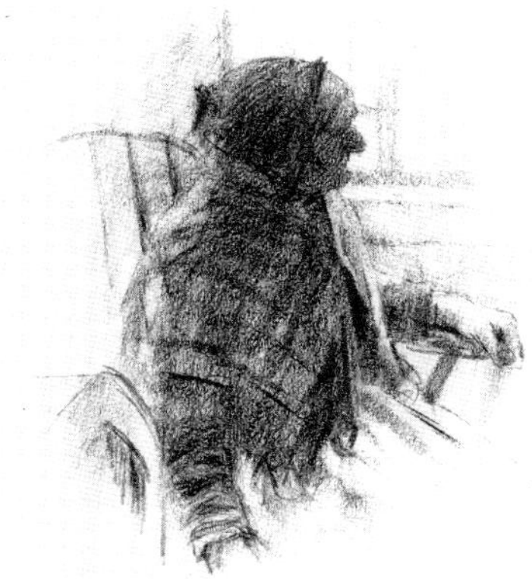

Study of an old woman late-1880s
chalk, 25.5 x 23cm

Motherhood
wc, 94 x 61
exh: RI00, WG00, RB01,
Exeter 1984
Berwick Club 1903, £41
(AP £105)

News from the Front
-,-
Fieldhouse (D) 1900, £32
and
wc, -
Luton (D) 1900, £65

News from the War
wc,-
Fieldhouse (D) 1900, £16

An Old Campaigner
wc,-
exh: RB00
sold RB Exh, £20
and
wc,-
exh: RI00
AP £15

On Dartmoor
wc,-
exh: RI00
AP £6

A Quiet Pipe
-,-
exh: WR00, NC01, PN01
sold PN Exh, £10

Reading the News
(c 1900)
o, 33.5 x 25.5
see: illustration p98

A Reverie
wc,-
exh: RI00
Luton (D) 1900, £28

A Signal of Distress
o,-
exh: RA00, WG00, YO00, HU01,
NC02, WR02, OL03, RB04, BR06
Paul (D) 1920, £50
(AP £250)
see: *Cornishman*,
March 29, 1900

A Street in St Ives, Cornwall
wc,-
exh: RI00, RB01
sold RB Exh, £15

War News
wc,-
exh: RI00, WG00, RB01
Siddons 1901, £52

1901

The Answer
wc, 61 x 56
Luton (D) 1901, £60

Awaiting the Boats
-,-
Williams 1901, £35

Between the Tides
o, 152.4 x 101.6
exh: RA01, WG01, RB02,
YO03, PN04
sold 1904, £150
(AP £350)
coll: Warrington Museum and
Art Gallery
see: illustration p26
and
o, 24 x 17

A Daydream
wc,-
exh: RB01
sold RB Exh, £19

An Interesting Book
-,-
Mawson (D) 1901, £25

In the Firelight
-,-
exh: PN01
sold PN Exh, £30
and
o,-
sold 1901, £75
coll: Leeds City Art Gallery

Local Critics
wc,-
exh: RI01, WG01, RB02
sold RB Exh, £47
(AP £84)

News of the Fleet
-,-
Williams 1901, £35

Pleasant News
-,-
Williams 1901, £42

A Quiet Pipe
-,-
exh: PN01
sold PN Exh, £10

Sympathy
o,-
exh: RB01, SO02, BR03, PN04
AP £80
see: *Cornishman* November
12, 1903

A Wanderer
-,-
Luton (D) 1901, £12

When One is Old
o, 78 x 45
exh: PL10
sold 1901, £53
coll: Plymouth Museum
and Art Gallery

1902

A Cornish Idyll
o, 132 x 122
exh: RA02, WG02
sold 1903, £300
(AP £400)
coll: Walker Art Gallery, Liverpool
and
wc,-
Luton (D) 1902, £50
see: illustration p114
and
wc, 28 x 27
exh: Exeter 1984

A Cornish Woman
wc,-
exh: RI02
sold RI Exh, £6

Interesting News
wc,-
exh: RB02
sold RB Exh, £38

Local News
wc,-
Mawson (D) 1902, £33

A Quiet Pipe
-,-
exh: PN02
Sold PN Exh, £10

A Sunny Afternoon, Newlyn
wc, 43 x 30
exh: RI02
AP £10
coll: Cornwall County
Museum, Truro
see: illustration p116

1903

Absent Thoughts
wc,-
exh: RB03
sold RB Exh, £25

A Cornish Woman
-,-
exh: PN03
sold PN Exh, £8

A Daydream
wc,-
exh: RI03
sold RI Exh, £30

Interesting News
wc, 69 x 53
Luton (D) 1903, £60

A Letter from Home
wc,-
exh: RB03, PN06
AP £42

Mending the Old Quilt
-,-
Luton (D) 1903, £35

Trouble
o,-
exh: RB03, PN04
AP £84

Waiting the Return of the Fleet
wc, 50 x 53
exh: RI03, WG03, OL04, RB05
sold RB Exh, £40
see: illustration p121

When the Boats are Away
o, 137 x 107
exh: RA03, WR03, SO04, BU04,
BR05, Exeter 1984
Marshall (D) 1906, £131
(AP £400)

1904

At Perranporth, Cornwall
wc,-
exh: RI04
sold RI Exh, £5
and
wc, 25 x 13

At Volendam
wc, 28 x 38

A Cornish Woman
wc,-
exh: RI04
sold RI Exh, £5

A Dutch Fisherman
wc, 32 x 23
exh: RB11, PN22
see: illustration p126

Evening Shadows
wc,-
exh: RI04
sold RI Exh, £10

Expert Opinion
wc, 56 x 75
exh: Exeter 1984
Luton (D) 1904, £50
coll: Birmingham Museums
and Art Gallery

A Fisherman's Daughter
wc,-
exh: RI04, WR04, OL05, PN05
sold PN Exh, £29
(AP £53)

The Greeting
o, 107 x 152
exh: RA04
Davis 1904, £300
see: cover and p30
and
wc, 26 x 31
exh: RI04
Luton (D) 1907, £21
and
wc, 18 x 11

Interesting News
wc,-
exh: RI04
sold RI Exh, £25

Meditation
-,-
exh: RB04, Birmingham 1923
AP £50

A Newlyn Fishwife
wc,-
exh: RI04, PN04
AP £8

An Old Dame
wc,-
exh: RI04, PN04
AP £5

The Old Quilt
wc,-
exh: RB04, NE05
sold NE Exh, £25

The Old Story
-, 38 x 51
Fieldhouse (D) 1904, £20

On the Cliff, Newlyn
wc,-
exh: RI04
AP £10

John Russell Pengelly
wc, 27 x 23

The Pink Bodice
-, 25 x 43
Fieldhouse (D) 1904

A Reverie
wc,-
exh: RI04, PN04
AP £5

A Sunny Day in Holland
-,-
exh: RB06
Fieldhouse (D) 1905, £21

1905

At Volendam, Holland
o, 61 x 41
exh: PO07, PN07, RB09, PL10
AP £42

By the Zuider Zee
wc,-
exh: RI06, RB07, Birmingham 1923
sold RB Exh, £24

A Chip off the Old Block
o, 91.5 x 81
exh: Hull 1984
Ford 1905, £84
coll: Ferens Art Gallery, Hull
see: illustration p133

A Cornish Fisherman
wc,-
exh: RB05, BR05, WR06
AP £35

A Cornish Maiden
-,-
exh: PN05
Jackson 1905, £17

A Dutch Boy
cc, 34 x 20

A Dutch Fishergirl, Volendam
wc, 23 x 32
see: illustration p127

A Dutch Fisherman
ch, 34 x 25

A Dutch Kitchen
cr, 34 x 24
see: illustration p124

Fisherfolk on the Pier, Volendam
wc, 23 x 24

A Fisherman of the Zuider Zee
wc,-
exh: PN05, RB05
sold RB Exh, £30

His Only Pair
wc,-
exh: RI05
Miller 1905, £60
and
cc,-

The Letter
wc,-
exh: RI05, SO06

Newlyn Fishwives
-,-
exh: RB05

An Old Dutchman
wc, 34 x 25
exh: PN22
and
wc,-
exh: PN05
Watney 1907, £25

An Old Dutchwoman
-,-
Luton (D) 1905, £30
and
wc,-
exh: RB15, PL17
AP £16

An Old Inhabitant
wc, 34 x 25
exh: PN05, RB11, PN11, PN22
see: illustration p122

An Old Inhabitant of Volendam, Holland
wc,-
exh: RI05, RB05, RI16
AP £25

The Old Jetty at Volendam
wc, 37 x 25

On the Dyke
wc,-
Leighton 1909, £10

On The Dyke, Volendam
wc,-
exh: RB05, RI05
AP £32

The Woman's Part
wc,-
exh: PN05
sold PN Exh, £27
and
o, 91 x 137
exh: RA05, PN05, SO06
sold 1907, £158
(AP £250)

1906

The Evening of Life
wc,-
exh: RI06
West 1906, £30
and
o,-
Ford 1906, £63

The Fisherman's Widow
o, 107 x 137
exh: RA06, RB06, SO07, ML07, PN07, OL08, RO11
Paul (D) 1919, £45
(AP £250)

A Little Dutch Girl
wc, 25 x 20
exh: RI06, PN06
sold PN Exh, £21

Memories
o, 99 x 122
exh: HU07, BU11, Bradford 1975, Hull 1984
T R Ferens 1907, £105
coll: Ferens Art Gallery, Hull
see: illustration p134
and
o, 65 x 76
Weiss 1907, £36

An Old Dutchwoman
wc, 25 x 20
exh: RI06
sold RI Exh, £21

An Old Dutchwoman of Volendam, Holland
wc, 25 x 37
exh: PL17
sold PL Exh, £21
coll: Plymouth Museum and Art Gallery

Thinking it Out
wc, -
exh: PN06
sold 1908, £27
and
o, -
exh: PO06
Hirst 1906, £74

Wandering Musician
wc, -
exh: PN06, PN14
Paul (D) 1918, £21

1907

A Belgian Interior
wc, 35 x 24.5
see: illustration p135

A Belgian Peasant Woman
wc, -
exh, RI07
AP £32

A Cornish Fisherman
o, 52 x 25
exh: PN07, Newlyn 1979

Crofthome
wc,-
exh: PN07

The Evening of Life
wc,-
exh: RB07, RI09
sold 1910, £26

A Flemish Peasant
wc,-
Latham 1914, £35
and
o, 102 x 137 (later 102 x 92.7)
exh: RA07, WG07, SO08, MA08, PN10, PL10
Paul (D) 1919, £45
(AP £210)
see: illustration p129

An Old Fisherman
wc,-
exh: RI07
AP £32

1908

At Polperro
wc, 36 x 26
exh: PN10
sold PN Exh, £24
see: illustration p140
and
o,-
Luton (D) 1909, £30

The Cliff Road, Newlyn
wc,-
exh: RI08, WR08, OL11
AP £32

Cornish Fisher Folk
o, 137 x 99
exh: RA08, WR08, OL09, BU09, RB10
sold 1911, £100
(AP £250)
coll: Waverley Borough Council
see: illustration p136

The Grandmother
o,-
exh: RB08, Birmingham 1923
Solomons 1908, £30

An Interesting Letter
wc,-
exh: RB08, RI11, OL12
Paul (D) 1915, £47

Motherhood
wc, 58 x 74
exh: RI08, RB08, WG09, SO11
sold 1911, £47
(AP £84)

Preparing Dinner
o,-
exh: RB08
sold RB Exh, £30

A Reverie
o,-
exh: PN08
sold PN Exh, £14

1909

The Answer
-,-
exh: PN09
sold PN Exh, £7

A Belgian Peasant Woman
wc,-
exh: RI09
AP £26

A Cornish Fishwife
wc,-
exh: RI09
AP £8

The Fisher Boy
-,-
exh: PN09, RB10
AP £10

The Fisherman's Widow
wc,-
exh: RI09
Lowndes 1909, £16

A Flemish Interior
-,-
exh: RB09, PN09, PN14
AP £30

In a Cornish Fishing Village
-,-
exh: RB09
AP £21

In a Devonshire Village
wc,-
exh: RI09
AP £26

A Newlyn Fisherman
wc,-
exh: RI09
AP £8

An Old Salt
wc,-
exh: RI09
AP £8

An Old Welshwoman
wc,-
exh: RI09, PN09
sold PN Exh £5
and
wc,-
exh: RB11
Luton (D) 1918, £10

Preparing Dinner
wc,-
exh: RI09
AP £42

A Reverie
o,-
exh: RB09, PN10
sold PN Exh, £19

The tender grace of a day that is dead, Will ne'er come back to me
o, 116 x 105
exh: RA09, PN09, WO09, RB10, OL10
sold 1910, £100
(AP £200)
coll: Oldham Art Gallery

1910

At Beer, Devon
wc, 25.5 x 13
see: illustration p47

At Beer, South Devon
wc, 33 x 25
exh: PN10, RB15

The Beach
(c 1910)
pa, 13 x 19

A Cornish Fisherman
-,-
exh: PN10
AP £10

The Fisherman's Widow
wc,-
exh: RI10
Jagger 1910, £32

In a Newlyn Court
wc,-
exh: RI10, RB11, OL11, PN13
Luton (D) 1915, £30

The New Arrival
o, 109 x 122
exh: RA10
Summers 1910, £210

A Quiet Time
-,-
exh: RB10
AP £25

A State Pensioner
wc,-
exh: RB10, RI11
Ap £42

1911

A Letter from Home
-,-
exh: OL11, PM11
sold PM Ex, £18

Maternity
o, 109 x 135
exh: RA11, PN11

1912

A Cornish Fishwife
wc,-
exh: RI12, RB12
sold 1915, £18

A Crown of Years
o,-
exh: RA12, OL13
AP £32

The Fairy Story
wc,-
exh: RI12, PN13
AP £45

An Interesting Letter
-,-
Williams 1912, £16

Mending the Quilt
o,-
exh: RA12, OL13
AP £35
and
wc,-
exh: RI12, RB12
sold RB Exh, £18

A Newlyn Byway
o,-
exh: PN12
sold PN Exh, £26

Preparing Dinner
o, 127 x 132
exh: RA12, RB12, OL13
Luton (D) 1918, £45
(AP £205)

1913

The Book
wc,-
exh: RI13, OL15
AP £32

Mending the Bodice
o,-
exh: RB13, RA19
AP £100
and
wc,-
exh: RI13
AP £26

Motherlove
o, 137 x 101.5
exh: RA13, RB15
Vincent 1915, £95

A State Pensioner
o,-
Mansell 1913, £85

The Widower
wc,-
exh: RI13, RB13
AP £50

1914

Daydreams
o, 122 x 130
exh: RA14, OL15
sold 1916, £90
(AP £200)
coll: Bristol City Museums and Art Gallery

The Pink Bodice
o,-
sold 1914 £26

Preparing Dinner
wc,-
exh: RI14, RB15
AP £50

1915

A Cornish Fishwife
-,-
exh: OL15
AP £40

The Letter
wc,-
exh: RI15
AP £21

The Pink Bodice
wc, 39 x 29
exh: RB15, RI15
Williams 1916, £25

1916

A Belgian Interior
o, 117 x 97
exh: RA16

The Letter
wc,-
exh: RB16, RI17
AP £32

My Old Dutch
-,-
exh: RB16
AP £26

The Pink Bodice
o,-
exh: RA16, WG16
AP £100

The Short Story
-,-
sold 1916, £25

1917

Anxious Thoughts
wc,-
exh: RB17, RI18
AP £32

A Cornish Fisherman
-,-
exh: RB17
AP £25

Eventide
wc,-
exh: RI17
AP £42

The Letter
o, 104 x 102
exh: RA17, RB17
AP £110

1918

A Bit of Old Newlyn, Cornwall
wc,-
exh: RB18
Paul (D) 1918, £12

A Cornish Stile
o,-
Paul (D) 1918, £13

Fading Light
wc,-
Gibbons 1918, £10

A Newlyn Fisherman
-,-
Paul (D) 1918, £12

A Reverie
o,-
Paul (D) 1918, £31

The Sacrifice
wc,-
exh: RI18, RB18
AP £35

War News
wc,-
Mawson (D) 1918, £15

1920

The News Sheet
-,-
sold 1920, £8

Peeling Potatoes
wc, 25 x 36
exh: RB20

Above Newlyn c 1884, wc
Absent Thoughts 1889, wc
1889, -
1899, wc
1903, wc
Adams, Rosa 1879, -
Admiration — see *A Cousin from Town*
After the Storm 1894, wc
Alone — Borne on the swift though silent wings of time, Old age comes on apace 1890, wc
Alone 1893, wc
Among the Missing — Scene in a Cornish Fishing Village 1884, wc
Answer, The 1886, wc
1887, wc
1901, wc
1909, -
Anxious Moment, An 1899, wc
Anxious Thoughts 1917, wc
Apprentice, The c 1884, wc
At Beer, Devon 1910, wc
At Beer, South Devon 1910, wc
At Blakeney, Norfolk 1893, wc
1893, wc
At Cadgwith, Cornwall 1893, wc
At Coverack, Cornwall 1891, wc
1891, wc
At Low Tide c 1893, wc
At Marston Green 1876, -
At Mousehole, Cornwall 1892, wc
At Paul, near Newlyn, Cornwall 1893, wc
At Perranporth, Cornwall 1904, wc
1904, wc
At Polperro 1908, wc
1908, o
At Porthgwarra 1896, wc
At Porthgwarra, Cornwall 1900, wc
At St Ives, Cornwall 1893, wc
At Sutton Coldfield 1880, -
At the Capstan, Southwold 1893, wc
At the Well 1876, -
At the Well, Brittany 1882, wc
At Volendam 1904, wc
At Volendam, Holland 1905, o
At Walberswick 1893, wc
1893, wc
At Walberswick, Suffolk 1893, wc
Authority, An 1882, -
Authority on Fish, An 1882, -
Awaiting the Boats 1901, -

Barking Nets 1882, -
1893, wc
Beach, The c 1910, pa
Beach, Newlyn, The c 1882, wc
Beached Boat, The c 1884, wc
Becalmed 1885, wc
Bedtime 1880, -
Belgian Interior, A 1907, wc
1916, o
Belgian Peasant Woman, A 1907, wc
1909, wc
Bell Tower, Evesham, The 1878, -
Best in the Market, The 1880, -
Betrayed 1887, wc
Between the Tides 1899, -
1901, o
1901, o
Bit of Old Newlyn, Cornwall, A 1918, wc
Blossom and Decay 1879, -
Book, The 1913, wc
Breadwinners 1881, wc
1896, o
Breadwinners [aka Fishwives] 1896, wc
Breton Mendicant, A 1881, wc
Breton Peasant Girl, A 1881, wc
1881, wc
Brittany Interior, A 1881, wc
But men must work and women must weep, Though storms be sudden and waters deep, And the harbour bar be moaning 1882, wc
1882,bw
1882,wc
1882, se
By the Church, Welford-on-Avon 1886, wc
By the Sea 1890, wc
By the Zuider Zee 1905, wc

Calm Day, Newlyn, A c 1887, wc
Cavalier, A 1881, -
Child of the Village, A 1883, -
Chip off the Old Block, A 1905, o
Cliff Road, Newlyn, The 1893, wc
1908, wc
Coming from the Shoot 1893, wc
Companions 1898, wc
Composure 1873, -
Confidences 1898, -
Consolation 1883, wc
Constancy 1884, wc
Contentment 1883, -
Contemplation 1876, wc
Convalescent 1881, wc
1888, -
1891, wc
1891, o
1894, wc
Cork Cutting 1884, o
Corner of the Kitchen, Brittany, A 1881, wc
Corner of the Studio, A c 1878, wc
1882, -
Corner of the Village, A c 1886, wc
Cornish Cottage, A 1894, -
Cornish Fisher Folk 1908, o
Cornish Fisherman, A c 1883, wc
1899, -
1900, wc
1905, wc
1907, o
1910, -
1917, -
Cornish Fishwife, A 1882, -
1882, wc
1889, pa
1889, wc
1909, wc
1912, wc
1915, -
Cornish Idyll, A 1902, o
1902, wc
1902, wc
Cornish Kitchen, A c 1881, wc
Cornish Maiden, A 1905, -
Cornish Stile, A 1918, o
Cornish Village Maiden, A 1883, -
Cornish Woman, A 1902, wc
1903, -
1904, wc
Cottage at St Paul, A 1881, wc
Cottage by the Sea, A 1893, wc
Cottage Home, A 1878, -
Cottage Home, Cropthorne, Worcestershire, A 1893, wc
Cottages at Fillongley, Warwickshire 1875, wc
Cottages at Marston Green 1880, -

Title	Date
Cottage Steps, Newlyn	c 1890, wc
Council of Three, A	1897, -
Country Inn, A	c 1886, wc
Country Lass, A	1876, -
	1895, o
	1898, o
Country Walk, The	c 1884, wc
Cousin from Town, A	1898, o
Cousin from Town, A [Study — aka Admiration]	1898, o
Critics of the Newlyn School	1892, wc
Crofthome	1907, wc
Crown of Years, A	1883, wc
	1898, wc
	1912, o
Daydream, A [aka A Fisherman's Daughter]	1884, wc
Daydream, A	1893, wc
	1901, wc
	1903, wc
Daydreams	1879, -
	1881, wc
	1882, -
	1886, -
	1898, wc
	1914, o
Deferred Hopes	1893, wc
Dingley, Miss	1880, -
Dionysus, a Study from Life	1877, wc
Disaster! Scene in A Cornish Fishing Village	1888, ch
	1889, wc
Dog and Duck Inn, Birmingham, The	1871, bw
Dreams by night and thoughts by day, Are with him that's far away	1880, -
Dutch Boy, A	1905, cc
Dutch Fishergirl, Volendam, A	1905, wc
Dutch Fisherman, A	1904, wc
	1905, ch
Dutch Kitchen, A	1905, cr
Early Cares [aka Sunshine and Shadow]	1888, wc
Early Reveries	1883, wc
End of the Story, The	1898, o
Entrez	1881, wc
Epps Door, The	c 1894, o
Evening at Coverack, Cornwall	1895, o
Evening Hour, The	1887, bw
	1887, wc
Evening, North Devon	1875, -
Evening of Life, The	1882, -
	1883, wc
	1887, wc
	1889, o
	1893, wc
	1899, -
	1906, wc
	1906, o
	1907, wc
Evening Shadows	1904, wc
Eventide	1917, wc
Eventide, Newlyn	c 1887, wc
Expert Opinion	1904, wc
Fading Light	1900, o
	1900, o
	1900, wc
	1918, wc
Fairy Story, The	1912, wc
Father's Boat	1884, wc
Fiction	1880, wc
Fish Cellar, The	c 1890, wc
Fisher Boy, The	1909, -
Fisher-girl, A	c 1877, wc
Fisherfolk on the Pier, Volendam	1905, wc
Fisherman, A	1874, -
Fisherman of the Zuider Zee, A	1905, wc
Fisherman's Courtship, The	1893, wc
Fisherman's Daughter, A — see *Daydream, A*	
Fisherman's Daughter, A	1904, wc
Fisherman's Home, A	1881, -
Fisherman's Pride	1879, -
Fisherman's Son, A	1884, wc
Fisherman's Son, The	c 1884, wc
Fisherman's Widow, The	1906, o
	1909, wc
	1910, wc
Fisher's Daughter, The	1886, wc
Fishing Boats, St Mawes	c 1884, wc
Fishing Fleet, The	c 1882, wc
Fishing Nets — Out to Dry	c 1888, wc
Fishwives — see Breadwinners	
Flemish Interior, A	1909, -
Flemish Peasant, A	1907, wc
	1907, o
Franks, Mr	1881, -
Gamekeeper, The	1879, -
Garden by the Sea, A	1884, wc
Gathering Seaweed	c 1882, wc
Gathering Storm, The	1883, cr
	1883, wc
	1883, wc
Gentle Craft, The	1893, wc
Going to Market	1885, wc
Good Catch, A	1893, wc
Gossip	1881, wc
	1881, wc
Grandfather, The	1899, -
Grandmother, The	1908, o
Greeting, The	1904, o
	1904, wc
	1904, wc
Hand-bell, The	c 1895, wc
Harborne Church	1881, -
Her Only Care	1895, -
High Tor, Matlock	1876, -
His Only Pair	1905, wc
	1905, cc
His Opinion	1882, -
Home from Market	1880, -
Idle Moments	1875, -
	1884, wc
	1894, wc
	1895, wc
I do remember an apothecary	1878, wc
Impromptu Exhibition, An	1898, -
In A Brittany Apple Orchard	1881, wc
In a Cornish Fishing Village	1881, wc
	1909, -
In A Cornish Fishing Village — Departure of the Fleet for the North	1886, wc
In a Cornish Fishing Village— Naval Manoeuvres	1891, wc
In a Cornish Village	1881, -
	1882, wc
	1891, -
In a Devonshire Village	1909, wc
In a Newlyn Court	1910, wc
Indecision	1896, wc
In faith and hope the world will disagree, But all mankind's concern is charity	1897, o
	1897, -
In Memoriam	1883, wc
	1883, o
	1887, wc
In St Ives Harbour	1889, wc
Interesting Book, An	1897, -
	1901, -
Interesting Chapter, An	1893, wc
	1899, o

Interesting Letter, An	1888, bw
	1908, wc
	1912, -
Interesting News	1902, wc
	1903, wc
	1904, wc
Interesting Paragraph, An	1900, -
Interesting Story, An	1886, wc
	1894, o
In the Cornfield	c 1884, wc
In the Firelight	1901, -
	1901, o
In the Fishing Season	1898, wc
In the Harbour, Coverack	1893, wc
In the Harbour, Newlyn	c 1888, wc
In the Hayfield	1877, -
In the Mackerel Season	1900, -
In the Net Loft	1885, -
In the Pilchard Season	1893, wc
In the Woods	1879, -
In Times of Trouble	1889, bw
I Think I'll be a Sailor — see *Wonderland*	
Jackdaw of Rheims, The	1882, wc
Jilted, — The fraud of man was ever so, Since summer first was leafy	1889, wc
Joanna	1879, -
Kitten, The	1878, -
Knitting	1884, bw
	1889, wc
	1890, wc
Kynance, Cornwall	1893, wc
La Blanchisseuse	1882, bw
Lamorna Cove, Cornwall	1880, -
Landing Fish, Newlyn	1884, -
Langley, Eleanore	1894, o
Langley, Mary Ann	c 1877, pe
Langley, Walter — Self Portrait	1897, o
Langley, William	1871, wc
La Pensiera	1873, -
Lass that Loves a Sailor, A	1882, -
	1893, wc
	1894, wc
Last Chapter, The	1884, -
Last Gleam, The	1888, wc
	1893, wc
Last Gleaning, The	1888, -
Left in Charge	1881, -
	1882, -
Leisure Moments	1889, -

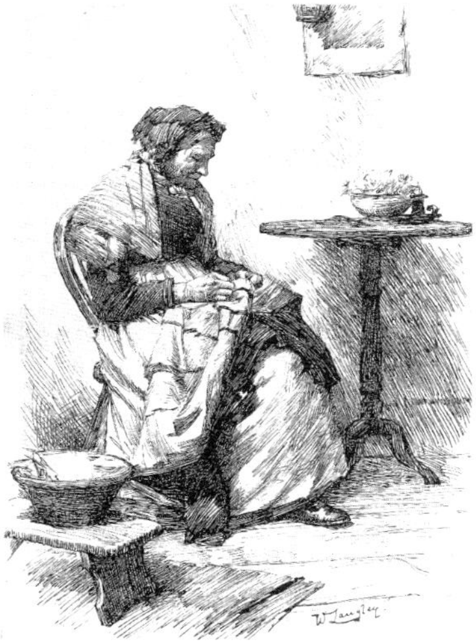

Study of an old woman late-1880s
ink, 37 x 25.4cm

This drawing was made for reproduction in an RI catalogue.

Letter from Home, A	1903, wc
	1911, -
Letter, The	1879, -
	1898, -
	1905, wc
	1915, wc
	1916, wc
	1917, o
Light in the Cottage	1881, -
Limpet Gatherer, The	1893, -
	1893, -
Lingering Hope	1882, -
Little Dutch Girl, A	1906, wc
Local Critics	1901, wc
Local News	1891, -
	1891, wc
	1891, wc
	1897, -
	1902, wc
Lover and his Lass, A	1884, wc
Lych Gate, Welford-on-Avon, The	1886, wc
Lynam, Mrs Kathleen	c 1883, wc
Maternity	1891, o
	1899, wc
	1911, o
Meditation	1904, -

Memories	1885, wc
	1906, o
	1906, o
Mending the Bodice	1913, o
	1913, wc
Mending the Net	1893, wc
Mending the Old Quilt	1903, -
Mending the Quilt	1912, o
	1912, wc
Mending the Sails	1882, -
	1882, bw
Midday Meal, The	1881, -
Milkman, The	1881, wc
Moment's Rest, A	c 1882, wc
Motherhood	1900, wc
	1908, wc
Motherless	1895, o
	1895, wc
Motherlove	1913, o
Mounts Bay	c 1882, wc
Mousehole Court, A	1881, -
Musing on the roaring ocean, Which divides my love and me	1879, wc
My heart is light and gay	1881, wc
My Neighbour	1893, wc
My Old Dutch	1916, -
My Youngest Son, Cecil	1886, wc
Near Coverack, Cornwall	1893, wc
Near Newlyn, Cornwall	1880, -
Near St Mawes	c 1884, wc
Never morning wore to evening, But some heart did break	1894, o
New Arrival, The	1881, wc
	1910, o
Newly Enfranchised	1886, wc
Newlyn	1880, -
	c 1882, wc
	c 1882, wc
Newlyn Byway, A	c 1883, cr
	1912, o
Newlyn Character, A	1893, wc
Newlyn, Evening	1893, wc
Newlyn Fisherlad, A	1884, wc
Newlyn Fisherman, A	c 1890, wc
	1893, wc
	1895, wc
	1909, wc
	1918, -
Newlyn Fishwife, A	1893, wc
	1895, wc
	1904, wc
Newlyn Fishwives	1905, -
Newlyn Harbour, Low Tide	c 1883, wc

Newlyn Woman, A	c 1882, wc
New Novel, The	1886, -
	1887, -
News from Abroad	1878, -
News from an Absent One	1879, -
News from the Front	1900, -
	1900, wc
News from the North	1885, -
News from the War	1900, wc
News of the Fleet	1893, wc
	1899, wc
	1901, -
News of the Sea	1883, wc
News Sheet, The	1920, -
Nothing Doing	1897, -
Obstruction	1881, -
	1882, bw
O! For the touch of a vanish'd hand, And the sound of a voice that is still	1888, wc
Old Age is Lonely	1896, -
Old Billy	1897, o
Old Breton Woman, An	1881, -
Old Campaigner, An	1887, wc
	1895, wc
	1900, wc
	1900, wc
Old Cornish Kitchen, An	1897, wc
Old Dame, An	1904, wc
Old Dutchman, An	1905, wc
	1905, wc
Old Dutchwoman, An	1905, -
	1905, wc
	1906, wc
Old Dutchwoman of Volendam, Holland, An	1906, wc
Old Fisherman, An	1889, wc
	1897, -
	1897, -
	1897, o
	1907, wc
Old Fishwife, An	1893, wc
Old Gardener, The	1884, wc
Old Grace	1894, wc
Old Inhabitant, An	1905, wc
Old Inhabitant of Volendam, Holland, An	1905, wc
Old Jetty at Volendam, The	1905, wc
Old Market Hall and Fountain, Birmingham, The	1884, wc
Old Pilot, An	1891, wc
Old Quilt, The	1904, wc

Old Resort for Young Gossips, An	1879, -
Old Sailmaker, The	1883, wc
Old Salt, An	1909, wc
Old Servant, An	1886, wc
Old Soldier, An	1896, wc
Old Story, The	1883, wc
	1893, wc
	1904, -
Old Well, The	1880, -
Old Welshwoman, An	1909, wc
	1909, wc
Old Windmill, The	c 1893, wc
Once upon a Time	1895, wc
On Dartmoor	1900, wc
One Man, One Vote	1892, wc
One of the Crew	1886, bw
	1892, wc
On Guard	1896, -
On the Alert	1877, -
On the Beach	c 1882, wc
On the Beach, Southwold	1893, wc
On the Cliff, Newlyn	1904, wc
On the Cliff, Southwold, Suffolk	1893, wc
On the Dart	1895, -
On the Dyke	1905, wc
On the Dyke, Volendam	1905, wc
On the Lookout	1895, bw
On the Lyn, Devon	1874, -
On the Moors	c 1882, wc
On the Rocks	c 1882, wc
	c 1884, wc
Orchard Scene	c 1892, pa
Orphan, The	1888, wc
	1888, ch
	1889, wc
Peeling Potatoes	1920, wc
Pengelly, John Russell	1904, wc
Pensive Maiden, A	1882, wc
Pensive Thoughts	1896, wc
Penzance, from Newlyn	c 1882, wc
Picture Book, The	1876, wc
	1881, -
Pink Bodice, The	1904, -
	1914, o
	1915, wc
	1916, o
Pleasant News	1901, -
Pleasant Reverie, A	1879, wc
Poor Weather	1893, wc
Prayer, The	1881, wc
Preparing Dinner	1908, o
	1909, wc
	1912, o
	1914, wc

Question of Quality, A	1882, -
Quiet Afternoon, A	1879, -
	1882, wc
Quiet Chat, A	1893, wc
Quiet Corner, A	1898, wc
Quiet Pipe, A	1884, -
	1898, wc
	1900, -
	1901, -
	1902, -
Quiet Time, A	1892, wc
	1899, -
	1910, -
Reading the News	c 1900, o
Rest and Rust	1882, -
Resting	1893, wc
Returning from Market	1883, -
Reverie, A	1883, wc
	1885, wc
	1889, -
	1893, wc
	1896, o
	1897, -
	1900, wc
	1904, wc
	1908, o
	1909, o
	1918, o
Road to the Village, The	1893, wc
Sacrifice, The	1918, wc
Sad News	1885, wc
St Ives, Cornwall	1893, wc
Sentinel of the Sea, A [aka Tol Pedn Rock, Lands End, Cornwall]	1895, wc
Shady Corner, A	1881, -
She gazed upon the golden gift, Absorbed in pleasant reveries	1879, wc
Shipping Intelligence	1882, -
Short Story, The	1916, -
Signal of Distress, A	1900, o
Silent Sorrow	1880, wc
Simple in structure but in bounty great	1879, wc
Son of Toil, A	1883, wc
Spring	1885, wc
State Pensioner, A	1910, wc
	1913, o
Steam Trawler, The	1888, wc
Stitch in Time, A	1883, -
	1895, -
Stories of the Battlefield	1898, o
Story of the Sea, A	1886, bw

Street in Clovelly, A	1889, -
Street in Newlyn, A	1880, -
	1880, -
	1893, wc
[aka Sunny Evening in Newlyn, Cornwall]	1893, wc
Street in Quimperlé, A	1881, -
Street in St Ives, Cornwall, A	1900, wc
Summer Morning on the Beach	1882, -
Sunlight and Shadow	1892, o
	1893, wc
Sunny Afternoon, Cornwall, A	1893, wc
Sunny Afternoon, Newlyn, A	1902, wc
Sunny Day, Cornwall, A	1885, -
Sunny Day in Holland, A	1904, -
Sunny Evening in Newlyn, Cornwall, A - see *Street In Newlyn, A*	
Sunny South, The	1885, o
Sunny South, The, a Study	1885, wc
Sunset of Life, The	1883, -
	1888, wc
Sunshine and Shadow — see *Early Cares*	
Sunshine and Shadow	1889, wc
	c 1890, wc
Sunshine, Brittany	1881, wc
Sympathy	1890, wc
	1901, o
Technical Instruction	1893, wc
Telegram, A	1881, wc
	1881, wc
	1881, -
Thatched Cottage, The	c 1886, wc
Their task being ended with declining day, Homeward the weary peasants wend their way	1880, -
The Old Gardener	1884, wc
The seas are quiet when the winds give o'er, So calm are we when passions are no more	1884, wc
	1884, ch
The tender grace of a day that is dead, Will ne'er come back to me	1885, wc
	1909, o

Thinking it Out	1906, wc
	1906, o
Time moveth not, our being 'tis that moves	1882, bw
	1882, wc
	1882, wc
	1882, wc
Tired Bacchanalian, A	1878, -
Tired Gleaner, The	1873, -
Tired Out	1889, wc
Toiler of the Sea, A	1883, -
	1890, -
Tol Pedn Rock, Lands End, Cornwall — see *Sentinel of the Sea, A*	
Trereife Avenue, Penzance	c 1892, o
Trouble	1892, o
	1898, -
	1903, o
Truant, The	1887, wc
View of Eckington, A	1880, -
View of Newlyn, A	1882, wc
	c 1883, wc
	c 1886, wc
Village Idyll — After the buoyant happy days of youth, Comes the calm eventide of age	1888, wc
Village Postman, The	1885, wc
Waif, The	1899, o
Waiting	1887, -
Waiting for the Boats	1885, wc
	1885, wc
	1893, wc
	1896, o
	1896, wc
Waiting for the Carrier	1880, -
Waiting for the Crew	1890, -
	1892, wc
Waiting for the Tide	1899, wc
Waiting the Return of the Boats	1896, o
Waiting the Return of the Fleet	1903, wc
Walberswick	1893, wc
Wanderer, A	1899, -
	1901, -
Wandering Musician	1906, wc
Wandering Musicians	1899, o
Wandering Thoughts	1882, wc
War News	1900, wc
	1918, wc
Washing Day	1881, -
	1893, wc
	1893, ch

Watching Father's Boat	1893, wc
	1893, wc
Watching for the Fleet, Cadgwith	1891, wc
Wayfarer, The	1881, -
Way to School, The	1892, wc
Weary Waiting	1882, -
Weston-on-Avon Church	1880, -
When One is Old	1895, wc
	1895, o
	1895, -
	1901, o
When the Boats are Away	1890, wc
	1891, wc
	1903, o
Whisperings of the Past	1888, wc
Widow, The	1891, -
Widowed	1887, wc
Widower, The	1897, -
	1899, o
	1913, wc
Woman's Part, The	1905, wc
	1905, o
Wonderland	1884, wc
[aka I Think I'll be a Sailor]	
Wonderland	1884, cr
Worcestershire Village, A	c 1886, wc
World Forgetting, The	1878, -
Yarn, The	1893, wc
Young Musician, The	1881, wc

APPENDIX 1: PRINCIPAL SOURCES OF INCOME

	YEARS	NO. OF WORKS	VALUE IN £
SALES VIA MAJOR DEALERS			
Cohen	1879-1904	42	284
Starkey (Birmingham)	1879-1899	95	2,037
Franks (Coventry)	1879-1888	22	871
Chamberlain (Birmingham)	1880-1890	54	395
Clarke	1881	31	318
Keeley (Birmingham)	1881-1898	116*	624
Ingram (London)	1883-1884	19	431
Luton (Birmingham)	1894-1918	40	1,184
Fieldhouse (Birmingham)	1899-1905	29	620
Paul (Penzance)	1915-1920	36*	466
SALES VIA EXHIBITIONS AND GALLERIES			
Royal Birmingham Society	1879-1914	35	1,458
Royal Inst of Painters in Watercolours	1885-1910	26	1,711
Royal Academy	1904	1	300
Fine Art Society	1893	21	397
Other exhibitions	1879-1918	45	1,770
MAJOR DIRECT PRIVATE COMMISSIONS/SALES			
Alldays (Birmingham)	1881-1882	43	500
Brunning (Birmingham)	1883-1884	5	378
Dearle	1883-1885	2	168
Wallis	1887-1888	2	235
Hill	1889	1	105
Lethbridge	1894	1	300
Jewell	1894	1	327
Black & White	1896	1	260
Booth	1896	1	315
Tooth & Son	1899	1	200
Ward	1904	1	150
Marshall Son & Hull	1906	1	131
Summers	1910	1	210
Other sales/receipts		292	4,510
Total recorded sales		965*	£20,655

Langley did not distinguish between dealers and private purchasers in his sales notebook and the analysis between categories should not be regarded as conclusive evidence of a purchaser's status.

An * against the no. of works sold indicates that the proceeds were recorded but not the exact number of works. Particularly in the years 1879 to 1882, Langley sold small unnamed works (not recorded in the catalogue raisonné). For example, in a letter in the *Birmingham Post*, January 13 1922, Keeley's son mentions that his father took 125 of Langley's works and the 54 works taken by Chamberlain included 20 unnamed pen and ink drawings.

	MEDIUM	PRICE IN £
1883		
But men must work	wc	105
The Gathering Storm	wc	105
News of the Sea	wc	105
1884		
Among the Missing	wc	420
A Lover and his Lass	wc	105
1885		
Going to Market	wc	105
Waiting for the Boats	wc	315
1886		
Departure of the Fleet	wc	420
1887		
Widowed	wc	200
1888		
A Village Idyll	wc	250
1889		
Absent Thoughts	wc	105
Betrayed	wc	158
The Orphan	wc	120
1890		
Alone	wc	150
By the Sea	wc	113
Disaster	wc	250
O! For the touch of a vanish'd hand	wc	150
1894		
After the Storm	wc	300
Never Morning wore to evening	o	328
1896		
Breadwinners	o	315
Motherless	o	260
1899		
A Cousin from Town	o	200
1904		
Between the Tides	o	150
The Greeting	o	300
1906		
When the Boats are Away	o	131
1907		
Memories	o	105
The Woman's Part	o	158
1910		
The New Arrival	o	210

APPENDIX 3: WORKS EXHIBITED AND SOLD

	WORKS EXHIBITED					WORKS SOLD	
YEAR	TOTAL	VENUES: RBSA	RI	RA	OTHER	NUMBER	SALES VALUE £
1873	3	3					
1874	2	2					
1875	3	3					
1876	4	4					
1877	4	4					
1878	5	5					
1879	5	5				66	288
1880	7	4			3	52	255
1881	13	5			8	102	723
1882	9	5			4	48	636
1883	17	2	2		13	49	951
1884	13	1	3		9	40	931
1885	10	3	3		4	22	797
1886	10	2	3		5	19	900
1887	7		4		3	42	714
1888	9	2			7	18	564
1889	14	2	3		9	33	905
1890	7	1	2		4	21	1,027
1891	4		2		2	9	294
1892	3	1	1	1		2	59
1893	66	1	1		64*	53	903
1894	8	1	2	1	4	27	938
1895	13	3	5	1	4	28	590
1896	8	1	4	1	2	29	1,052
1897	7	2		1	4	13	315
1898	10	4	2	1	3	21	431
1899	10	5	1	1	3	19	718
1900	13	2	8	2	1	17	416
1901	5	2	1	1	1	18	533
1902	5	1	2	1	1	15	331
1903	7	3	2	1	1	23	711
1904	15	2	10	1	2	19	698
1905	11	3	3	1	4	14	420
1906	9	1	4	1	3	15	540
1907	8	1	2	1	4	8	428
1908	7	3	2	1	1	6	121
1909	14	3	8	1	2	15	178
1910	8	2	2	1	3	10	476
1911	2	1		1		9	273
1912	6		3	3		6	135
1913	5	1	3	1		8	243
1914	2		1	1		7	169
1915	4	2	1		1	6	197
1916	5	2	1	2		3	140
1917	5	2	1	1	1	-	no record -
1918	2	1	1			27	357
1919	-					22	200
1920	1	1				4	98
1921	1				1		
1922	1				1		
Totals	407	104	93	28	182	965	£20,655

* *In 1893 Langley exhibited over 60 works in his one-man show at The Fine Arts Society.*

The picture sales recorded by Langley from 1879 to 1920 and his exhibitions from 1873 to 1922 are here summarised. He did not record every sale and sometimes he sold a bundle of sketches without listing them individually. On the other hand, these sales results do include some unnamed sketches which are not listed in the catalogue.

To give a clearer indication of the volume of new work by Langley, the exhibition details relate only to the first occasion on which each work was shown. In some years the number of works re-exhibited exceeded that of works shown for the first time.

The most important exhibition venues for Langley were the Royal Birmingham Society of Artists (RBSA), the Royal Institute (RI) and the Royal Academy (RA).

Notable omissions from Langley's records of sales are two Academy oils, *Charity*, 1897 and *A Cornish Idyll*, 1902, though the records of the Walker Art Gallery indicate the latter was sold for £300.

BIRMINGHAM

1852
151 Irving Place, Irving Street

1861
9 Brunswick Place, Irving Street

1871
2 Court 32, Irving Street

1873
2 Highfield Place, Irving Street

1875
Studio — 87 Holloway Head (above the shop of Emund Wright)
Studio — 12 Great Colmore Street (above the shop of Miss Harriet Bird, dressmaker)

1876
19 Grant Street
78 Wynn Street

1878
2 Monument Street, Waterworks Road
4 Beaumont Place, Cregoe Street

1879
Studio — 29 ½ Paradise Street (shared with Edwin Harris)
Studio — Grosvenor Chambers, 11 Broad Street Corner

1881
Studio — 321 Broad Street
High Street Harborne

1882
Studio — Grosvenor Chambers, 11 Broad Street Corner
19 Lea Crescent

CORNWALL

1882
Pembroke Lodge, Newlyn

1886
Bay View House, Newlyn
From 1882 to 1886, Langley rented studio space in the village (addresses unknown). For a while he also shared Ralph Todd's studio.

BIRMINGHAM

1886/87
168 Bristol Road, Edgbaston
Studio accommodation rented (address unknown)

CORNWALL

1887
Holbein House, Penzance
Studio purchased, the Fradgan, Newlyn

1890
Pembroke Lodge, Newlyn

1892
Morrab Road, Penzance

1894
6 St Mary's Terrace, Penzance

1896
'Westbourne', Alexandra Road, Penzance

1919-1922
18 Clarence Street, Penzance

APPENDIX 5: SIGNATURES

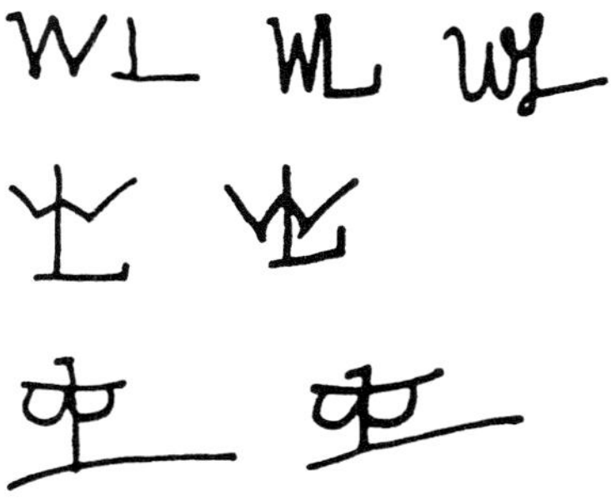

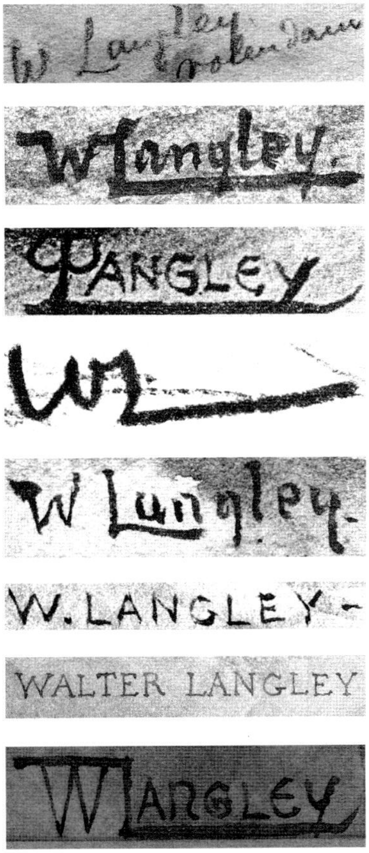

Walter Langley used a variety of styles of monogram and signature on his work. These styles changed through different periods but not in a traceable development from one to another. Several styles might therefore appear on works of the same date, or a style might be reverted to in later years. These examples represent the most common forms of Langley's signatures. (The monograms are reproduced from Peter Nahum *Monograms of Victorian and Edwardian Artists*, Victoria Square Press.)

1852
Born June 8, Birmingham

1857
Attended Hurst Street Unitarian Mission School

1863
Attended evening classes at Birmingham School of Design

1865
Apprenticed to A H Biermann, lithographer
First exhibited work, Midland Counties Exhibition, Birmingham

1866
Earliest surviving work, School of Design exercise

1871
Earliest dated art work — *Dog and Duck Inn, Birmingham*

1872
Scholarship to South Kensington Schools to study design

1873
First exhibit at Royal Birmingham Society of Artists (RBSA)
First sketching tour, to South Devon

1875
Partnership with A H Biermann

1876
Marriage to Clara Perkins, August 26, Birmingham

1877
Son, Lorraine, born September 8

1879
First year as 'professional' artist
Daughter, Eleanore, born March 15
Founder member of Birmingham Art Circle

1880
First visit to Newlyn

1881
Visit to Brittany
Second visit to Newlyn
Elected Associate Member of RBSA
Son, Gabriel, born November 21

1882
Thrupp/Allday commission for £500
Settled in Newlyn

1883
Time moveth not, our being 'tis that moves shown at Dudley Gallery, London, January
RI — *'But men must work .....'*
Son, Cecil, born February 17
Elected Member of Royal Institute of Painters in Water Colours (RI), March 12
In Memoriam shown at Institute of Painters in Oils (IPO)

1884
RI — *Among the Missing*
Elected Member of RBSA

1885
IPO — *The Sunny South*
RI — *Waiting for the Boats*
Return to Birmingham

1886
RI — *Departure of the Fleet*
Exhibition of watercolours at Birmingham Art Gallery
Elected Associate Member of IPO

1887
RI — *Betrayed*
President of the Easel Club, Birmingham
Return to Newlyn and purchase of studio

1888
RI — *Village Idyll*

1889
RI — *Disaster!* and *O! For the touch of a vanish'd hand*
Gold Medal for watercolours at Paris Exhibition

1890
RI — *Knitting*
President of Sutton Coldfield Art Class for 1890 (SAC)

1891
RI — *An Old Pilot*
Presidential Address at SAC, January

1892
Sunlight and Shadow, first painting exhibited at Royal Academy (RA)

1893
One man show at Fine Art Society
Gold Medal for watercolours at World's Colombian Exposition, Chicago

1894
RI — *After the Storm*
RA — *Never morning wore to evening*
Exhibition at Nottingham Art Gallery and Museum, 'Painters of the Cornish School'

1895
RA — *Motherless*
Invitation from Uffizi Gallery to donate self-portrait
Death of Clara, aged 44

1896
RA — *Breadwinners*

1897
RA — *In faith and hope the world will disagree* and this work selected by Tolstoy as example of good art in his essay 'What is Art?'
RBSA — Self portrait occupies place of honour at Spring Exhibition before despatch to Florence
Marriage to Ethel Pengelly, June 24, Penzance

1898
RI — *In the Fishing Season*
RA — *A Cousin from Town*
Son, John, born September 19

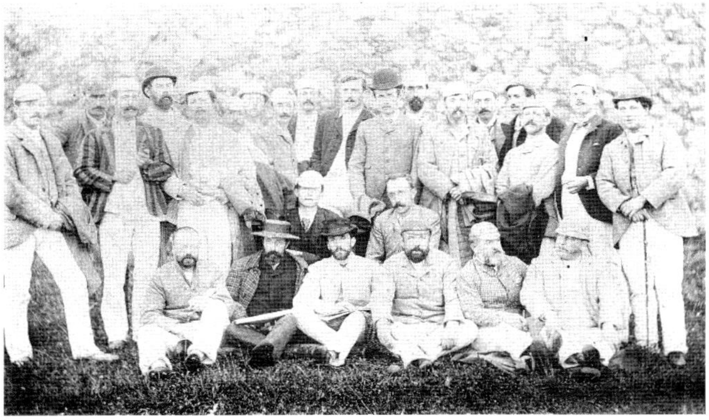

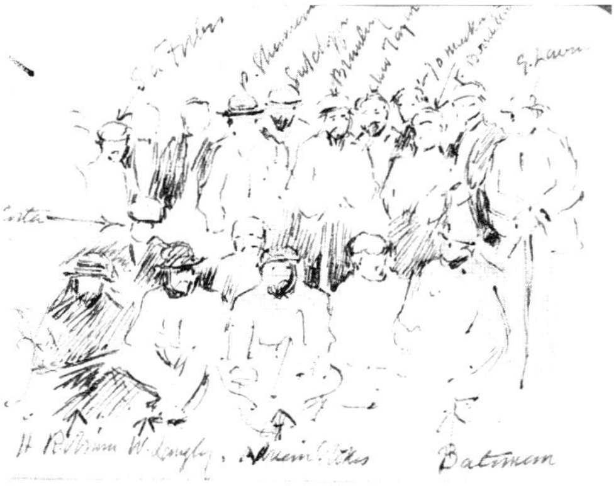

Photograph of the Cornwall artists' cricket team, see pp 85–88, with a key drawing and annotations by Stanhope Forbes.

1899
RA — *Wandering Musicians*
RBSA — Retrospective at Spring Exhibition

1900
RA — *A Signal of Distress*

1901
RA — *Between the Tides*

1902
RA — *A Cornish Idyll*

1903
RA — *When the Boats are Away*
Honorary Associateship of Royal College of Arts

1904
RA — *The Greeting*
First visit to Holland

1905
RA — *The Woman's Part*
Second visit to Holland

1906
RA — *The Fisherman's Widow*
Visit to Belgium

1907
RA — *A Flemish Peasant*

1908
RA — *Cornish Fisher Folk*
Member of Royal British Colonial Society of Artists

1909
RA — *The tender grace of a day that is dead*
Death of Cecil, November 1

1910
RA — *The New Arrival*

1911
RA — *Maternity*
International Fine Arts Exhibition, Rome

1912
RA — *Preparing Dinner*

1913
RA — *Motherlove*

1914
RA — *Daydreams*

1916
RA — *A Belgian Interior*

1917
RA — *The Letter*

1920
RBSA — Last exhibited work in Birmingham, *Peeling Potatoes*

1922
Died, March 22, Penzance

Breton Folk, Henry Blackburn and Randolph Caldecott, Sampson, Low, Marston, Searle & Rivington 1884
City of Birmingham, Proceedings of the Council, 1891-92
The Avon and Shakespeare Country, A.G.Bradley, Methuen 1910
The Art of Walter Langley, William Wainwright, Clarendon Lecture 1923
Dictionary of British Sculptors, Rupert Gunnis, The Abbey Library, London 1951
Victoria County History of Warwickshire Vol VII, W.B.Stephens 1964
Work and Struggle — The Painter as Witness, Edward Lucie-Smith and Celestine Dars, Paddington Press 1977
Americans in Brittany and Normandy 1860-1910, Phoenix Art Museum, Arizona 1982
The Making of Victorian Birmingham, Victor Skipp 1983
Pont Aven 1800-1914, Bertrand Queinec 1983
The Good and Simple Life, Michael Jacobs, Phaidon 1985
Jacob Smits, een portret, Fernand van Gompel, Bert Nuyts, Ivo Verheyen, VZW Vrienden van het Jacob Smitsmuseeum 1988
Birmingham Working People, George J Barnsby, Integrated Publishing Services, Wolverhampton 1990
100 Years of Newlyn — Diary of a Gallery, Melissa Hardie ed, Patten Press and Newlyn Art Gallery 1995

EXHIBITION CATALOGUES:

Artists of the Newlyn School 1880-1900, Newlyn Art Gallery 1979
Painting in Newlyn 1900-1930, Newlyn Art Gallery 1985
Painting in Newlyn 1880-1930, Barbican Art Gallery with Newlyn Art Gallery 1985
The Hague School, Grand Palais, Paris, the Royal Academy and Haags Gemeentemuseum 1983
Walter Langley, Birmingham Museums and Art Gallery 1990
Hard Times — Social Realism in Victorian Art, Manchester City Art Gallery 1987
The Birmingham School, Birmingham Museums and Art Gallery 1990
British Watercolours from Birmingham, Birmingham Museums and Art Gallery 1991

NEWSPAPERS AND PERIODICALS 1870-1923, INCLUDING:

Birmingham Daily Post
Birmingham Mail
Birmingham Graphic
Sutton Coldfield and Erdington Times
Circle (Birmingham Art Circle)
Edgbastonia
King's Heath and Moseley Journal
Cornishman
Cornish Telegraph
The Times

OTHER SOURCES:

Walter Langley correspondence and papers in the family archive
Stanhope Forbes correspondence, Tate Gallery Archive

PHOTOGRAPHIC CREDITS

Christie's Images
6, 38, 63 *below*, 102 *right*, 106

A C Cooper
21 *below*, 73 *left*

The Courtauld Institute of Art
17 *below*

Jeff Darken, Woking
77

James Dee
120

Serge Domingo/Marco Rabatti, Florence
Frontispiece

Richard Hagen Fine Paintings, Broadway
46, 87, 90 *below*, 94, 103 *above*

Locke and England, Leamington Spa
68, 69 *main picture*

David Messum Fine Art, London and Marlow
18, 23, 35, 39, 59, 67, 78 *below*, 80, 82 *below left*, 87, 93, 94, 107, 112

John Mills, Liverpool
24

Peter Nahum at the Leicester Galleries
62

Sotheby's
cover and 30, 43, 45 *above*, 50, 54 *right*, 56 *below*, 77 *top right*, 79, 85 *main picture*, 90 *top*, 95 *above and below*, 97 *left*, 105, 109, 113, 114, 118, 119, 129, 140, 148

Sotheby's, Sussex
70 *main picture*

Steve Tanner
42, 86

Unless otherwise stated here or at the illustration, all photographs are by Colin Mills.

Works in public collections are noted at the illustration and in addition we are grateful to all those noted here for the use of their transparencies and photographs.

Study of a Welsh mine, c1909
watercolour, 20.3 x 12.6cm

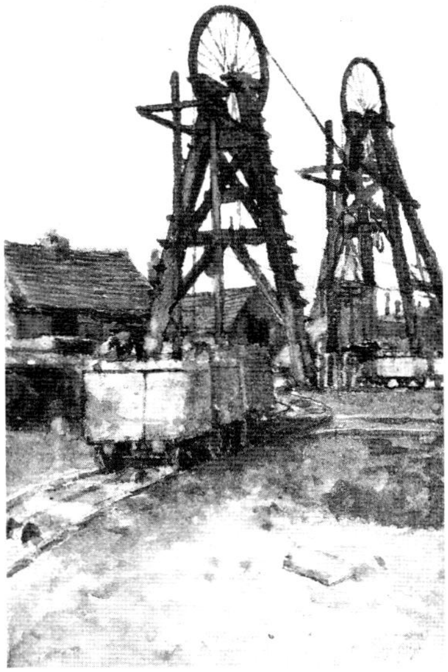

All references are to text and illustrations which appear in the Introduction and the Life of Walter Langley. Page numbers in *italic* refer to marginal notes; those in **bold** indicate illustrations. Place names which recur regularly throughout the text, e.g. Birmingham, London, Newlyn, Paris and Penzance, are not included.

PAGE 192
The Hand-bell c1895
watercolour, 20.4 x 12.7cm

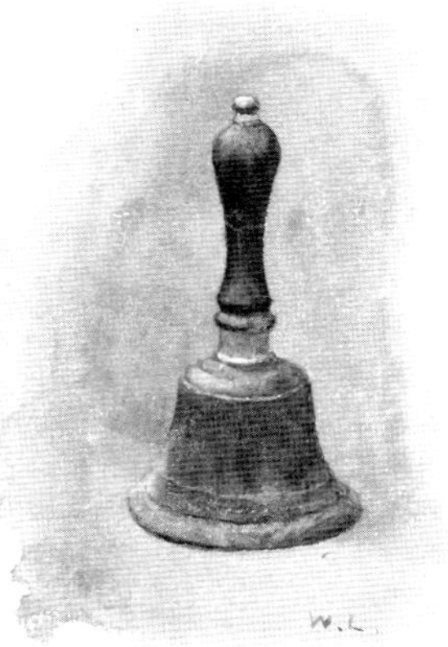